Edging Women Out

Edging Women Out

Victorian Novelists,
Publishers,
and Social
Change

Gaye Tuchman with Nina E. Fortin

Yale University Press
New Haven and London

Designed by Sonia Laniado and set in Perpetua with Bodoni display type by Rainsford Type, Danbury, Conn.
Printed in the United States of America by Vail-Ballou Press, Binghamton, N.Y.

Tuchman, Gaye.
   Edging women out : Victorian novelists, publishers, and social
change / Gaye Tuchman, with Nina E. Fortin.
     p. cm.
   Bibliography: p.
   Includes index.
   ISBN 0-300-04316-3 (alk. paper)
   1. English fiction—19th century—History and criticism. 2. Women and literature—Great Britain—History—19th century. 3. Literature and society—Great Britain—History—19th century. 4. Novelists, English—19th century—Social conditions. 5. Novelists, English—19th century—Economic conditions. 6. Literature publishing—Great Britain—History—19th century. 7. Sex role—Great Britain—History—19th century. 8. Women—Employment—Great Britain—History—19th century. 9. Great Britain—Social conditions—19th century. I. Fortin, Nina E.   II. Title.
PR115.T8 1989
823′.8′09—dc19

88-21595
CIP

The paper in this book meets the guidelines for permanence and durability of the Committee on Production Guidelines for Book Longevity of the Council on Library Resources.

10   9   8   7   6   5   4   3   2   1

For Ethan Raphael Tuchman

Contents

Contents

Contents

Illustrations

Tables

Preface

Twenty-five years ago a friend whose father was a university dean said to me, "There's something so masculine about sitting at a typewriter and writing, don't you think?" I remember being surprised by her statement, for I had never thought of writing as a particularly masculine activity. This research has helped me learn that members of our culture have historically characterized writing a book as a job for men.

This book uses perspectives derived from the sociologies of occupations and gender to analyze a literary problem—the changing status of women writers, especially novelists, during the Victorian era. It is informed by women's studies, especially the feminist concerns that are encompassed by that interdisciplinary area. I should like to think that this book is an exception to the rule that interdisciplinary books frequently displease scholars in the two or more fields that they straddle.

I started working on this study in 1978. I was particularly fortunate to have Nina E. Fortin as my research assistant for more than three years. During our daily discussions she contributed so much to my own thinking that, as is frequently the case in a close collaboration, it is often difficult to determine who offered which conceptualization. After a fierce fight with cancer, Nina died on 2 October 1987.

I am grateful to literary critic Elaine Showalter, who suggested that I look at two sets of archives housed at the British Museum: the Macmillan papers and the papers of the Society of Authors. She also read an early draft of the manuscript and suggested some additional and valuable sources to examine.

Visiting London during the summers of 1978 and 1982, I spent a total of four months copying records at the British Library (handcopying was cheaper than ordering microfilm). The staff of the Students Room was superb. Its personnel did not flinch even when, on the last day of my stay, a bank holiday with fewer people than usual working, I ordered more than twenty volumes of records to check and cross-check materials. Michèle Barrett kindly supervised a British student who copied more records while I returned to New York to teach. Chris and Linda MacDowell, Elizabeth Wilson and Angela Weir, Gill Davies and John McCarthy, and a feminist collective generously provided me with places to stay during my visits.

Over the years Nina Fortin and I were blessed with good friends and colleagues who listened, criticized, and helped us come to terms with our material. We were ably assisted by Nancy Naples, Martha Ecker, Phyllis Houvos, Kathleen Kramer, and Lisa Master. We received guidance on statistical matters and computer glitches from Roberta A. Cohen, Jack Hammond, Audrey Blumberg, and John Van Hoek. Since 1983 Steven Cohen, Harry Gene Levine, Dean Savage, and Lauren Seiler have helped with problems in computer programs, read bits of an ever-changing manuscript, or offered useful comments.

When we began this project, neither Nina nor I would have identified ourselves as personally inclined to quantitative research. Indeed, in many ways this book uses quantitative methods to substantiate a qualitative argument. Christine Bose provided valuable reassurance about how we reasoned with our data. We have not followed all of her advice; sociologists who work with large samples and use advanced statistical techniques to analyze contingency tables, as Chris does, use a different method to identify the number of cases in the cell of a table than do some other sociologists, who apply such relatively simple techniques as chi-square to relatively small samples. We followed the latter practice; in our tables the raw numbers reported in a cell refer to the number of cases that served as the denominator when we calculated percentages.

I am most grateful for the mainframe facilities of the City University and the magnificent microcomputer laboratory of the Queens College Department of Sociology. I am also grateful to my department for doing everything possible to facilitate this research, including providing me with an ideal teaching schedule. Queens College granted me a course off for two semesters and a semester sabbatical in spring 1987 to complete the manuscript.

In the early years, our research was funded by grants. I received a grant from the Ford Foundation (Mariam Chamberlain was then their program officer), two grants from the National Endowment for the Humanities, and three grants from the Professional Staff Congress–Board of Higher Education Program of the City University of New York. The bibliography lists the articles and reports that Nina and I wrote with their support. The views in these earlier efforts and in this book are mine and Nina's and do not reflect on the funding agencies. We appreciate the permissions of *Signs: A Journal of Women in Culture and Society,* the *American Journal of Sociology*, and *Media, Culture and Society* to include portions of our articles. We also appreciate comments on drafts of early papers from members of the Proseminar on Women and Work, which convened at City University of New York Graduate School and University Center from September 1980 through August 1983.

I cherish the encouragement and toleration of my friends in New York, who put up with me when I became obsessed with analytic problems. I value the goodwill, prods, and superb editorial advice proffered by my friends and editors, Gladys Topkis of Yale University Press and Gill Davies of Routledge. Mary Evans offered loyal friendship and magnificent comments on the two drafts. Woody Powell's comments on the manuscript were splendid.

I am additionally indebted to the day-care center and babysitters without whom I could not have completed this book. Gladys Valdivie, Rosa Bautista, and the Gardens Nursery School and Kindergarten helped me to maintain an equilibrium while my son taught me in a substantial way what feminists mean when they discuss the problems of mothers who write.

Gaye Tuchman

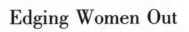

Edging Women Out

1
Gender Segregation
and the Politics
of Culture

Before 1840 the British cultural elite accorded little prestige to the writing of novels, and most English novelists were women. By the turn of the twentieth century "men of letters" acclaimed novels as a form of great literature, and most critically successful novelists were men. These two transitions—in the prestige of novel writing and the gender distribution of lauded novelists—were related processes, constituting complementary elements in a classic confrontation between men and women in the same white-collar occupation.

Why does some literature supposedly transcend the ages and so constitute "culture" while other once-popular books languish in disuse? Why and how does an occupation shift from having a preponderance of female practitioners to being performed mainly by men? These seemingly dissociated questions are fundamental to the fields of academic inquiry that they straddle.

The definition of culture is basic to historical, critical, and sociological discussions of literature, including the novel. Yet scholars rarely agree about the meaning of culture or about why some books are lasting and others not. Humanistic critics still tend to view literary culture as comprised of honored works that supposedly speak to the human condition across the centuries. Although they no longer identify a unitary great tradition, they nonetheless continue to argue about which authors and works merit analytic attention. Thus, they continue to enshrine some authors as mighty progenitors and to claim implicitly that great authors create great culture.

Cultural sociologists tend to believe that even humanistic debates about the merits of specific authors are acts of sanctification that ignore the social and institutional conditions that give books life and govern their reception. Such controversies are the self-justifying activity of specific groups within powerful social classes. Drawing distinctions between high and popular cul-

1

ture, ascendant groups (or class fractions) articulate a set of values about money, art, and the relation between them that they then use to support claims about their own activities and way of life— what anthropologists term culture. Among those claims may be that the cultural activities of other, less elite groups scarcely qualify as culture. To the cultural sociologist, then, the issues of quality, popularity, and neglect require a stance outside the ongoing humanist debate about which authors and books are worthy of analytic consideration, which are high culture, and which, popular culture.[1]

The topic of shifts in the gender concentration of an occupation is basic to recent social science inquiries inspired by the desire to integrate a labor force now largely segregated by gender, ethnicity, and race. Some of these studies emphasize processes reinforcing occupational gender segregation. Others explore shifts in occupational gender segregation to learn how women can gain access to the better-paying jobs held largely by men.[2] Sometimes these studies have difficulty untangling processes associated with race or ethnicity from processes associated with gender. In such complex multiracial, multiethnic societies as the United States and Great Britain, the strands of these separate social processes sometimes seem intertwined because white women, minority women, minority men, or members of all these groups may assume jobs once held by white men.

This case study unites cultural sociology with the sociology of work to ask, Who defined Victorial literary culture? What was the impact of that activity on women novelists, who at the turn of the nineteenth century had constituted most of the writers of fiction? To answer these questions, we pose others: What was the impact of processes associated with industrialization on the creation, production, distribution, and reception of novels—on conditions all novelists faced? How were such processes implicated in transforming

---

1. The distinction between high culture and popular culture is an expression of ideology (Bourdieu 1984 and Williams 1977). We use the terms to point up their implication in the (re)production of class and gender relationships. We make no claims about the merits of either type of culture, for the debate about innate quality treats potentially invidious distinctions as accurate renditions of aesthetic "essences" (Bourdieu 1984). Griswold (1986) also argues that the relevant sociological issue is which books are considered high culture in which historical periods and for what reasons.

2. Most studies consider women entering male-dominated occupations. Reskin and Roos (1987) provide a good review of this literature. Studies of race and ethnicity, such as Lieberson's (1980), speak as though their findings apply to both men and women. But their data concern only the behavior of men in the paid labor force and so are not applicable to women. Of course, many of these generalizations probably apply to such female-dominated occupations as domestics and clerical workers in which ethnic groups have succeeded one another (see Kessler-Harris 1981).

the job of novelist from one practiced primarily by women to one performed primarily by men? We intend our answers to contribute to several fields.

To literary critics, we offer discussions relevant to recent historically based feminist literary criticism.[3] Frequently resting on generalizations derived from the lives and texts of either canonized or highly popular women novelists, much of this literature insists that women writers came into their own in Victorian England. Delineating changes in the material conditions of all novelists, including men, we tell a different story, which may affect how critics interpret the orientation of women novelists toward the dominant literary tradition. By discussing how men's hegemony over expanding literary opportunities enabled them to define the novel as a genre suitable for elite men and to dismiss novels by women as merely popular, we suggest how women novelists may have appeared to have come into their own and yet have experienced an "anxiety of authorship" (Gilbert and Gubar 1979).

To cultural sociologists, we offer a discussion of a critical period in the development of the distinction between high and popular culture. At the turn of the nineteenth century literary critics and novelists distinguished among the literary qualities of novels and implicated gender in those distinctions. By and large they assumed that the novel had a lowly status because of its association with women, as many novelists were and most novel readers were thought to be. By 1870 men of letters were using the term *high culture* to set off novels they admired from those they deemed run-of-the-mill. Most of these high-culture novels were written by men.

Others (for example, DiMaggio 1982) have stressed how class interests infuse the identification of high culture. We hope to show how definitions of culture are imbued with gender interests as well. Neither all men nor all elite men have the same interests. Yet even when their short-range interests conflict, men of different class fractions may agree on common standards of high culture. We hope to establish how those common standards encode gender interests and to link those interests to the material conditions of all writers.

---

3. Since 1975 American feminist criticism has taken two complementary directions (Showalter 1984b). Both qualify as close readings of texts. One, termed *gynesis* by Alice Jardine (1982), has adapted French theories to explore "sexual consequences and representations of sexual differences." The other, termed *gynocritics* by Showalter, is "roughly speaking, historical in orientation; it looks at women's writing as it has actually occurred and tries to define its specific characteristics ... within a cultural network that includes variables of race, class, and nationality" (Showalter 1984, 36). Our study is germane to criticism with a historical orientation, including such important texts on nineteenth-century female writers as those by Moers (1976) and Showalter (1977).

To sociologists of work and gender, we offer a detailed historical analysis of an important process rarely discussed in the sociological literature: how men gradually invade, redefine, and come to dominate what had primarily been a women's occupation. Complementing discussions of how physicians assumed tasks once performed by laywomen, our analyses of how men gradually edged women out as high-culture novelists develop a new concept, the "empty field phenomenon." We use this term rather than the more neutral terms "invasion and succession" to stress the power of men to define their own and others' occupational experience.

This power is stark in male-dominated professions, in which men clearly influence perceptions of the rare token woman in their midst. Writing about the social expectation that women would fill some jobs and men others, Everett Hughes (1956) pointed out that when a woman entered a job normally held by men, she was treated as an anomaly. In classes at Brandeis University (fall 1963), he spoke of the problems caused by the first woman to sit on the British bench. How was she to be addressed? Hughes pointed out that she became an "honorary man." Dressed in wig and robe, she was addressed as "sir," and the traditional decorum of the court was preserved. Perceptually, it remained a male preserve; no women were there.

Elite men may define others' occupational experience in less dramatic contexts as well. To understand this aspect of the empty field phenomenon, consider a common situation—how people frequently perceive a room full of others as empty. Envision how people experience a party where they expected to meet friends but find that they do not know anyone. Describing the party to friends the next day, they will invariably say, "No one was there," as if the room had been empty. Aspiring male authors, we argue, viewed writing novels as attending a party without their friends.

The perception of emptiness in a crowded area also occurs in other social settings, for example in the gentrification of inner cities. In such a case, a neighborhood starts with a poor and frequently minority population. According to the white middle class, no one lives there. Then some members of the white middle class decide that proximity to work and entertainment facilities warrant buying and improving dilapidated housing. They also speculate that they could benefit economically by buying a house in this empty neighborhood. As news of their activity spreads, sometimes through the media, more middle-class whites invade the neighborhood, causing real-estate prices to rise and pushing the minority population elsewhere. At the end of the gentrification process, white professionals predominate in the neighborhood, and those minorities who remain are also mostly members of the middle class.

Applied to female-dominated white-collar occupations, the empty field phenomenon implies that when people realize that a job entails social or economic rewards, they may find it desirable. Additionally, some men may find the competition of women so insignificant that they may view a job where women cluster as an unoccupied terrain ripe for the taking. We say "some men," because not all Victorian men active in literary enterprises harbored such feelings about women who wrote. Some of the publishers who earned significant profits on novels by women were perfectly content to continue doing so. Such publishers, of which Tinsley was one, seem to have viewed themselves as specialists in popular fare.

Women may have abetted men's successful invasion of the high-culture novel. As more occupations became open to women, some able and talented women who might once have become novelists probably turned to other fields (Neff [1929] 1966; Vicinus 1985). Assessing the quality of the competition between literary men and women is difficult. Although some very able women wrote fiction at the turn of the twentieth century, it is possible that literary women posed less competition to men of letters in the 1890s than in the 1840s.[4] But we argue here that in the late nineteenth century men used their control of major literary institutions to transform the high-culture novel into a male preserve.

Some of our findings contradict theories derived from studies of women entering men's occupations. Those theories suggest that the status of an occupation changes *during* a shift in gender concentration. We find that the rise in prestige occurred *after* an improvement of the status of novelists. The temporal order matters. To design programs that can integrate the work force by gender, social analysts require accurate descriptions of how the empty field phenomenon unfolds. Finally, since the authors we study are from similar ethnic and socioeconomic backgrounds, we provide a base from which others may analyze more complex cases.

The Historical Context

Most other studies dealing with the exclusion of women of talent from valued cultural spheres have identified crucial practices through which men excluded women from full participation. Often men exercised raw power by denying women access to training. In the nineteenth century (and earlier) art

---

4. Showalter (1977, 193–94) suggests that in the 1890s many feminist novelists were "engaged in the kind of quarrel that, according to Yeats, leads to rhetoric but not poetry. Thus, the [feminist] writers of this period have not fared well with posterity," because they may have been inferior novelists.

academies barred women from such vital training as life-drawing classes.[5] Nineteenth-century music masters taught women to play music but did not provide them with instruction in music theory (Wood 1980).

But women artists and musicians in the nineteenth century encountered obstacles different from those of women novelists. In music and the fine arts the key question is how men *maintained* exclusionary practices, whereas in the case of the novel it is how men *introduced* them. Additionally, upper- and middle-class norms about women's domestic roles had a more direct application to music and art than to literature.

In nineteenth-century England and America, social custom drew a rigid dichotomy between men's and women's public and domestic activity. Applied to activity in the arts, this distinction also incorporated ideals about social class.[6] Middle-class men and male artisans monopolized the public sphere; they might earn their livelihood as artists or musicians. Both women and men might sketch or paint, sing or play music in the privacy of their homes and in the homes of their friends. Indeed, the ability to do so was one mark of a cultured lady or gentleman of the upper classes.[7] Ultimately, this disparity between public and domestic practice helped reinforce men's existing dominance over the occupations of artist and musician. A lady whose class background permitted at least rudimentary training was neither to perform in public nor to display her work outside her limited domestic circle.

Some practices crucial to barring the professional involvement of ladies in music and the fine arts did not apply to literary activity. In the eighteenth and nineteenth centuries as today, an author did not need formal training to write a good novel. And although few women novelists had sufficient privacy to write without interruption for extended periods, by writing in their homes or by publishing anonymously or pseudonymously, they could prevent others from learning that they had contravened cultural mandates against earning money.[8]

5. An early portrait of the French Academy of Art shows the male members in a life-drawing class and depicts the female members as pictures on the wall (Nochlin 1971). See also Harris and Nochlin 1977, Peterson and Wilson 1976, Parker and Pollack 1981.

6. For example, women acted in public theaters, but even when successful, actresses were déclassé.

7. Nochlin (1971) argues that elite members of the aristocracy did not produce great art because to do so would contravene class-based understandings about the role of art in the life of a gentleman. She notes an exception who proves the rule: Henri Toulouse-Lautrec, whose physical deformity barred him from full participation in his class.

8. To avoid interruptions, some of them wrote while other members of their households slept. See Moers (1976) and Showalter (1977).

Before 1840 at least half of all novelists were women; by 1917 most high-culture novelists were men. The year 1840 is a useful (and necessarily reified) benchmark to date this changeover, because literary historians often claim that the decade of the 1840s marks the emergence of both the Victorian novel and the production and distribution system with which it was associated.[9] Our benchmark is the first year of that decade rather than the last because such important Victorian authors as Charles Dickens and William Makepeace Thackeray were publishing novels before 1840. (The first installment of Dickens' *Pickwick Papers* appeared in 1836 and of Thackeray's *Catherine* in 1839.)

We argue that as the Victorian novel emerged as the prototypical genre of the bourgeois age,[10] men realized anew a lesson that Sir Walter Scott had taught in the 1810s and 1820s with his Waverley novels: some novelists could earn profit and popular glory.[11] Many of these men may have recognized that while publishers amass profits most novelists eke out a living at best. Yet like today's teenagers who, dreaming of riches and celebrity, form rock groups, they too may have hoped for exceptional success. Most aspiring male novelists must have realized that in many countries, including England, some of the most popular and acclaimed novelists were women. They may have also been familiar with the "critical double standard" (Showalter 1977) explicit in nineteenth-century literary theory and rampant in literary reviews, which claimed that women could not hope to write either as powerfully or as thoughtfully as men could. Thus, the occupation of novelist seemed ripe for invasion.

The empty field phenomenon unfolded in three stages, as we will demonstrate with data derived from the Macmillan Archives at the British (Museum) Library. We have derived dates for those stages by analyzing submission rates to Macmillan and acceptance rates by Macmillan in the context of other literary activity.

We term the first stage, from 1840–1879, *the period of invasion*. Most novelists were probably women, but men began to value the novel as a cultural form. During the period of invasion, women submitted appreciably more

9. See Collins (1928), Gettmann (1960), Griest (1970), Gross (1970), Mumby (1974), Sutherland (1976), Tanzy (1961), Tillotson (1962). Tillotson (1962) and, following her, Showalter (1977) suggest that between 1840 and 1880 the novel was the dominant literary form.

10. On the realistic novel as a prototypical bourgeois form, see Lukács (1964), cf. Tillotson (1962), Showalter (1977), and Colby (1970).

11. Though Scott's novels were profitable, his status in the literary community derived from his poetry.

novels to Macmillan than men did, and women's fiction was more likely to be accepted than men's.

We call the years 1880–1899 *the period of redefinition*, when men of letters, including critics, actively redefined the nature of a good novel and a great author. They preferred a new form of realism that they associated with "manly" literature—that is, great literature. During the period of redefinition, men submitted more novels to Macmillan than women did, but women and men were equally likely to have their fiction accepted.

The years 1901–1917 are *the period of institutionalization*, when men's hold on the novel, particularly the high-culture novel, coalesced. The Macmillan Archives indicate that in these years men submitted less fiction than women but enjoyed a higher rate of acceptance.

Historical materials enable us to infer much about how these stages followed one another, for the shift in the gender concentration of novelists was but one aspect of the multifaceted impact of industrial capitalism on the creation, publication, dissemination, and reception of literary materials.

Men's eventual domination of the high-culture novel was abetted by a series of gradual transformations, many of which independently grew out of the increasing industrialization of England. For instance, industrialization brought a marked rise in literacy.[12] Before the nineteenth century, literacy was largely confined to middle- and upper-class men, although some women from these classes and some servants read, too. At first, industrialization and urbanization led to a decline in literacy. Peasants who had learned in church schools to decipher at least their names lost even that much formal training when they first became an urban proletariat. But gradually, as free schools increasingly opened to the poor and to women of all classes, literacy grew rapidly, especially among women (Graff 1987). A signal of a new industrial age, this increased literacy brought an expanding market for reading matter, particularly novels. The ability to read books, and even to write them, was no longer a mark of privileged status. And so the elite men who had once claimed this mark of distinction began insistently to differentiate their literature from the literature of others.[13] (At the time, the term *literature* included

12. No accurate figures on national British literary rates exist. For a general discussion, see Altick (1957). For a discussion of specific regions, cities, and parishes, see Graff (1987).

13. Bourdieu (1984) provides the most theoretically sophisticated discussion of "taste cultures." DiMaggio (1982) provides a useful analogy, the establishment of Boston museums. When the urban elite established cultural institutions in the nineteenth century, they actively sought to distinguish their tastes as high culture and dismissed the tastes of others as merely popular. For a discussion of how the novels of an individual author may be "promoted" from popular to high culture, see Jane Tompkins (1985) on Nathaniel Hawthorne.

fiction, what we might now term creative writing, the humanities, the social sciences, as well as aspects of the natural sciences.)

In addition to the growth of literacy, industrialization brought new printing technologies and the rationalization of the publishing industry, as it both expanded and centralized in London. To profit from increased literacy, publishers expanded their wares. They brought out more periodicals; in each decade they issued more books than in the last. After a temporary contraction of the industry caused by the general economic malaise of the 1820s, newly established publishing houses sought venture capital. By the 1830s both these new firms and the older ones specialized. No longer general publishers, houses identified themselves as specialists in such areas as library fiction, travel, or education. Different sorts of firms had different kinds of stakes in the novel.

Industrialization also had an impact on patterns of migration and settlement. London clearly became the center of the British financial world and attracted new publishing houses, as successful firms established elsewhere in the United Kingdom opened London offices. A bureaucratic center as well as a financial hub, London became a more important site in English intellectual life as more aspiring young men with elite educations migrated to that city. These and other men helped forge the social and economic role of that grand nineteenth-century generalist, the English man of letters. We will argue that some men used this role to redefine valued fiction as a male preserve. But having a position from which to dominate does not mean that men either chose to do so or achieved their ends.

We have already suggested that after 1840 some men may have become novelists because writing fiction increasingly brought status. Additionally, after 1840 the job conditions of novelists improved. Novelists struggled to gain more autonomy from both publishers and Mudie's Select (circulating) Library, which from roughly 1845 through 1890 dominated the distribution of fiction (Griest 1970). During the late 1880s (near the end of the period of redefinition) writers organized the Society of Authors to work collectively toward better terms in the standard contract for novels and better protection against American publishers' ongoing infringement of British copyrights. This attempt to control an important aspect of their working conditions—remuneration—is a basic component of professionalization.[14]

Another basic component of professionalism developed between 1840 and 1890—an ideology about how the work of the novelist was to be done. Literary theorists termed that ideology "realism" and located it in the texts

---

14. Two important discussions of professionalization are Larson (1977) and Freidson (1986).

of great male novelists. Realism was not a new concept. Critics trace the origin of the novel to the mid-eighteenth-century notion of realism and distinguish between the realism of those fictions and the improbabilities of the earlier romances, most of them by women (for example, Watt 1957; Spender 1986).

By the 1880s realism had come to indicate a serious fictionalized depiction of plausible actions of socially and psychologically individuated characters in a stratified society. Realism was to be revelatory. "The essence of the [realistic] novel is, and has always been ... reporting the news of life, *fact*—but fact related to a rational, ordered universe, such as indeed the Victorian world still gave the illusion of being" (Colby 1970, 13; compare Lukács 1964). Stressing that the mission of the novel was to reveal, not merely to entertain, this ideology made writing novels seem an important enough activity to engage the best, the brightest, and the most talented—men.

An ideology facilitates some activities and hampers others. The ideology of realism led some critics, including Macmillan's editorial consultant John Morley to confuse what we now call modernism with the abstraction of the earlier romance. For instance, both Morley and Frederick Macmillan initially characterized Maurice Hewlett's *The Forest Lovers* (1898) as "fantastic" and therefore an affront to realism.

The ideology of realism may also have turned some talented—and potentially literary—middle-class women away from the novel. To prove themselves as serious people, able to address some ugly facts and situations marring the supposedly rational, ordered Victorian universe, some middle-class women turned toward real action rather than literary realism. During the decades when men invaded the novel, some bourgeois women expanded their traditional nurturing roles within the home into new jobs for women outside the home, including nursing, social work, and eventually social activism. "They captured unclaimed [occupational] areas and pushed out from there" (Vicinus 1985, 15). These middle-class women claimed new arenas— empty fields—to call their own.

New literary conditions—transformations in the production, distribution, and reception of fiction—and new opportunities for middle-class women nourished the shifting gender concentration of novelists. Placing this particular change in its historical and sociological context carries two implications. First, to understand a significant transformation in any occupation, one must understand its social and historical circumstances. Second, the occupation novelist may be viewed as just another white-collar job, subject to the same social pressures and processes as other white-collar jobs. To be sure, the work conditions of free-lance authors, including novelists, differ significantly from those of most other white-collar workers. Writers determine their own schedules and so may create more flexible hours than the often rigid arrival and departure times of many other white-collar workers. And highly successful authors may be lionized, as were Scott and Dickens, whereas even the most esteemed secretary or schoolteacher may never be socially acclaimed. Furthermore, the product of a novelist's work—books—may be lauded as cultural hallmarks that speak to the present and to the future, a form of praise never extended to a secretary's work. But a novelist still does white-collar work.

By analyzing the occupation of novelist as merely another job rather than as the culturally lauded endeavor of a few gifted people, we hope to learn about aspects of the literary experience that were previously inaccessible to scholars.[15] The literature about occupational sex-typing guides our attempt at desanctification.

Occupational Gender Concentration

Since the resurgence of the women's movement in the late 1960s, social scientists have been trying to understand how the gender typing of an occupation changes. They do not yet have a satisfactory theory to explain this phenomenon (Reskin and Roos 1987), in part because most studies consider the transformation of jobs held mainly by men to jobs in which women are increasingly prevalent. By and large, these studies are ahistorical.[16] Studies, such as ours, which examine in historical detail the shift in occupational gender concentration from female to male are rare indeed.

Nonetheless, existing studies on the reverse shift of an occupation, from

15. This book belongs to a relatively new sociological approach termed "the production of culture perspective." It seeks to understand how social processes associated with art worlds, including both loosely organized and formal institutions, both limit and facilitate cultural endeavors. See Becker (1982) and Wolff (1981).

16. For example Epstein's work on women lawyers (1981) points to one mechanism of social change: civil rights legislation and litigation mandated law schools to accept women and elite firms to employ them. Epstein cannot, however, discuss the long-term trends in women's participation as attorneys because when she interviewed her informants they were so recently employed that most had yet to be considered for partnerships in their firms. To discuss how an occupation's gender-typing shifts, one must have quantitative and qualitative data spanning several decades. A dearth of historical data also afflicts sociological studies of female doctors (for example, Lorber 1984) and academicians (see Rossi and Calderwood 1973). To date, convincing historical discussions of accomplished transformations exist only for jobs that were once male but are now female—namely secretaries and elementary schoolteachers (see, for example, Davies 1983 and Tyack and Strober's preliminary analysis published in 1981).

male to female, provide a valuable insight. Using a variant of queuing theory,[17] such studies suggest that when more desirable jobs become available to them, men decamp from fields that they have virtually monopolized. Assessments of the value of jobs are determined by such factors as remuneration, autonomy, and the social meanings of the technologies associated with tasks. If a job is socially valued and correspondingly rewarded, men do it. If a craft becomes deskilled and thus devalued, men leave it. These studies lead us to expect that, if a relatively unvalued white-collar "woman's occupation" gains sufficient social and economic status, men will enter it and may even try to monopolize it.

Three occupations illustrate how men decamp when they no longer believe a job is desirable. Two of these positions, secretary and schoolteacher, are in white-collar jobs, and one, newspaper typesetter, is in a craft. Aspects of a fourth job, physician, reveal how men may come to assume tasks once performed by women.

Consider the transformation of the job of secretary in the United States. The historical connotations of the title give a notion of the power and prestige with which that job was once associated. Americans speak of the "secretary of state" and the "secretary of the treasury," not of the "foreign minister" and the "finance minister," as done in other nations. Until roughly 1890 most secretaries were white men drawn from the educated business classes. In her study of class transformation in New York State during the nineteenth century, Mary Ryan (1981) documents how the former mercantile elite put their family resources into training sons to enter into such jobs as clerk and secretary. But when American manufacturers introduced increasing supervision of industrialized workers around 1890 firms needed more middle managers. As described in Robert Lynd's and Helen Lynd's *Middletown* ([1929] 1956), they lured these managers from the social classes that had previously sent their sons into clerical and secretarial work. Thus, firms needed to locate a new and suitable pool of workers to perform clerical tasks.

At the turn of the twentieth century social understandings of the newly invented typewriter helped managers to define that labor pool. The typewriter contributed to the deskilling of secretarial work (Davies 1983). Once that machine had a standard keyboard to be tapped with standardized fingering, secretarial work became more routine and less remunerative. White Anglo-Saxon managers then hired white Anglo-Saxon women to be secretaries.

17. Queuing theory analyzes how ethnic groups enter a work force stratified by race, ethnicity, and class. It describes how they locate and sometimes create occupational niches. See Lieberson (1980).

Drawing on cultural notions of gender-appropriate behavior, managers demanded that the women behave in ways that had not been required of male secretaries. For instance, female secretaries were supposed to smile—to cast sunbeams around the office environment. Managers could make such demands because women who entered the occupation, unlike the former male incumbents, did not have something more powerful, more prestigious, and better paying to do.

A comparable process occurred in England between 1850 and 1914, as the percentage of women clerks increased from two to twenty (Zimmeck 1986). Men and women were not equally distributed throughout the clerical labor force. Rather, "clerical work was divided into two clear-cut spheres of activity for men and women. Although the boundaries between the two spheres moved from time to time, the separation between them remained constant and absolute" (ibid., 159). Men supposedly did clerical work that required a "wide-ranging, bold, and penetrating" intelligence; women "were only good for tying up the loose ends of execution" (ibid., 158). Working in offices where they were surrounded by other women, including female supervisors, women acquired new sorts of work that either did not have a tradition of male occupancy or that were "transferred (downgraded) to them from the male sphere" (ibid., 159).

The job of elementary teacher reveals that occupational gender segregation may shift without the introduction of new technologies. On the American frontier most schoolteachers were men (Tyack and Strober 1981), farmers who doubled as schoolteachers during their off-season. As compulsory elementary education and a longer school year became the norm in the United States, these men could no longer hold both jobs. Because farming paid better, the men decamped, leaving the less desirable job to women.

The nineteenth-century ideology about women's proper roles was also implicated in this change (Lerner 1969). According to the cult of domesticity, white women were supposed to civilize men and children. They were to be "mothers of civilization" (Ryan 1975). Thus, when such writers as Catharine Beecher urged white, middle-class, Protestant women to fulfill their mission by becoming schoolteachers on the western frontier, men welcomed them with open arms, so to speak (Sklar 1973). There was a shortage of women in the western towns.[18] In both these instances white middle-class women

18. The situation in nineteenth-century England was somewhat different. Women had been underpaid governesses. In midcentury their pay averaged £25 per year and ranged from £10 to £65 (Holcombe 1973, 14). As more elementary schools opened after the Education Act of 1870, women crowded into teaching.

took over jobs previously held by men because the men no longer wanted those jobs. Their departure created a void—an empty field—that women regarded as an arena of opportunity.

Although some occupations in the United States that are currently experiencing a shift from male to female, such as typesetting, are blue-collar rather than white-collar, the processes they are undergoing uphold these generalizations about the empty field. Women have been typesetters in both the United States (Kessler-Harris 1982) and Britain (Hunt 1986) since the nineteenth century. Despite women's often fierce attempts to join the emerging unions, men succeeded in keeping them out of their powerful unions and their workplaces. But in the 1970s and 1980s most newspapers shifted from linotype composition to computerized typesetting. In New York (Hochwald 1981) the powerful newspaper unions insisted that linotype operators who wished to be retrained to perform the less skilled and less autonomous job should be permitted to retain their previous high wage rates. The contract also provided incentives for men for retirement, so that "others" could enter the job at a lower rate. Those others were mainly women, whom the newspapers were encouraged to hire because of successful settlements of affirmative-action suits. Again the men decamped, leaving behind an empty field that had been devalued in their eyes. As Angela John (1986, 10) sums up the historical evidence, "The very real threat which workers have faced (and still face) in deskilling via technology and the lower status traditionally accorded to female labour have helped ensure that when work has become feminized it has been seen as losing status. Paternalistic employment practices have enhanced these processes."[19]

Finally, the converse possibility—men entering and monopolizing a field once dominated by women—also involves shifts in the social and economic rewards accruing to workers. All the familiar examples involve male physicians who used their professional power to monopolize what they claimed to be tasks requiring their technical expertise, although there is little reason to believe that their technology at the time was superior to that of the women they displaced. In Britain and the United States, midwifery is the classic example (Ehrenreich and English 1973; Rich 1976; Wertz and Wertz 1977).[20]

19. The occupation of bread baker also illustrates these principles (see Reskin and Roos 1987). Once a highly valued and organized craft, bread baking has been technologically transformed to an activity accomplished on the assembly line, a mode of work less esteemed than craft-activity. In individually owned and operated bakeries, bread bakers are predominantly men who do their jobs at night. On the assembly line, they are mostly women.

20. Male doctors pushed out midwives by claiming that childbirth required medical intervention. Male physicians drove women doctors out of obstetrics and gynecology by

These examples should not be taken to mean that women never practice "men's jobs" or men, "women's jobs." Some men are elementary schoolteachers and secretaries (though generally called administrative assistants). Some men use computers to set type at newspapers. A few women perform neurosurgery. One or two lady novelists—for example, Virginia Woolf— assumed important cultural positions after men had successfully invaded the high-culture novel.

These are the exceptions that prove the rule. As in the case of urban gentrification, when one group replaces another, some of the former occupants remain. Those who stay tend to share salient characteristics with the new group. Until recently, women's occupational alternatives were very limited, and so women from different fractions of the middle class entered many of the same occupations, including elementary schoolteaching and secretarial work. Today significant numbers of minority women from working-class backgrounds continue to experience both teaching and secretarial work as a personal advance. Men who become either secretaries or elementary schoolteachers often feel that their jobs represent upward mobility, for they too tend to come from backgrounds that provide few occupational alternatives. Similarly, when middle-class professionals gentrify a poor, nonwhite neighborhood, some members of racial or ethnic minorities remain or move in. They tend to hold lucrative white-collar jobs.

Virginia Woolf is comparable to the members of nonwhite minority groups who remain in gentrified neighborhoods. Although she was an unorthodox woman belonging to an unconventional social set, she, her family, and her friends were from elite backgrounds that both social and literary arbiters would find more than acceptable. Woolf's father, Leslie Stephen, was a major Victorian man of letters. Her husband, Leonard, was a journalist and political essayist. Her brother and other members of the Bloomsbury Group had attended Cambridge. But not all lady novelists of impeccable literary lineage become acclaimed high-culture novelists. And not all start their careers as members of what was to be seen as a significant set.[21]

---

defining obstetrics as a surgical specialty and so appropriate for men (Myra Strober, personal communication 1984). In the 1970s and 1980s many women reentered that field.

In the mid- and late nineteenth century, physicians removed issues involving abortion from lay debates about the morality of the procedure by converting it into a question of their expertise about medical indications (Luker 1985).

Finally, in the 1920s American physicians used their power with legislators to monopolize well-child care, a function previously served by women social workers allied with settlement houses (see Rothman 1978).

21. See Williams (1980) on the general issue of social set versus class fraction.

Another key to Woolf's exceptional status is that her literary vision did not challenge men's domination of the realistic novel. Rather, she "defied that central demand of serious bourgeois fiction—that it be realist" (Mary Evans, letter, 30 January 1987b). Plotless in the ordinary sense, some of Woolf's novels explore stream of consciousness, unfolded through interior monologues, and transform impressionistic moods developed through symbols and imagery into a coherent whole.

Gender and literary proclivities made Woolf seem doubly deviant and in that sense a "safe neighbor." Praise for Woolf did not connote acceptance of women as novelists. Through most of the twentieth century, Woolf reaped accolades not as a novelist but as a "woman novelist"— "the best woman novelist of our century," some said (for example, Blotner 1958, 1172; on the term "woman novelist," see Showalter 1984a). Like the middle-class women who turned to social work and social action, by abjuring literary realism Woolf located an empty field to call her own.

The Data and Plan of the Book

To understand in a historical context how men edged women out of the high-culture novel, we require information about the literary competition between an array of women and men. We need to know whether women and men were as likely to submit fiction manuscripts, to have their work accepted, and to receive recognition because the cultural elite deemed their books important—either very popular or critically well received.

Four unique sets of data enable us to discuss aspiring authors (who submitted manuscripts to a major London publisher, Macmillan), published authors (whose manuscripts Macmillan accepted), and posthumously acclaimed authors (listed in the *Dictionary of National Biography*).[22] These data also facilitate comparisons between novelists, nonfiction authors, and poets. Such comparisons illuminate the changing situation of novelists. To emphasize how authors of diverse literary forms faced disparate problems and oppor-

22. Because of its status in the nineteenth century and because its records are available, Macmillan provides an ideal case for examining how the empty field phenomenon applied to Victorian writers. The firm was so elite that analyzing its treatment of male and female novelists is theoretically akin to studying affirmative action at elite universities. Pacesetters for other American educational institutions, elite universities employ faculties whose professional standards frequently embody professional ideologies about merit. Elite universities lay bare the problems encountered by women who would enter their faculties, as well as the structural problems women face should they join those faculties. Issues of merit and ideology also permeate nineteenth-century literary milieus.

tunities, we will depart from literary convention and identify novels, poetry, and nonfiction as *genres*[23].

These data sets[24] include information about:

1. the editorial disposition of a sample of fiction and nonfiction submitted by women and men to Macmillan and Company (London) from 1867 through 1917;[25]
2. the publications of a sample of authors of rejected manuscripts, as listed in the *Catalogue to the British Museum (BMC)*;
3. the family background, education, friends, and careers of all women listed in the first twenty-three volumes of the *Dictionary of National Biography (DNB)* who published imaginative literature and were born between 1750 and 1865, as well as of a sample of comparable men; and
4. the publications of these authors, including translations of their books and treatments of their lives and work, as listed in the *BMC*.

These four sets of data make complementary inquiries possible because the Macmillan archives concern a sixty-year period at the end of the historical span in which the "*DNB* authors" lived. Analyses based on the Macmillan archives illustrate the processes of invasion, redefinition, and succession. They also demonstrate that these patterns were peculiar to the novel.

The Macmillan archives also contain reports about manuscripts prepared by editorial consultants (readers) for Macmillan. (The firm tended to hire as its readers noted literary critics and scholars. These were almost invariably men, for Victorians tended to denigrate women's critical abilities). These reports support the notion of a male invasion. As the high-culture novel emerged, Macmillan's readers first decried romance, then emphasized variant

---

23. Commonly, the term *genre* is used to refer to a type of novel, such as a mystery. Following Baym (1984b), we use the term to refer to a broader category of literature, such as the novel or poetry. We shall use her term "subgenre" to refer to kinds of novels, such as mysteries, historical novels, and gothic novels. On the problem of defining genres, see DiMaggio 1987.

24. Appendix A describes our sampling procedures. Because of the nature of our procedures and because tests of statistical significance are intended to enable generalization from a sample to a population, such tests are inappropriate for our data, and so we do not report them. Rather, we draw inferences from the direction of trends.

25. By and large, we found it unnecessary to check how we coded gender because the ledgers almost always use "Miss" or "Mrs." to identify women; they give initials as in "F. A. Smith" only when identifying men, as we learned by looking for some accepted and rejected authors in the *BMC*. As discussed in chapter 3 and appendix A, pseudonyms were not a problem.

types of realism, and finally found the mid-Victorian novel old-fashioned. The consultants applied a "critical double standard" (Showalter 1977), the contents of which differed in each of the three stages of the empty field phenomenon.

Information about the publishing careers of authors whose work Macmillan rejected permit us to make crude comparisons between the literary experience of women and men, novelists and nonfiction writers. We can ask whether the judgments of Macmillan's readers seem justified by an author's past and future publication record. We can learn, too, whether the women and men whose novels were rejected received contracts from less prestigious houses.

Analyses based on the *DNB* and *BMC* affirm the operation of the empty field phenomenon. Using these data, we ask whether and how, *relative to women*, men gained from the centralization of the publishing industry in London. We examine the lives and careers of four groups of authors, defined by gender and year of birth. These are early women and early men (those born between 1750 and 1814 and who mainly began publishing before 1840) and late women and late men (those born between 1815 and 1865 and who mainly began publishing during or after the 1840s). Our benchmark for salient changes in both the Victorian novel and the publishing system with which it was associated is 1840. After 1840 men, compared to women, increasingly exercised literary authority. Additionally, after 1840, being a novelist contributed more to the fame of men than to the fame of women. Indeed, being a novelist hampered recognition of the accomplishments of women authors, for the *DNB* favored women who wrote nonfiction, not novels.

Using Macmillan's records and correspondence, including contracts with novelists and records of print runs, we argue that gender also affected novelists' earnings. By the 1880s Macmillan paid men more than women—even for novels that sold as well and, within the confines of the critical double standard, were as well received. Concentrating on novels by authors in both the Macmillan and *DNB* samples, we analyzed reviews in the *Athenaeum* and the *Edinburgh Review*. In each stage of the process of invasion and succession, the contents of the critical double standard shifted.

Although our data about the literary opportunities of most women novelists are substantial, our conclusions are based on inferences. For, as we have noted, since the turn of the twentieth century critics have praised a few "exceptional" women as high-culture novelists.

We start by establishing that the eighteenth- and nineteenth-century literary terrain encouraged the empty field phenomenon. We ask, What was women's participation in literature when the novel was a lowly genre, paid authors an ignoble lot, and publishing a despised trade? In chapter 2 we discuss salient characteristics of the pre-Victorian publishing industry and firms' relationships with their authors. Often scurrilous, eighteenth-century publishers took for granted procedures that would thrust twentieth-century publishers into costly litigation. Authors, we argue, have never been professionals. Historically, they have had few rights and even less autonomy.

Mid-nineteenth-century publishers profited from novels by depending upon a distribution system that they could not control. They issued novels in small hardback editions and profited by selling fewer than half of the copies to Mudie's Select Library. Rather than seek the massive profits of a runaway best-seller, firms sought to accumulate modest returns by publishing many novels attractive to Mudie's. Thus, many Victorian houses accepted manuscripts by relatively mediocre novelists.

This system prevented authors from developing autonomy. As long as many aspiring authors queued to supplant weak but published novelists, all but the most eminent (and profitable) fiction writers were at the mercy of publishers. In chapter 2 we also define Macmillan and Company's place within this system.

In chapter 3 we consider the special problems confronting women novelists. Scholars affirm that the novel has historically been associated with women and even that at one time a majority of novelists were women. But affirmation is not proof, and literary histories portray an ephemeral victim: the apparitions of the lady novelists loom before us and fade from view, only to rise again.

And so in chapter 3 we turn to a mode of argument that permeates the rest of our book—inference based on original data. Analyzing the submissions of fiction and nonfiction to Macmillan and Company between 1866 and 1917, we surmise that in the mid-nineteenth century most aspiring novelists were women. The data also permit inferences about when that situation changed.

To write a novel is one thing, to have it accepted for publication another. In chapter 4 we draw inferences about the empty field phenomenon by analyzing the fate of fiction manuscripts submitted to Macmillan. How were they reviewed? Did the Macmillans and their editorial consultants have the same expectations of male and female authors? Did they favor men? Were the readers' recommendations justified? We use statistical analysis to address some of these questions. To answer others, we interpret manuscript reports submitted by Macmillan's editorial consultants.

But whether based on statistics or on archival documents, facts in and of themselves are meaningless. We therefore delve again into the nature of nineteenth-century publishing. What did it mean for a house to aspire to leadership within its industry? Why, after 1880, did Macmillan shun the work of women novelists, even though women's novels sold well? How did the Macmillans and their editorial consultants inject the Macmillans' vision of the firm into nineteenth-century debates about the high-culture and the popular-culture novel? Our answers to these questions permit inferences that men were invading the high-culture novel.

Like all generalizations, ours need reexamination. In chapter 5 we review salient characteristics of our second major source of data, the *DNB*. Then we ask about the books and lives of the four groups of authors we have delineated: early women (born between 1750 and 1814), late women (born between 1815 and 1865), early men, and late men. After the centralization of publishing in London, were male authors more likely than women to move there? Through family contacts and school ties, could these men take advantage of the increased literary opportunities? We infer that women in London lacked school ties and were less able than men to convert family contacts into literary opportunities. But were men more likely than women to convert their influential positions into ascendance over the novel?

In chapter 6 we ask how men's literary authority may have contributed to the empty field phenomenon. We interpret our data about authors' publications to imply that men of letters increasingly stressed the virtues of the realistic novel. Men began to identify being a novelist with cultural accomplishment. A listing in the *DNB* indicated cultural recognition: more late than early authors wrote novels. Additionally, we infer from multivariate statistical analyses that late men could more readily transform their accomplishments, especially the publication of novels, into social recognition than could late women.

Posthumous recognition, such as is conferred by inclusion in the *DNB*, may indicate an author's status during his or her life, but it usually reveals little about an author's earnings.[26] Historically, men have earned more than women of equal status for work of equivalent or similar quality. Did male novelists earn more than their female peers? Some literary historians have claimed that women earned less (for example, Tanzy 1961), but they were not comparing authors whom the Victorians felt to be of equivalent quality. We do not know of any systematic data concerning the contracts for novels received by the women and men listed in the *DNB*. Again we must make inferences.

---

26. See Jane Tompkins (1985) on the fame, reception, and earnings of nineteenth-century American novelists.

To explore the relationship between the empty field phenomenon and novelists' pay, we examine in chapter 7 Macmillan's contracts with novelists in the latter half of the nineteenth century. We show that from one stage of the empty field phenomenon to the next Macmillan altered the terms of the contracts customarily offered. These contracts supposedly contained standard provisions. Yet, comparing the contracts, reviews, and print runs of two popular novelists, F. Marion Crawford and Margaret Oliphant, we infer that between 1870 and 1905 male novelists received better contracts than women of roughly comparable ability and popularity.

Why did women receive less favorable contracts? One obvious possibility is that either publishers, critics, or readers valued their work less than that of men. Showalter's (1977) discussion of mid-nineteenth-century reviews in leading literary periodicals supports this contention. Examining reviews of selected authors in two very different leading Victorian periodicals, the *Athenaeum* and the *Edinburgh Review*, we argue in chapter 8 that after 1880 critics continued to apply a critical double standard. But the contents of that standard had shifted. The standard expressed a salient assumption of the empty field phenomenon: Novels by men embodied the features that critics now valued.

In chapter 9 we ask, What do all these inferences mean? How are they relevant to an understanding of nineteenth-century literature? What do they teach us about shifting occupational gender concentration? Our study may illuminate some connections between literature and the material conditions confronting all authors, may resolve some contradictions in feminist literary criticism, and may provide a new yardstick with which to gauge the transformation of white-collar occupations.

2
Writers
and the Victorian
Publishing System

o grasp the opportunities and obstacles that women novelists confronted, one must understand the position of all Victorian authors, especially their dependence on publishers. Then as now, authors needed to locate a publishing house willing to invest its capital to transform their manuscripts into books.[1] Especially when not well established, an author may be financially at the publisher's mercy, for publishers do not issue books for the sheer pleasure of doing so.

Book publishing is a culture industry. By this we mean that publishers and those with whom they are associated—writers, printers, and, in the nineteenth century, circulating libraries—deal in books to make money. To earn profits, they produce books that they expect will appeal to contemporary readers and perhaps to posterity as well. Even when a publisher invests in a book that he suspects will have a limited *immediate* audience, he probably has some kind of future profit in mind.[2] He may believe that the book will take off in the near future and yield a profit then. He may feel that the talented author's next book will be profitable and hope that the author will stay with the publisher who previously expressed faith in his or her abilities. Or he may suppose that even if the book brings no immediate profit and limited future profit it will somehow credit his list—his catalogue of wares—and so

1. Through the early decades of the nineteenth century, authors might publish by subscription, with as many as one hundred family members, friends, or strangers providing the funds necessary to set type, print the text, and bind the pages between covers. A rare author might pay what we today call a vanity press to issue a book.

2. Since publishers have historically been men and men continue to dominate the industry (Coser, Kadushin, and Powell 1982), we shall refer to them as men.

benefit the firm by enhancing its prestige and attracting other, potentially successful authors.

This interpretation of publishing as a business is explicit in the writings of Pierre Bourdieu (1984). He explains that the publishing industry is stratified by "culture-type." That is, some firms specialize in avant-garde books directed to a limited immediate audience of educated, upper-middle-class readers who possess a fair amount of cultural capital (familiarity with the great literature of the past). These firms expect to make a profit in the future, when the books on their backlists become classics. Other firms search for the immediate profit of best-sellers, appealing to the middle class. These books may flood the bookstores for three to six months and then disappear from the shelves. Still other firms, notably the American and Canadian companies issuing the ro-mances sold in North American drugstores, airports, and dime stores, have taken the search for immediate profit to an extreme.[3] They market their wares as if they were detergent or toothpaste. Emphasizing their "name brand," they issue new titles monthly, rapidly retiring the older ones (Radway 1984).

Lewis Coser, Charles Kadushin, and Walter Powell (1982) had this series of options in mind when they spoke of the distinction between production-oriented publishers and consumer-oriented publishers. This distinction cap-tures not only aspects of the market for books but also of class structure. Roughly speaking, production-oriented publishers seek to deal in high cul-ture—"aesthetically legitimate" work that may bring profit in the long run, to paraphrase Bourdieu (1980)—for class fractions with a high investment in cultural capital. Consumer-oriented publishers care more about short-run profit, mass appeal, and mass culture. They aim to appeal to class fractions that seek entertainment, not enlightenment, in novels. Necessarily, consumer-oriented publishers need a harmonious relationship with the distribution system that brings their books to readers. Today, for example, the sales forces of textbook publishers court faculty who teach large introductory courses in the hope that these professors will assign their texts as required reading (Coser, Kadushin, and Powell 1982). To quash the market for used books, whose sales bring no profit to the original publishers, these firms bring out new editions of texts every few years.

In mid-nineteenth-century Britain, the distinction between consumer-oriented and producer-oriented publishers was not as marked as, say, the

---

3. Such books currently comprise 28 percent of all the paperback books sold in Canada and 10–12 percent of all the paperbacks sold in the United States (Jensen 1984).

contemporary American distinction between Lyle Stuart and Farrar, Straus and Giroux or between Harlequin and Vintage paperbacks. Indeed, publishers did not assume that a popular book was unworthy of critical praise. Conversely, they believed that some critically esteemed novels could gain large audiences.

To be sure, the publishing industry was stratified. Such publishers of literary novels as the seven houses largely responsible for the works still read today were distinct from those that brought out penny-installment fiction. Those bringing out literary works were further stratified. Although both firms published Charles Dickens (1812–1870), the bookseller-publisher Chapman and Hall might have claimed superiority over the printer-publisher Bradbury and Evans. Because printer-publishers were more common in the eighteenth than the nineteenth century, bookseller-publishers felt themselves more modern and hence superior. Because of the "quality" of the books it published, Bentley claimed to be and was considered a better house than Tinsley or Newby, although Tinsley published Thomas Hardy's first novel and Newby, Anthony Trollope's. But even at the top of the heap, the seven "best" houses— Bentley, Blackwood, Bradbury and Evans, Chapman and Hall, Longmans, Macmillan, and Smith, Elder—merged consumer and production orientations, as most houses do today. They sought both to make an immediate profit and to claim some distinction for the books and authors on their list.

In their public self-presentation, the emphasis that these seven firms placed on distinction was such as to make one think that publishing concerned simply art. Official house biographies listed the house's famous writers and splendid books so that future readers would appreciate the firm's contribution to literature. Now and then a literary historian departs from the formulaic emphasis on quality and issues a reminder that publishing is a business and that in the nineteenth century writing was called a profession. Writing about the relationships between Bentley and other literary institutions of the Victorian age, Royal Gettmann (1960) examines the firm's financial records to see what pieces had to fall into place for that company to make a profit. But like others willing to recognize that publishers need to make money if they are to continue to publish he writes of publishing as half-business and half-art, as if business and art made competing claims on publishers. Literary critics and historians seem to avoid a view of publishing as a culture industry, as though to recognize it as such would denigrate its products.

The attitudes of the house biographers must capture how the leaders of the elite firms wished to see themselves. Charles Morgan's (1943) book about Macmillan and Company, Arthur Waugh's (1930) treatment of Chapman and Hall, and Margaret Oliphant's (1897) book on Blackwood are, after all, commissioned biographies. Their emphasis on famous books and authors underscores the odiousness of making a profit on literature, an important part of that elite enterprise termed the cultural heritage. Echoing the attitude dominant at the middle of the eighteenth century, these biographies seem to say that gentlemen are not supposed to make money, especially not by contributing to the general (cultural) welfare.

One can appreciate how much that attitude is itself a historical tradition by considering the class origins of the major Victorian publishers. Such publishers as Daniel and Alexander Macmillan, described by Charles Morgan as Scottish peasants, started their firm after working in a bookstore. Others, such as Richard Bentley, were apprenticed to the trade. Still others, such as the founders of Bradbury and Evans, were originally printers. To be sure, these were middle-class and upper-middle-class trades, but their practitioners were not gentlemen. In the nineteenth century, gentlemen did not establish publishing houses.

That gentlemen were supposed neither to write nor to publish for a profit is not surprising. The eighteenth-century book trade was a barter industry that had once been associated with the stationers' guild. Booksellers frequently commissioned volumes, particularly novels, and paid by the word. Many treated writers so badly that near the turn of the nineteenth century Charles Lamb spoke of booksellers as "Turks and Tartars when they have poor authors at their beck and call" (quoted in Collins 1928, 11). Because of the practice of commissioning works and frequently paying by the word, writers—even some novelists now called great—were spoken of as "hacks." The term is reminiscent of hackney carriages hired for a short journey by people who might not own a carriage or choose not to use their carriages. Also, to be paid by the word was to engage in "piece work," as in the sweatshops of London's East End clothing industry.

Literary histories abound in stories of how ladies and gentlemen sought to avoid the opprobrium of having their names on their poems or novels. They did not want it known that they had written for money. One familiar example is related by Frank Arthur Mumby (1974): In 1751 Thomas Gray wrote to Horace Walpole that he had learned from "certain gentlemen" who had recently taken over a magazine that they were going to print his "Elegy Written in a Country Churchyard." To avert the shame of being paid for his work, Gray dispatched Walpole to see the bookseller Dodsley, who had previously issued anonymously Gray's "An Ode on a Distant Prospect of Eton College." Dodsley immediately issued the "Elegy" as a pamphlet of anonymous authorship. According to Edmund Gosse's biography of Gray, "The success of the poem brought [Gray] little direct satisfaction, and no money. He gave the right of publication to Dodsley, as he did in all other instances. He held a [Q]uixotic notion that it was beneath a gentleman to take money for his inventions from a bookseller, a view in which Dodsley naturally coincided" (quoted in Mumby 1974, 157).

By referring to Gray's action as quixotic, Gosse suggests that it was idiosyncratic and ran counter to the practice of his day—receiving money for work. Indeed, several years later in June 1757 Gray accepted forty guineas from Dodsley for the copyright to two poems. But the story does tell us that gentlemen were expected to avoid an association with trade. Publishers were tradesmen.

That moral is also easily drawn from the class boundaries that separated gentlemen from professionals, even in the countryside, where the social classes were more likely to mix than they were in the cities (Davidoff, 1973).[4] Socially, paid authors and bookseller-publishers were akin to others who worked for their livelihood. The most noted writers might be included in the large dinner parties of polite society, but by and large gentlemen did not mingle socially with those who wrote for money, as Thackeray affirmed in *Vanity Fair* (1847– 1848) and George Gissing echoed decades later in *The New Grub Street* (1891). (The condemnation of women who wrote for money was greater still.)

For now, let us simply note that by emphasizing their contribution to the cultural heritage and detracting attention from their profits the major Victorian publishers claimed to be gentlemen. They were expressing their aspirations for upward social mobility, a hope fulfilled by some of their descendants, such as Lord Harold Macmillan, first Earl of Stockton.[5]

Publishers' Profit in Literature

For most of the nineteenth century, literature was profitable, although then as now publishing was not an easy way to make money. It was affected by social unrest, responses to revolutions in other countries, wars, and depressions. When banks failed during the depression of the late 1820s, many publishing houses failed too. Like other manufacturers, publishers operated on a credit system. When other tradesmen and manufacturers could not quickly determine which firms should receive credit, solvent houses found their credit frozen.

4. Jane Austen's *Pride and Prejudice* illustrates the class antagonisms among the gentry at the turn of the century. In order to marry the aristocrat Darcy, Elizabeth Bennett must overcome her class background: her father is a gentleman, but her maternal uncle is in trade. On gender and class in Austen's work, see Evans (1987a).

5. These aspirations were also played out in the Bentley family. In the 1890s Richard Bentley's son sold the family firm to Macmillan so that he could become a gentleman-farmer.

The industry remained in the doldrums as England underwent the political, economic, and social turmoil that forced the Reform Bill of 1832. William Blackwood wrote in 1831, "There never has been so slack a year in our trade ever since I have been in the business" (quoted in Gettmann 1960, 10). In November of that year, the *Athenaeum* reported that "six hundred London printers were jobless because publishers were holding back on long promised books" (ibid.).

Historians also say that in the 1820s trade in the book business suffered because the nature of literature was changing; no great novelist was emerging to become a cultural hero comparable to Sir Walter Scott, whose first novel, *Waverley*, had appeared in 1814. Following the practice initiated with the publication of Scott's *Kenilworth* in 1821, the selling price of a three-volume hardback novel was high, 30s. (It was to become 30s. 6d. for most of the century.) "Books are a luxury," a printer had told a committee of the House of Commons in 1818 (quoted in Altick 1957, 260). The price of a novel made its purchase comparable to buying a television set in the 1960s (Showalter, telephone conversation with Tuchman, 1980).

The price of the novel had been high since its inception in the mid-eighteenth century. Altick translates that price into the value of wages and commodities in the 1770s:

> If a man in the lower bracket of the white neck-cloth class—an usher at a school, for instance, or a merchant's clerk—had a taste for owning books, he would have had to choose between buying a newly published quarto volume and a good pair of breeches (each cost from 10s to 12s), or between a volume of essays and a month's supply of tea and sugar for his family of six (2s 6d). If a man bought a shilling pamphlet he sacrificed a month's supply of candles. A woman in one of the London trades . . . could have bought a three-volume novel in paper covers only with the proceeds of a week's work. (1957, 51–52)[6]

Given the cost of novels in both the 1770s and the nineteenth century, when the cost of these hardcover volumes initially rose relative to wages, it is not surprising that the first edition of a novel generally ran between five hundred and a thousand copies. Scott's *Waverley* was one of the few British novels to be printed in large editions.

The price of novels did not prevent people from reading them, thanks to circulating libraries, the first one founded in the 1740s in the corner of a London bookstore. These libraries specialized in making novels available to

6. Note that Altick (1957) sex-typed literary interests. He supposes that men read essays and women, novels.

subscribers for a fee. The fee varied over time, but by 1840 it had risen to as much as two guineas. The libraries were sufficiently important that the founders of the *Athenaeum* in 1828 supposed that the roughly fifty thousand members of the "accessible reading public" rarely purchased fiction but rather obtained novels through circulating libraries (Sutherland 1976, 12).

Circulating libraries were synonymous with novels, as were some of the publishing houses with whom they did business. Because they carried only novels, the libraries as well as the publishing houses that fed them were disparaged by the male literary elite. An apt example is William Lane's Minerva Press, which from 1790 until its failure in 1820 issued mainly romances written by women and designed for women readers.[7] By the time of its failure, the phrase "Minerva Press" had become a term of condemnation among literary circles. That condemnation encompassed novel readers. Indeed, literati who despised the run-of-the-mill novel and sneered at the Minerva Press identified novel reading with women and servants.[8] They were not sneering at the profit; rather, they were expressing disdain based on class and gender. Much as future literati were successively to condemn comics, then movies, then television, and finally video arcades, they blamed novel reading for social ills. Some of the literary elite discussed the novel reader as a lady reclining on a chaise lounge in her boudoir. Some feared that the common worker who learned to read would read novels and would no longer be satisfied with his station in life.[9]

The articulation between the libraries and the publishers helped to maintain the price of both library subscriptions and novels. Readers who could not afford to buy novels would have to pay a library-subscription fee to read them. Circulating libraries could encourage or discourage subscribers by the size of their fees. These were set low enough to permit a subscriber to read more books in a year than would be possible if she or he purchased

7. Lane even established his own circulating libraries, which naturally enough purchased the novels he published.

8. Ian Watt (1957) draws upon this identification to explain the rise of the novel; but Richard Altick (1957, 62) suggests, "If we are to believe the constant burden of contemporary satire, domestic servants attended [circulating libraries] in great numbers on their own account; not merely to exchange books for their mistresses; but it is possible that they were singled out for blame because the effects of novel-reading were most irritating when errands went unfulfilled, a roast burned on the spit, or an imperiously pulled bell rope went unanswered." We know from such novels as Jane Austen's *Northanger Abbey* that, drawing careful distinctions about quality, gentlemen also read fiction.

9. Lowenthal (1961) reviews the mid-eighteenth-century controversy about literacy. Some essayists clearly believed that increased literacy would benefit both individuals and society.

books but high enough for circulating libraries to turn a neat profit. Publishers profited too, counting on reliable sales to libraries rather than small sales to bookstores or chancy retail sales to readers.[10]

By the mid-nineteenth century, one circulating library—Charles Edward Mudie's Select Library, founded in 1842—held sway over the publication of novels and so over publishers' profits. Mudie's subscription fees were lower than those of other libraries. Charles Mudie carefully distinguished his library from its competitors by stressing how select his choices were; he emphasized that he purchased more than novels. Indeed, Guinivere Griest (1970) estimates that only one-third of Mudie's purchases were novels. Yet, at one point, Mudie was buying as many as 120,000 copies of novels a year, which made him the largest purchaser of novels in the world. His patronage was crucial in an era when of every five novels published one was a financial failure, three broke even, and only one was a financial success (Gettmann 1960); it made publishing novels in the Victorian era less financially risky than it is today.

In the mid-nineteenth century, the economics of novel publishing diverged from the earlier system. Rather than commission works as was done in the eighteenth century or share the net profits with the author as was done by less prestigious houses, the leading publishers either leased the author's copyright for a limited time—say a year—or purchased the copyright to a specific edition.[11] But British publishers continued to issue expensive books in limited editions of five hundred to a thousand copies for both the libraries and the relatively few well-to-do readers who had the means and the taste to buy them. To break even on a first edition, a publisher might have to sell only half the available stock—if he had bought the copyright for that edition at less than £ 350. Charles Mudie supposedly purchased books that suited his taste; at mid-century his taste was that of a religious fundamentalist and a patriarchal Victorian. If he thought a novel would be popular, he bought

10. To some extent, the increase in literacy after the Reform Bill of 1832 fed this system. As is usually the case, in England literacy increased relatively slowly—generation by generation. After 1832 literacy increased among members of social classes who could not hope to buy newly issued books but could hope to subscribe.

11. Today if a book is reprinted and its contents are the same as those of the previous printing, one says that it has gone through several printings. If a publisher issues a version of the book revised by its author, the publisher is said to issue a second edition. In the nineteenth century, the term *edition* was very often used to mean an additional printing of a unrevised edition. For instance, Sutherland (1976; 38) writes that Dickens' *Great Expectations* went "through five editions in a year." Then, as now, even when the contents of a printing were identical, publishers distinguished between hardcover and paperbound editions.

Table 2.1: Financial Breakdown of *The Three Clerks*, First Year

	Debits				Profits		
	£	*s.*	*d.*		£	*s.*	*d.*
1000 Printed	130	5	6	38 presented			
Paper	91	0	6	500 Mudie	288	0	0
750 Bound	47	10	3	210 sold	227	8	9
A. Trollope							
(payment in full)	250	0	0	119 sold	115	12	6
Advertising	63	7	8	23 sold	24	19	
				890			

Source: Sutherland 1976, 14.

over half of the initial edition for the many branches of his library. Indeed, the assumption that every three-volume hardback set was destined for Mudie's was so strong that it was termed the "library edition." Even at the preferential financial terms it received, Mudie's Select Library frequently meant the difference between profit and deficit on a book.

In table 2.1 we show the importance of Mudie's purchase to the profits of Anthony Trollope's *The Three Clerks*, which Bentley brought out in an initial edition of one thousand in 1857. Note that if Mudie's had not purchased five hundred copies the novel would have failed financially. Profit on that first year was £ 74 9s. 7d. "Of the 123 left on hand 97 were sold off at cut price the next year, yielding £ 32 16s. 7d. for the publisher" (Sutherland 1976, 14).

By today's standards, that £ 100 profit on an investment of under £ 600—roughly 17 percent[12]—is slight, but the expensive "three-decker" still presented less commercial risk than trying to sell "5000 copies at half a crown or 50,000 at a shilling" (ibid., 15).

Presumably that less predictable path would also require the publisher to spend more on advertising than the 11 percent of costs (£ 63 7s. 8d.) that Bentley invested in *The Three Clerks*. Mudie also advertised the books he had in stock, thus decreasing the publishers' need to do so. This articulation between the production and distribution of novels—including promotion by Mudie's—was so advantageous to publishers that in 1856 Blackwood covered his costs on "an obscure and unsuccessful novel of the period, *Zaidee* by Mrs.

12. Gettmann (1960) and Sutherland (1976) arrive at close but not identical estimates of this book's monetary profit.

Oliphant," even though at the end of the year he had sold only one-third of the initial edition of 1,578 copies (ibid., 16).

To appreciate how Victorian publishers' dependence upon circulating libraries encouraged conservative practices, consider the problems of present-day American publishers of fiction. The ex-chairman of the board of a major production-oriented American publisher describes the present system as a "lottery" (telephone interview, April 1987).[13] To be sure, he notes, the large American chains Waldenbooks and B. Dalton may together buy up to 60 percent of the print run of a novel. But their favor does not guarantee the economic success of even a so-called blockbuster, the prized novel of a well-established and popular author. Other costs, especially those connected with promoting a novel, have risen dramatically. The authors of these prized novels command very large advances—although some late Victorians received extraordinarily high sums, too, sometimes as much as £ 1,000 (roughly $4,600). For blockblusters and even for other novels, the sale of subsidiary rights, especially to movies and television, spells the difference between economic success and failure.

Less likely to attract the sale of subsidiary rights, the ordinary novel, particularly a first novel, may be even riskier than the blockbuster. According to this ex-chairman of the board, the minimum run on a contemporary American novel is 5,000 copies. To break even, 3,000 must be sold. Large bookstore chains are not interested in purchasing a "small book," although they are more inclined to do so when a publishing house promotes it extensively—"greases the wheels," as the ex-chairman put it. Such promotion involves not only advertising but wide distribution of review copies—well beyond the 4 percent of the print run of Trollope's *The Three Clerks* (38 of 1,000 copies) that Bentley had "presented" to reviewers. The chains are also more likely to carry a book if a publisher's sales representatives can convince the buyers that his or her past recommendations have been correct. Then, the ex-chairman emphasizes, the chains might buy 1,300 copies of which they sell 943 copies and return 357. The publishing house, which must absorb shipping costs for returns as well as the cost of unsold books, takes a loss. As publishing lore credits Alfred Knopf with saying, publishing is the only business in which the merchandise is "gone today and here tomorrow."

The occasional exceptions receive so much publicity that aspiring authors

---

13. Executives of other contemporary culture-industries, such as television and records, also speak of their inability to predict which particular item will make a profit. (See Hirsch 1978; Gitlin 1983.)

might fantasize that they too can achieve fame, glory, and financial security.[14] This informant again stressed the possibility of earning more through the licensing of subsidiary rights than through the sale of a book. This year his firm did so on a first novel and thus enjoyed a significant profit. But no one at his house can determine why this first novel caught on whereas others for which they had also waged extensive promotional campaigns did not. A publisher, he stressed, must hope that an author stays with the firm and establishes a significant following by the time it issues that author's third novel. However, most publishers would drop an author whose second novel did not produce a return on their investment. Victorian publishers enjoyed a more reliable yield on their capital.

The failure of Victorian publishers to challenge their dependence on Mudie's Select Library involved more than conservative business practices. Marketing larger quantities of books at a lower initial price was unappealing in terms of class. A publisher might feel that to sell that many copies he had to select manuscripts of potential interest to less elite readers—to reach the "lowest common denominator."[15] To a British publisher who identified with the educated elite, pandering to mass tastes would be denying his own class position. As defined by the elite, mass tastes included penny fiction, especially thrillers, and some works of religious fundamentalism.[16] Publishers who took this route were criticized by their peers. For instance, Bentley was criticized for "puffery" of his firm's novels in order to build a large readership of mainly women. Their gender disqualified women for membership in the educated elite (Gettmann 1960).

Griest (1970) stresses that Mudie's did not invent circulating libraries and was responsible for neither the pricing system nor the practice of initially issuing the novels in a small three-volume library edition. Rather, Charles

14. The *New York Times Magazine* (Shear 1987) devoted an article to lawyer Scott Turow's first novel, *Presumed Innocent*, which Farrar, Straus and Giroux purchased for an advance of $200,000. They printed 135,000 copies; bids for the paperback rights started at $670,000. Farrar, Straus and Giroux also printed 5,000 paperbound reviewers' copies, roughly 4 percent of the hardbound first edition, and comparable to the number of reviewers' copies of Trollope's *The Three Clerks* that Bentley's had distributed.

15. "Lowest common denominator" is the term used to describe the predominantly blue-collar television audience, but it is also pertinent to American book publishing. Critics of the contemporary American industry charge that publishing houses select novels with such chains as Waldenbooks and B. Dalton in mind. As would have held in Victorian times, marketing to chains affects reader's selections. They cannot buy novels that their local (chain) bookstore does not stock.

16. Thus, in *Culture and Anarchy* 1960 [1869] critic Matthew Arnold was to condemn both the barbarians (who preferred thrillers) and the religiously moralistic philistines.

Mudie took advantage of a system that existed and did his best to make sure it would be maintained. So that he might sell used copies of that first library edition to avid readers at prices determined by the book's popularity with subscribers, he pressed publishers to withhold larger and cheaper editions of successful novels until at least a year after their initial appearance. He also urged them to issue novels in three volumes rather than one or even two so that he might simultaneously circulate one novel to three families.[17]

Mudie's Select Library also owed some of its success to the rising literary status of the novel after 1840, the beginning of the age of the novel, according to such literary historians as Kathleen Tillotson (1962). By midcentury, marketing strategy and literary ideology were becoming fused. By the time Mudie's institution opened its doors in 1842, the novel was well on its way to dominance, supported by the literary ideology of realism and specificity. In the sense of a "conscious commitment to understanding and describing . . . the movement of psychological, social or physical forces" (Williams 1976, 219), realism was particularly appealing to the bourgeoisie. As Tillotson (1962, 13) notes, a contemporary critic spoke of the novel as "the vital offspring of modern wants and tendencies." Satirists no longer portrayed the typical reader as a chocolate-eating lady reclining on a chaise lounge in her boudoir. By then novels were commonly read *en famille*, the father intoning them to his assembled wife and children, much as earlier Puritan patriarchs had read the Bible to assembled family and servants after dinner. Or mother and children might read and discuss novels together, as is captured in Charlotte Yonge's *Heir of Redclyffe*. To the dismay of the emerging high-culture novelists, by midcentury the genre was to conform to a Victorian father's notion of what his sixteen-year-old daughter should be allowed to read and hear. Those standards, too, resonated with Charles Edward Mudie's sensibilities.

Finally, technological improvements in the printing press and in the manufacture of paper had made it cheaper to make books. The English publishing industry had started the century at least twenty years behind other English industries in technical developments. By midcentury, it was no longer outmoded.

By midcentury the components of what historians now speak of as the Victorian publishing system were in place. They had developed through a series of homologies; that is, they had descended independently from earlier social formations (Williams 1977; cf. Bourdieu 1980). Industrialism, increased

17. Mudie's Library also had another important impact. Sutherland (1976) gives particularly valuable evidence that publishers ordered novelists, even the acclaimed George Eliot, to rewrite their manuscripts to satisfy Mudie's preferences (cf. Griest 1970).

social mobility, new publishers, new technologies, and revamped distribution systems all arose at the same time and for some of the same reasons, but they did not cause one another. The publishing system had not caused the rise in literacy, which was created by the social mobility of an industrializing society. It had not introduced such periodicals as the *Athenaeum*, which assiduously reviewed newly issued books. It did not introduce the new technologies that facilitated the growth of publishing houses, which now issued books independently rather than in concert, as they had once done to minimize the economic risk. It did not give Charles Edward Mudie the idea for a select library different in kind from the despised but still extant circulating libraries that operated much as their eighteenth-century predecessors had done. It could not account for Mudie's tastes, which were themselves class-based and shaped by the concerns of developing industrial England.

Profit and the Professionalization of Writers

The publishing system we have described had literary consequences. First, it encouraged the growth of the novel; firms specializing in fiction actively sought novels to buy. Seeing more novels issued, more aspiring authors were encouraged to try their hand at this developing genre. Much like many of today's teenagers who against all odds hope to become rock stars and so form rock groups that practice in homes and garages, each of these aspiring novelists may have dreamed of fame and economic success. By midcentury, novels replaced religious works as the largest category of book issued. Second, the more novels published, the greater the likelihood that some would be memorable, as a large pool of authors—like a large pool of musicians—constitutes a critical mass that will necessarily contain some people of great talent and skill. Third, because there was a large pool of authors, most novelists were potentially replaceable (Becker 1982). This possibility of replacing published authors with aspirants meant that for much of the nineteenth century *most* novelists could not dare to challenge the terms of contracts that publishers had established.[18] Put somewhat differently, nineteenth-century novelists

18. Both publishers' inability to predict sales of most novels and their ability to replace an average author on their list with any one of many aspiring authors continue to have economic consequences for authors, especially when production costs are high. For instance, Lewis and Maude (1953) claim that in the 1940s the cost of book production escalated in England. Authors were urged to accept cuts in their royalties, and many did so. Nonetheless, publishers instituted additional practices to increase the probability of a profit, such as backing "the minority of best-selling authors even more fully, leaving the average author to abandon his [sic] profession or turn

could not achieve the criteria that sociologists identify with professionalism. Most of them were at the mercy of publishers.

Sociologists specify that members of a profession collectively and frequently individually control key aspects of their work by defining:

1. what their work is—and what it is not;
2. how the work is to be done—that is, setting professional standards;
3. who will do the work—controlling access to the profession and expulsion from it; and
4. how much they will be paid—that is, establishing an economic monopoly that does not appear to be economic (a common example is how doctors invoke their training to justify their fees).[19]

Looking back to the nineteenth century, sociologists speak of three classic professions: medicine, law, and the clergy. In each group members controlled their collective fate and were able to force the state to recognize their claimed license, even as they sought to extend their mandate.

People who are not sociologists speak of professions and professionals quite differently. Not only do members of unlicensed occupations, whose work is directed by others, speak of themselves as professionals, but also the term *professional* has become synonymous with competence. Someone might praise a plumber or secretary by saying that he or she did a "really professional job." Today so many occupations are claiming professional status, among them such semiprofessions as nursing, teaching, and librarianship, that sociologists now recognize professionalism as an ideology and speak of the "professionalization of everyone" (Wilensky 1964).[20]

Today's authors are among those who like to speak of themselves as professionals. Although some contemporary writers influence the careers of other authors, contemporary writers do not control entry to or expulsion from their profession. Thus, they do not meet even a watered-down definition of professionalism. Sometimes, though, twentieth-century authors retrospec-

---

from craftsmanship to cheap-jackery" (Lewis and Maude 1953, 158).

In the 1950s for a novelist "to get £ 1000 a year [a middle-class income] demands the writing of at least two and possibly four modestly successful books a year—that is books which sell from 3,000 to 4,000 copies." (ibid., 155).

19. For valuable discussions of professionalism, see Freidson (1971; 1986) and Larson (1977).

20. Occupations are gender-segregated. The classic professions are "male" work; the semiprofessions, such as nursing, "female" work, although women are increasingly entering the professions and men are trickling into some of the semiprofessions.

tively justify their claim to professional status by applying the term professional to earlier authors who got paid for their work.

Nineteenth-century writers used the term professional in yet a different sense to mean those pursuing "literature as a mean of living, independent of all others" and working "for high ideals" (Collins 1928, 7). But nineteenth-century writers were not professionals either by the classic sociological criteria; they did not control significant elements of their work.

Nor did paid nineteenth-century authors emerge from a professional heritage. In the eighteenth century writing was either a hobby or an occupation. By examining the conditions under which eighteenth-century novelists wrote, we can see that the working conditions of nineteenth-century novelists were substantially improved, but still not professional. Nineteenth-century novelists did not control their fee structure, training, recruitment, or expulsion. But with critics, and sometimes as critics, they began to define the nature of their work. And as was true of the classic professions many nineteenth-century writers viewed writing as a possible avenue for upward mobility. Among men, being an author came to be seen as a socially approved and even prestigious job, although only the most noted among them might be invited to the dinner parties of the social elite.

The occupational status of eighteenth-century novelists was low because they lacked power, even over their own work. Not only were they paid by the word, but publishers rarely honored their words. Until late in the eighteenth century, publishers freely altered manuscripts. They also freely altered books; if a book had not sold well under one title, some publishers would quickly reissue it under another. They were able to engage in this and similar practices because, having paid the author for a manuscript, they owned it.

Charles Lamb wrote about dependence upon booksellers this way: "Throw yourself on the world without any rational plan of support, beyond what the chance employ of booksellers would afford you!!! Throw yourself rather . . . from the steep Tarpeian rock, slap-dash headlong upon iron spikes. If you had but five consolatory minutes between the desk and the bed, make much of them, and live a century in them, rather than turn slave to the booksellers" (Collins 1928, 11). He continued, "I have known many authors [writing] for [their] bread, some repining, others envying the blessed security of a counting-house, all agreeing they would rather have been tailors, weavers—what not, rather than the things they were" (ibid.).

Such vituperation is not surprising. Dealing with the booksellers, the author had no rights. Consider again the example of Thomas Gray's "Elegy Written in a Country Churchyard." Gray literally could not prevent unauthorized people from printing his poem. He could have his own publisher, Dodsley, print it first, but Dodsley beat the rival bookseller by only a day.

Gray purportedly asked Dodsley to add "a line or two to say it came into his hands by accident" (quoted in Mumby 1974, 157). Since Dodsley quickly concurred with this request, one must suppose that he did not feel he was putting himself in a bad light by claiming to have published the poem without the author's permission. Some contemporary contrasts emphasize the point. To publish an author's work without the author's or the publisher's permission today infringes upon the copyright and is legally actionable.

Gray wanted to have his poem published anonymously. And the prevalence of literary anonymity throughout the eighteenth century and well into the nineteenth is well known. But more was involved than the attempt of gentlemen to dissociate themselves from trade. First, women were condemned for writing for money even more than men were. In *The Minerva Press, 1790–1820*, Dorothy Blakey (1939) records that women so insisted on anonymity that William Lane sometimes communicated with his authors through advertisements in newspapers. "Will the Lady who sent me a mss. called . . . please communicate with me immediately," an ad might read. The history of Fanny Burney's *Evelina*, published in 1778, presents another familiar example. Not only did Burney write her novel at night, so that her father and stepmother would not know of her literary activity, but she dispatched her brother in disguise to a local coffee house to fetch the note that would tell her whether the novel had been accepted (Hemlow 1958, 60).

Second, to write a novel was akin to announcing financial need. In the eighteenth century and even the early nineteenth, the literary world assumed that women who wrote did so because they needed the money. Joyce Tompkins ([1932] 1961) tells us that in the 1790s impoverished industrialists turned to novel writing to earn money quickly. Aside from discussions of such famous novelists as Jane Austen, Fanny Burney, and the Brontës, literary historians rarely mention authors' writing novels for the fun of it—although Arthur Collins notes, "Those who have been greatest in the practice of letters have rarely been those to whom letters was their supporting profession." Significantly, Collins' examples are male poets, and he asks rhetorically, "Of the poets, of whom can we say that he wrote for money? Not of Wordsworth, nor Coleridge, nor Shelley, nor Keats, nor Byron, nor Rogers, nor yet Scott" (Collins 1928, 8).

When literature is described as the "avocation" of a man writing before 1800, as is frequently done in the *DNB*, the term *literature* connotes essays, reports of scientific experimentation, and other sorts of nonfiction. The *DNB* differentiates carefully between hobbyists and hacks. To quote Collins again: "In the fifty years that followed the death of Johnson [1784], only one truly great man lived, 'whose whole estate was in his ink stand.' Others were clerks, and secretaries, and sheriffs, and bankers, and [poet] Robert Southey [1774–1843] was the one general in the army of letters who had no other resource than the sums in his pay-book. Most of the great captains were free lances who marauded among the public in occasional sallies" (ibid, 8). The man who wrote for money, and even more the woman who did so, was at worst condemned, at best condoned.

As literacy increased, literary journals multiplied. In the first quarter of the nineteenth century, "as far as the profession of authorship was concerned, there was constantly more for a writer to write and more people for him to write to" (ibid., 134). Collins lists some men of the time whom he considers both "professional" and "first class": Leigh Hunt, William Hazlitt, Samuel Coleridge, William Gifford, John Galt, Washington Irving, and Sir Walter Scott. Except for Scott, only Gifford and the American Irving wrote fiction as well as essays. The others wrote essays or poetry. Collins had included Scott on the list with a qualification: at the turn of the century Scott's famous works were poems. After Scott's first years as an author, "the money which he earned he was compelled to earn by the necessity of ambition and later of debt, and he had in truth, despite the competency of his clerkship, not more freedom than the man whose compelling necessity was for money to live" (ibid., 135).

The inclusion of Scott is particularly significant to a consideration of the occupational status of nineteenth-century authors. As Lewis A. Coser (1965) has convincingly argued, by contrasting Scott with Dickens one can appreciate how much the job of novelist had changed in the intervening years. The contrast is meaningful because each was the most popular novelist of his era, although Scott was critically acclaimed and Dickens was not.

Coser points out that Scott started with a sinecure, his clerkship, and then turned to literature, notably poetry. Scott used the fortune he earned from this work to buy and maintain a country home, Abbotsford, where he sought to live in the manner of established eighteenth-century gentry. That is, he sought to transform his profits into the life-style of a member of a higher social class and to live in a manner associated with graciousness and largess. Abbotsford sucked up money. So did his secret partnership in John Ballantyne and Company, publishers started in 1802. Therefore, in 1814,

> Scott, turning to prose when he found his poetry losing some of its vogue after Byron's arrival, had founded the nineteenth-century school

38

of romance with *Waverley*. Published anonymously...it opened up at once the new career which was to eclipse Scott's reputation as a poet and, for a time, restore his embarrassed financial affairs. Abbotsford was now making dangerous inroads into his income, and the demands for more capital from his printing and bookselling partners, the Ballantynes, were insatiable. (Mumby 1974, 192)

As the silent partner in a publishing firm, Scott was not a canny capitalist; he went bankrupt. Mumby puts it kindly, "How deeply involved were his affairs, even when he was drawing something like £15,000 a year [well over $67,000] as the author of the Waverley Novels, no one knew" (Mumby 1974, 192).

Dickens, by contrast, started as a poor, aspiring journalist (what Scott might have called a "hack"). His father was sufficiently embarrassed for Dickens later to support his parents as well as his own wife and children. Dickens put his name on his novels. He turned extra profits by reintroducing methods of publication that had fallen by the wayside, such as publishing by parts, a mainstay of eighteenth-century publishers. With this method, a novel was issued and sold a chapter at a time, each chapter costing as little as a penny. This practice made each chapter accessible to the common reader, who was essentially buying a novel on a layaway plan. The reader also did not have to purchase unwanted material, as might be the case when a novel was serialized in a magazine. By reintroducing publication by parts Dickens was able to bypass the power of Mudie's Select Library—no mean feat at the time.

When in April 1859 Dickens started his own magazine, *All the Year Round*, he too became a publisher. Unlike Scott, he did not insist on anonymity. And unlike Scott, he was a canny publisher with an innate feel for what readers wanted and a fine editor of other authors' manuscripts. By nineteenth-century standards he was also a capricious purchaser of manuscripts, paying more to those whom he admired and using his power as publisher to overrule the commercial department.[21] The magazine prospered as long as Dickens gave it his primary attention. Unlike Scott, Dickens was also canny in his dealings with book publishers, reducing them "to the purely functionary status of printer," an ability made explicit when he left bookseller-publishers

---

21. According to Sutherland (1976, 169), "As if to demonstrate his power, Dickens was arbitrary about prices. Lytton, whom he admired immensely, had £ 1,500 for an eight-month story; Mrs. Gaskell, whom he did not admire immensely, was offered £ 400, for the same length of narrative at exactly the same period." Sutherland does not indicate whether an author's gender influenced the degree of Dickens' admiration.

Chapman and Hall for the printers Bradbury and Evans (Sutherland 1976, 167).

As Coser (1965) points out, Dickens wrote for money, but not in order to maintain the aura of a country gentleman, as Scott had done. Rather, he sought funds to support an upper-middle-class urban life-style, replete with town house and carriage. At points in his career, he too was financially in debt. He solved those problems with his pen, writing on installment several books at a time and complaining of a sense of "something hanging over him like a hideous nightmare" (Mumby 1974, 212).

Finally, Dickens sought to alter the profession of letters. In his typescript "History of the Society of Authors," which recounts how Sir Walter Besant and other journalist-novelists founded that organization in 1883, G. H. Thring (n.d.) says that in the 1850s Dickens had tried unsuccessfully to found a comparable group to improve the position of authors.

What had happened to the publishing industry and the job of author between the 1820s and 1840s, the years when Scott and Dickens were active? We have already reviewed some of the major changes, including the introduction of new technologies, growing literacy, and new configurations of the old library-publisher relationship. Additionally, more elementary and secondary schools opened and mechanics institutes were established for workers. Although the price of newly issued novels (as opposed to reprints of eighteenth-century work) remained high, the price of other books decreased. According to Charles Knight (summarized in Altick 1957, 286), "Between 1828 and 1853, . . . the average price of a complete book declined from 16*s* to 8*s* 4–1/2*d*, or, in terms of single volumes, from 12*s* 1*d* to 7*s* 7–1/2 *d*." Three-decker novels were relatively less dear, too.

The state also played a role. In the second quarter of the nineteenth century, it had removed the taxes on newspapers, advertisements, and paper. In 1851 it removed the window tax as well, which Dickens had seen as "an even more formidable obstacle to the people's reading" (Altick 1957, 92) because poor lighting and the expense of candles prevented the average man and woman from reading. Indeed, the average English home did not have adequate lighting until late in the nineteenth century.

Still, the average person could not afford to buy Dickens' books. Indeed, the inability of most middle-class families to purchase books is what makes Dickens' scheme of serialization in parts such a financial masterstroke. (It also, as we have seen, prompted the success of Mudie's Select Library.) As long as people could find a way to read novels, there could be profit in issuing them and even some profit in writing them. Judging from the Macmillan Archives, a typical, mediocre novelist might receive from £ 50 to £ 100, equivalent to $225 to $450, for the sale of a novel's copyright. If an author published a book a year, this sum was sufficient to maintain a family in the middle class—not prosperous, but wealthy enough to keep more than one servant. Thus, in an age when writing for money was no longer socially condemned, increasing numbers of people would not have written novels had they not expected some modest profit.

Where Macmillan and Company Fit In

Macmillan and Company differed in one significant way from other companies publishing the novels we remember today: it was an academic house; novels were a sideline.[22] It was founded in 1843 by two Scots brothers, Daniel and Alexander, then ages thirty and twenty-four. The brothers were from a peasant family originating on the Island of Arran and were largely self-educated. First Daniel and later Alexander migrated to London and then to Cambridge seeking work. They found jobs in a bookstore and by taking silent partners, whom they bought out as quickly as possible, purchased a well-established bookstore in 1844. Daniel died in 1856. Alexander led the firm until roughly 1890, gradually ceding authority to his sons and nephews.

From its inception Macmillan had academic associations. In 1843, while still employed by others and with a pharmacist as a silent partner, the brothers published their first book, the ninety-two-page *The Philosophy of Training* by A. R. Craig. It gave "suggestions on the necessity of normal schools for teachers of the wealthier classes, and strictures on the prevailing mode of teaching languages" (Morgan 1943, 2). Some of the firm's early authors were scholars who frequented the Cambridge bookstore that the brothers opened in 1844. Like the brothers, some were advocates of "muscular Christianity," among them the divine F. D. Maurice (1805–1872), who had befriended the impoverished Daniel while Daniel was looking for a job in the London book trade. Others included novelist and historian Charles Kingsley (1819–1875) and his brother the novelist Henry Kingsley (1830–1876), whose work the Macmillans were to publish, and Charlotte Yonge (1823–1901), devotee of poet and divine John Keble (1792–1866). The Macmillans eventually published her novels, and she edited a religious series for them. But despite their loyalty to Maurice and their belief in his views, the firm's publications were not sectarian. Daniel and Alexander knew how to admire authors with whom they disagreed.

Macmillan published prize essays and poems. From 1843 until they came

22. This discussion draws heavily upon Charles Morgan's *The House of Macmillan, 1843–1943*, as well as the Macmillan Archives.

to a "friendly parting of the ways in 1881," Macmillan and Company was the home of Oxford's Clarendon Press. From the first, only a small proportion of the firm's books were fiction, although the fiction offerings expanded in 1863 when the house purchased John W. Parker's list upon his bankruptcy. Its fictional choices tended to be good guesses reflecting Alexander Macmillan's taste. Among those guesses were Charles Kingsley's *Westward Ho!* accepted in June 1854, and Thomas Hughes' *Tom Brown's School Days*, issued in 1857.

Like Charles Edward Mudie's literary preferences, Alexander Macmillan's taste represented a significant portion of the novel-reading public. Today, and even in the nineteenth century, many would question Alexander's critical judgments. For example, Alexander Macmillan disliked the acclaimed novels of William Makepeace Thackeray (1811–1863), as Alexander explained to Thomas Hardy in 1868 while rejecting Hardy's first novel, *The Gentleman and the Lady*. Alexander argued that Thackeray's approach was, roughly, " 'Dukes and duchesses and all the kit are humbugs, society is based on humbug, but it's rather pleasant and amusing, when you can get pleasant dinners and nice wines . . . ' That was his tone . . . I don't think Thackeray's satire did much good; indeed, I fear it did harm. He was in many respects a really good man, but he wrote in a mocking tone that has culminated in the *Saturday Review* tone, paralyzing noble effort and generous emotion" (Morgan 1943, 41–42). Macmillan liked Charles Kingsley's novels. As Morgan puts it, "He succeeded because, being loyal to his own taste and conscience, he made himself publisher to those who, in the widest meaning of the phrase, 'preferred Kingsley' " (ibid., 42).

Although Alexander Macmillan made all decisions to publish, after the firm moved to London in 1863 its success in publishing fiction rested partly with its atypical and elite literary advisers, including the successive editors of *Macmillan's Magazine*, whose selections of novels to serialize were later issued as books. Among them were David Masson (editor 1858–1868), one of the first professors of English literature in Britain, who successively held the prestigious posts of Professor of English literature at University College, London, and the University of Edinburgh; Sir George Grove (1863–1883), editor of the famed *Dictionary of Music*, still selling in revised editions under the name *Grove's Dictionary*; John Morley (1883–1885), a friend of John Stuart Mill, Leslie Stephen, and George Lewes, to whom, upon his retirement from that position, Lewes had turned over the editorship of *Fortnightly Review*; and Mowbray Morris (1885–1915), a minor Victorian critic. Alexander Macmillan had founded the magazine for the firm to have its own literary vehicle, as often done by prestigious London firms.

As the firm expanded after Daniel's death, business manager George

Lillie Craik was taken in as a partner. Craik brought with him his own ties to the British literary world through his wife, novelist Dinah Mulock Craik, though he opposed her writing novels after their marriage (Showalter 1975). Alexander's sons, Malcolm and George, and Daniel's sons, Frederick and Maurice, also entered the family business, some directly after Eton, some after university. Frederick became president of the firm in Alexander's waning years. As Macmillan's head in the late 1880s and early 1890s he led the Publishers Association during a "war" over the discounts that bookstores could offer on their merchandise.

Alexander Macmillan was sufficiently foresighted to have founded an American branch in 1869. The company's American agent, George Edward Brett, led it, and after his health declined in the late 1880s his post was assumed by his son, George Platt Brett. The American branch was incorporated as Macmillan and Company of New York in 1890, when the British firm became a limited company. Macmillan founded the American branch after a trip to the States during which he decided he must find a way to protect his interests in that country. He made a business rather than literary decision. As Morgan (1943, 83) tells it, Macmillan saw that in the United States the sale of his books and books issued by other English firms "was handicapped by high tariffs and the absence of international copyright. The only compensating advantage was that the English costs of production were less than the American, but that might change; if so, he would be shut out of the [profitable] American market unless he had 'manufacturing and distributive power on the spot.' "

This recital of intelligent business moves may not seem like literary credentials. It does not indicate a transformation of Macmillan and Company from a house specializing in monographs and texts to a literary one. That transformation never took place, for Macmillan continued to profit mightily from academic trade in England and the British colonies, especially India. But it does indicate that Macmillan and Company was a major Victorian firm, ever expanding, ever profiting, at first following and later leading the pattern of business among Victorian publishing firms.

Charles Morgan's *The House of Macmillan* proudly recites the famous authors and books that the Macmillans published. Many of the names belong to nonfiction writers; the titles extend from the field of mathematics, represented by Isaac Todhunter's *Differential Calculus*, to Alfred Marshall's *Principles of Economics* and such anthropological classics as Sir James Frazer's *The Golden Bough*. Macmillan issued Matthew Arnold's criticism and his poetry as well as Henry James' criticism and novels. In the area of fiction, we have already mentioned *Westward Ho!* and *Tom Brown's Schooldays*, the Kingsleys, Tom Hughes, and Charlotte Yonge. The Macmillans also published such major Victorian authors as Mrs. Oliphant, Mrs. Humphrey Ward, F. Marion Crawford, William Blackwood, J. D. Shorthouse, Thomas Hardy, and Rudyard Kipling. They also published the poetry of George Meredith, Thomas Hardy, and Rudyard Kipling, as well as the collected works of Alfred Lord Tennyson. When the heir to the House of Bentley decided to sell the firm in 1894, Macmillan and Company purchased it and thus gained copyright to such well-known and profitable books as Mrs. Henry Wood's *East Lynne*, which despite its sensationalism had fared well at Mudie's Library in the early 1860s.

Elite status and respectable profits do not prevent editors and publishers from evaluating the manuscripts of women and men differently. Rather, to help their firm retain its success leaders may alter their practices to conform to changing notions of quality, including shifting evaluations of women's contributions to literature. In chapter 3 we shall see that in the nineteenth century Macmillan and Company slowly grew less likely to accept fiction manuscripts by women. To understand how Macmillan exhibited the empty field phenomenon, we turn to the history of women's association with the novel.

3
Novel Writing
as an
Empty Field

o prove that men invaded the novel, we must first establish that before 1840 at least half of all novelists were women. Many literary historians claim that well into the nineteenth century novelists were mainly women. But their evidence is not definitive because it is impossible to learn how many novels were published, let alone what proportion of them women wrote. But it seems likely that from the late eighteenth century through the mid-nineteenth century at least half of the published novelists were women.

As we have mentioned, if a novel did not sell well an eighteenth-century publisher could change its title and reissue it. Both title pages often announced that the book was "By a Lady." But that pseudonym may have been intentionally misleading. Although Virginia Woolf claimed, "Anonymous was a woman," some of the novels supposedly by a lady were written by men. As *Gentleman's Magazine* informed its readers in June 1770, "Among other literary frauds it has long been common for [male] authors to affect the stile and character of ladies" (273, quoted in Spender 1986, 118).

The identity of some anonymous and pseudonymous novelists can be discovered. The *BMC* assiduously provides cross-references of known pseudonyms. Such tomes as Samuel Halkett's and John Laing's seven-volume *Dictionary of Anonymous Literature* (1971) can lead scholars to modest authors. We have used these sources to verify the gender of some of the authors who submitted manuscripts to Macmillan and Company. But these sources cannot parse the convoluted record constructed by eighteenth-century publishing practices.

Lacking sufficient accurate information to satisfy the requirements of sociological generalization, we use several strategies. First, we will review what little is known about the prevalence of women authors and women's occupational opportunities. Then we will develop new data, derived from the Macmillan Archives, that suggest more about the occupation of novel writing as a job associated with gender. Our analysis of these data, Macmillan's records concerning the submission and acceptance of fictional manuscripts, indicates that slowly, from 1866 through 1917, men did edge women out of the occupation of novel writing.

Our research strategies draw on what literary historians take to be a fact: In the eighteenth century and for the first quarter of the nineteenth-century, perhaps until 1840, the novel was a lowly genre. That status arose from men's association of the novel with women, for many novelists and most novel readers were thought to be women. England's traditional readers and authors were elite men. In the late eighteenth century the genres that they favored, poetry and essays, had high status. The novel's lowly status may have also resulted from the genre's extensive concern with the theme of love, a topic thought to be dearer to women than to men. Thus, relative to the tastes of elite men, the novel seemed a weak form.

In the year of its one hundredth birthday, 1902, the *Edinburgh Review* confirmed this judgment of the novel's status in the eighteenth century. An article on "The English Novel in the Nineteenth Century" stated:

> No one will wish to assert that the "Edinburgh Review" has been consistently inspired in its judgments; but probably no one will care to deny that it has represented more than adequately the normal standard of well-informed criticism. In the first ten years of its existence, or in the first forty-eight numbers, the editor only devoted ten reviews in all to novels; and of these, five were concerned with stories by Miss Edgeworth, an authoress "whose design of offering 'instruction' entitled her novels to more consideration than is usually bestowed on works of this description." ... Yet, let it be remembered, almost every issue of the Review devoted one article at least to some work in verse, even thought the poets to be reviewed were of no greater merit than Mrs. Opie or Joanna Baillie, and often, indeed, were writers whose share has been a still more perfect oblivion. (1902b, 487–488)

The anonymous author emphasized, "The plain fact is that the novel was excluded because the novel had fallen into the deepest disrepute . . . Yet among a wide circle of readers the vogue of the novel was, relatively speaking, as great as at present" (ibid., 488).[1]

---

1. The essay is presented as a review of Walter Raleigh's *The English Novel: Being a Short Sketch of its History from the Earliest Times to the Appearance of 'Waverley'* (Edinburgh Review 1902b, 487–506).

Like many other literary critics and historians, this unnamed author suggests that the status of the novel began to improve in 1814, when Scott published *Waverley*. Perhaps some potential male authors mused that if a great poet (and country gentleman) could write a critically acclaimed and financially successful novel, then the occupation of novel writing must be less disgraceful and more remunerative than they had thought. But although some men tried to imitate Scott the novel did not seem to attract the most talented. Rather, English literature continued to experience "those great outbursts of poetry which attended, and, in part were inspired by the first and second French Revolutions" (ibid., 487). Status is a relative matter. Compared to poetry, the novel still seemed weak.

In the 1840s, as summarized in chapter 2, the novel became the pro-totypical genre of the bourgeois age. In subsequent chapters we will argue that partly as a reaction to women's prominence as novelists, partly as a reaction against the bourgeois library-subscribers who crowned the "queens of the circulating library," and partly because of the clear economic oppor-tunities that the novel offered writers, men began to define the high-culture novel as a male preserve. They began to edge women out of literature. For now, let us concentrate on discovering how well ensconced in the novel women were before the distinction between popular culture and high culture became widespread.

The Prevalence of Women Authors

The eighteenth century. According to standard literary histories men—Defoe, Richardson, Fielding, Smollett, and Sterne—invented the modern realistic novel. Standard histories do not recognize earlier prose fictions as novels. They term them romances, partly to indicate that so many improbabilities permeated those early prose fictions that they neither captured nor presented real life. Standard histories call Aphra Behn's *Oroonoko*, published in 1688, a romance.

Some feminist critics demur from this standard literary history. For instance, Dale Spender (1986) claims that some women, whom she terms "mothers of the novel," anticipated the techniques and topics that were to be credited to the "fathers of the novel." She identifies *Oroonoko* as the first novel. But mainstream literary criticism continues to associate the early novel with male authors.[2]

---

2. In *Mothers of the Novel* (1986) Dale Spender challenges this interpretation. She claims that in the eighteenth century, the novel was not a despised genre. Many men,

According to that same mainstream literary history, the association of men with the authorship of novels broke down in the late eighteenth century. In the 1790s women as well as men of the educated classes wrote novels (Tompkins [1932] 1961). The novels thought to be written by women and "male hacks" in the late eighteenth century were dull and borrowed freely from the early "male progenitors" of the genre. Standard literary histories either ignore these novels or dislike them so that one almost infers that most late eighteenth- and early nineteenth-century novels were weak because they were written by hacks and female autodidacts. Many of these despised novels were published by the Minerva Press, which generally assigned authorship to an anonymous lady, although men parading under a female pseudonym may have written some of them.

The extent of female authorship is virtually impossible to document. Ian Watt (1957) states that women wrote most of the two thousand novels that he estimates were published in the eighteenth century. Spender (1986) has collected the names of one hundred eighteenth-century women who wrote almost six hundred of these two thousand novels. Assuming that she has not located every woman novelist, she too estimates that at least half of all eighteenth-century novelists were women.

The early nineteenth century. We have not been able to locate estimates of the extent of female authorship in the first four decades of the nineteenth century.

---

including Samuel Johnson and the fathers of Fanny Burney and Jane Austen, read novels. Johnson even helped some women authors to find publishers. According to Spender, the literary achievements of eighteenth-century women novelists were recognized in their own time but ignored or denigrated in the nineteenth century when elite men began to invent the great tradition.

Spender's defense of the novel's status in the eighteenth century does not seem sensible. That some esteemed literary figures read novels does not mean that novels had high status relative to other literary genres. It might simply mean that these esteemed figures had interesting foibles or secret vices. That one noted British philosopher has been said to be an avid reader of mediocre detective novels does not make such fiction acceptable to the contemporary literary elite. Consider another analogy: As much as 25 percent of the American audience for soap operas is male, but American culture deems soap operas a female genre. Suppose it was suddenly revealed that Harold Bloom and Jacques Derrida daily set their VCRs to tape a favorite soap opera that they customarily view as soon as they finish the day's work. Although some people might sample that soap in order to share experience with these literary figures and some might watch it to smile at the quirks of great critics, the status of the genre would not necessarily improve.

For an extended discussion about the connotations of the terms *romance* and *novel*, see Williams (1976).

Even books that concentrate on the profession of writing or on popular literature during these decades do not provide estimates of the proportion of female novelists. Arthur Collins (1928) dates the transformation of what he termed the "the profession of letters" to 1832, when increased literacy brought new readers, prompted more and new publications, and so produced more outlets for writers. But Collins never explicitly discusses what this expansion of opportunity meant for women who wrote.

Writing about mid-nineteenth-century popular fiction, Margaret Dalziel (1957) gives the decade of the 1840s as the date of a literary revolution. She emphasizes the meaning of that revolution in terms of the social class of an expanded readership, some of whom must have been women. "For the first time in the history of England," Dalziel writes, "anyone could for the price of a penny buy up to sixteen large pages of reading matter, large pages of very small print, often illustrated" and so a bargain (Dalziel 1957, 2–3). That nominal price made novels available to "the half or more of [the English masses] who could read." But Dalziel does not specify the proportion of writers who were women or even how many women wrote. Nor does Q. D. Leavis, who discusses expanded literacy and popular fiction in her acclaimed *Fiction and the Reading Public* (1932).

There are other literary historians who agree that the nineteenth-century novel encompassed a variety of types, including the one-shilling gothic shocker (as opposed to the three-volume gothic romance), the juvenile thriller designed for boys, the "penny dreadful" or mystery issued in parts for a penny a part, and assorted novels printed in the *Family Herald* and *London Journal*. Some of these probably never made their way into circulating libraries, which preferred the three-volume form. Men and women wrote tracts issued by religious societies.

The sheer number of novels printed in these excluded categories was probably quite high. For instance, Dalziel estimates that "each year's volume [of the *London Journal*] contain[ed] 832 big closely printed pages, about two-thirds of which on the average consists of fiction" (1957, 3). Many of these stories were "family literature" and must have been written by women. At least after 1840, perhaps earlier, women did write for such newspapers as the *Family Herald* and the *London Journal*. In the 1870s several women writers asked Macmillan to reissue as books novels previously published in these newspapers.[3]

---

3. Macmillan rejected them. Indeed, as we will see in chapter 5, Macmillan's readers—

Excluding family literature and religious tracts, men probably wrote most of the novels excluded from the circulating libraries, especially the thrillers. Men probably also wrote most of the literature designed for the working classes. Although it is possible that he succumbed to the tendency of twentieth-century male critics to ignore women writers, Louis James never mentions a woman author in his classic *Fiction for the Working Classes* (1963). But Martha Vicinus, a feminist, notes in *The Industrial Muse* (1974) that she could find few works written by women for the working class.

These sources cannot tell us much about the gradual emergence of the high-culture novel and how men edged women out of a canonized literary culture. Literary historians did not have thrillers and novels serialized in newspapers in mind when they generalized about the queens of the circulating library, nor have they referred to these works when speaking of the advent of the high-culture novel and the development of the middle-class popular novel into the prototypical genre of the Victorian age. But both the existence of these novels and their exclusion from circulating libraries indicate that in the first part of the nineteenth century popular novels were already differentiated by the age and social class of their readership.

Novelists at midcentury. To determine exactly what proportion of all three-decker novelists were women after 1840, when the Victorian literary system began to coalesce, is also impossible. Conrad Tanzy's (1961) economic analysis of nineteenth-century publishing assumes that more women than men published novels. In essence, he argues that what might now be termed "shlock publishing houses," including vanity presses, accepted women's novels at minimal fees and then sold them at a heady discount to Mudie's Circulating Library. Mudie's, in turn, preferred to stock these weak novels bought cheaply to superior novels published by more elite firms and sold to Mudie's at a smaller discount.[4]

Estimates about the prevalence of women novelists among the authors of Bentley's, a firm specializing in the three-volume novel, are contradictory. Citing Jeanne Rosenmayer Fahnestock (1973), Elaine Showalter (1977) tells us that in the 1840s most of the novels issued by the house of Bentley were

---

the Victorian equivalent of editorial consultants—spoke of novels appearing in the *Family Herald* and the *London Journal* with a sneer.

4. Additionally, Tanzy (1961) feels, other factors promoted popular novels by women. Such firms as Routledge specialized in reprinting novels to sell cheaply. They were more likely to issue weak work for minimal fees to their (frequently female) authors; better (male) authors whose books were priced at 33*s.* 6*d.* by elite firms were not as likely to have their work reprinted for as small a fee to the author and as cheap a cost to the reader.

by women. But according to Royal Gettmann (1960, 249), "In the 'thirties and 'forties approximately 20 percent of the books published by the House of Bentley were by women, whereas in the 'seventies and 'eighties the proportion was more than doubled." After 1840 many women must have published novels, since half of the 441 works of fiction featured in Mudie's 1871 clearance sale were by women (Griest 1970).

The best source of information is probably the British census. At mid-century it underscored two phenomenon: a surplus of women and few occupational alternatives. So many men had migrated to far-flung portions of the empire to seek new lives that by 1851 there were over half a million more women than men in England (Harriet Martineau, quoted in Holcombe 1973, 10). Never married or widowed, these redundant women were concentrated in the middle classes. Uneducated and undereducated, they had few occupational alternatives. According to W. J. Reader,

> Apart from teaching and prostitution, there were very few occupations by which an early Victorian middle-class woman could support herself— let alone any children she might have.... She might keep a shop or run some other kind of business, if she had the capital for it. She might write ... though whether that was quite proper was debatable. She might go on the stage, though throughout a large range of middle-class society that would be considered quite definitely improper: more or less equivalent to prostitution, in fact. Domestic service was out of the question, though formerly its upper reaches had been quite an acceptable middle-class occupation. The kind of industrial work by which many working-class women earned money were certainly not likely to attract anyone who had the remotest opportunity of anything better. Altogether the openings for women of decent social standard were few, precarious, and apt to be tinged with social disapproval or contempt. (1966, 167)

In 1865 for the first time the British census listed separately the numbers of men and women found in several occupations grouped under the general rubric "professions." In table 3.1 we present an enumeration by gender of those professions in which women were found. Mainly, women were teachers: 72.5 percent of all educators, including college professors. They were barely 9 percent of all declared authors. The paucity of women admitting that they were authors affirms that even as late as the 1860s middle-class norms prevented respectable women from acknowledging that they wrote for money. But the census probably underestimated the number of all authors, male and female, because writers, then as now, supported themselves through other jobs.

All we can reliably know is that writing was one of the few acceptable

Table 3.1: Population Engaged in Selected Occupations in the 1860s,
by Gender

	Women	Total	Percent Female
Occupations			
Schoolmasters,			
teachers, professors*	50,565	69,745	72.5
Stage performers	891	2,202	40.5
Painters and sculptors	1,652	6,901	23.9
Authors	145	1,673	8.7
Musicians[†]	1,618	9,466	17.1
Midwives	1,913	1,913	100.0

Source: Reader 1966, 153, 172–173.
*Holcombe (1973, 203) states that there were 110,260 schoolmasters, teachers, and
  professors in England and Wales in 1861, 72.5 percent of them women.
†Reader (1966) suggests that some musicians may have been listed as music teachers.

ways that middle-class women could support themselves if they were forced
to. Norms stressed that only force of circumstances should drive them to
write, and then they were certainly to write novels.[5] In the *DNB*, first issued
in 1888, one finds very few women identified as nonfiction writers, just as
one finds very few men identified as novelists. Since the *DNB*'s pattern of
identification captures the norms of the late 1880s (see chapter 5), it seems
safe to assume that the norms about what women should write—if they
transgressed the norms and dared to write for money—were even stronger
in the earlier periods, when fewer people could read and men were more
likely than women to be literate. It also seems safe to assume that when
relatively few women could read, even fewer wrote. But we cannot be sure
how many women published or aspired to publish. To have a better idea of
the prevalence of women novelists in the nineteenth-century, we must examine
the cultural expectations that insistently identified women with the novel.

Novelists. Eighteenth-century readers could hardly have surmised that all novelists were women. Literary reviews assumed that any person of even modest
culture knew of Defoe, Richardson, and Fielding. A typical turn-of-the-century
novel-reader probably knew that some prominent London intellectuals, such

5. Many forms of writing cultivated by women, such as diaries and letters, are
commonly not even identified as literature and therefore are not in the college curriculum,
except for courses in women's studies. See Williams (1976) on the way the meanings of the
terms *literature, fiction,* and *novel* have been transformed historically.

as Godwin, had written novels. Still later, most novel readers knew of Scott's *Waverley*.

Nonetheless, the authors and publishers of the late eighteenth century and early nineteenth century seem to have assumed that novelists were supposed to be women, as revealed by the simple and common pseudonym "By a Lady." If it had been assumed that novelists were supposed to be men, the phrase "By a Gentleman" might have graced title pages more frequently. The use of female pseudonyms may have been intended to attract female readers by suggesting that these pseudonymous authors saw the world as women did. A contemporary parallel is the practice by many men who write gothic novels and historical romances of using female pseudonyms to appeal to female readers.

Literary historians have usually ignored the use of female pseud-onyms by men. Rather, they have generally discussed the use of male pseudonyms by women to emphasize the theory that nineteenth-century authors were expected to be men or that women novelists felt that pub-lishers gave preferential treatment to male authors. The most common examples of male pseudonyms are George Eliot, who first published a novel in the late 1850s, and Acton, Ellis, and Currer Bell (the Brontës), all of whom first published in the 1840s. In the 1890s such women as Violet Martin (Martin Ross) and Pearl Cragie (John Oliver Hobbes) as-sumed easily pierced male disguises.[6]

But solid data seem to support the assumption that many male writers masqueraded as women in the novel's heyday. In chapter 1 we described the material in the Macmillan Archives on which the rest of this chapter and chapter 4 are based. By coding the gender of authors who submitted novels to Macmillan and subsequently locating some of their names in the *BMC*, we found a phenomenon that contravenes standard assumptions about the mid-nineteenth century use of pseudonyms. (That catalogue cross-lists multiple pseudonyms.)

Although pseudonymous submissions in general were rare, in the 1860s and 1870s men submitting fiction were more likely to assume a female name than women were to use either a male or a neuter name. Although pseudonyms

6. Showalter (1977, 58–63) assumes that later women assumed disguises to imitate George Eliot and the Brontës. She also suggests that since childhood a male *persona* had been "part of the fantasy life of these women." Women adopted pseudonyms because they feared discrimination and were anxious not to offend friends or to betray affection or because their publishers felt their novels would stand a better chance if they appeared to be by a man (ibid., 58–59).

were even rarer in the 1880s, the pattern in the Macmillan records changed: women were more likely to assume a male disguise than men a female nom de plume. During the 1880s and 1890s, a few women submitted novels to Macmillan under a male pseudonym, and to the best of our knowledge no men used a female nom de plume. We did not discover pen names among the twentieth-century Macmillan authors. This pattern indicates to us that through the 1870s cultural expectations were that novel writing was largely a female occupation. Later cultural expectations emphasized that novelists were mainly men.

The mid-Victorians assumed that women wrote novels simply because they needed the money (Showalter 1977). They did not bother to ask what other reason would drive women to break middle-class norms against earning their livelihood. Earlier, we pointed out that people may take cultural expectations—what everyone knows or believes to be true—as guides to action. According to W. I. Thomas' famous explanation of the *definition of the situation*, when they do so, their expectations might as well be based upon fact. As he put it, "When people believe a situation to be real, it is real in its consequences." Thus, some women may have said that they wrote for money rather than self-satisfaction so that they would appear socially acceptable; stating that they worked because they liked to do so would have challenged the social norms against earning money. Others may have wished to convey that they worked for money but did not expend the intellectual effort associated with manly accomplishment. Showalter explains: "This strategy was partly a way of minimizing the professional and intellectual aspects of the work, and partly a way of describing the powerful drives for self-expression that especially for feminine novelists like Mrs. Oliphant, made the act of writing initially a possession by the muse: 'I have written because it gave me pleasure [said Mrs. Oliphant], because it came naturally to me' " (Showalter 1977, 83). By assuming that women wrote because of financial need, these mid-Victorians also assumed that a novelist might earn enough to remain in the comfortable middle class. Thus, they implicitly ignored the financial plight of authors in their own day. For then as today, a few novelists earned substantial incomes while others barely got by.

Since cultural expectations are a guide to behavior, they enable other inferences as well. It is very likely that most eighteenth-century novelists and early nineteenth-century novelists were women. Additionally, through at least 1840 and probably even later, novels were associated with women's topics, women readers, and most likely women novelists. Thus, many men may have perceived the occupation of novelist as a potentially remunerative empty field and accordingly behaved as though it were one. Our reading of the Macmillan records leads us to believe that men invaded that field.

Patterns of Female Authorship: the Macmillan Records

The Macmillan Archives begin in November 1866—three years after the firm had moved to London, two decades after the advent of the Victorian literary system, and two decades after the novel became the dominant genre of the bourgeois age. They give us an idea of how many men and women wrote novels that they hoped to publish. The records are particularly important because they tell a story that goes against the common wisdom.

Rather than presenting a literary scene increasingly open to women, the Macmillan Archives tell of a literary world closing its gates to them. First, in all three of the periods that we examined (the period of invasion, 1866 and 1877; the period of redefinition, 1887 and 1897; and the period of male institutionalization, 1907 and 1917), women submitted the same proportion of all the manuscripts Macmillan and Company received—30 percent. Second, especially in the 1860s and 1870s, the Macmillan records show, women constituted a very high proportion of all those trying to publish fiction—62 percent. Third, as the novel became even more established, men increasingly tackled the genre. During the 1880s, the very decade when women were supposedly the queens of the circulating library, men such as those described by George Gissing in *The New Grub Street* (1891) besieged Macmillan with fiction manuscripts. Fourth, when the three-decker disappeared and the "modern" novel emerged, women authors were edged out.

Before examining women's and men's patterns of manuscript submission and acceptance, we will consider the increased submission of manuscripts to Macmillan from November 1866 to 1917. The overall pattern enables us to see women's literary activities in the more general context of a veritable surge in novel writing.

General submission patterns. The pattern of submission to Macmillan and Company seems to match literary historians' insistence that the novel flowered in the late nineteenth century, when fiction became the largest category of books published. Thus, it tends to support the credibility of the Macmillan data as a source of information about male and female authors. That credibility is enhanced by Macmillan's concentration on educational—that is, nonfiction—books, for we may suppose that the pattern of submission to Macmillan and

Company necessarily *understates* the growth of the novel. We will accept these data on their face value.[7]

In November 1866 Macmillan's clerks began to record each manuscript and proposal submitted in special ledger books. These entries reveal a pattern of continuous expansion. To some extent the growing flood of manuscripts announced the ever-increasing success of the firm as it solidified its position in the publishing world, started its magazine, added overseas branches, and inaugurated such special series as the Colonial Library. But the flow of manuscripts depended primarily on the growth of the entire British book industry. Without the general expansion of both English and overseas markets, Macmillan and Company could never have grown as it did.

The yearly increase in manuscripts is remarkable. In its first full year in London—1867—Macmillan and Company received 102 manuscripts. In 1872 it registered 143 submitted manuscripts and proposals; in 1877, 216; in 1882, 243; in 1887, 384. Despite wars and recessions, submissions continued to increase. In 1897 Macmillan and Company received 586 manuscripts and proposals; in 1907, 627. And although paper was rationed during the Great War, in 1917 authors sent 522 manuscripts and proposals to Macmillan. This remarkable growth in the number of all submissions is roughly akin to the extraordinary expansion in novel publishing in an earlier fifty-year period, 1837 to 1887. In 1837 the *Publishers' Circular* listed 31 novels; in 1887, 184 novels, a six-fold increase (Sutherland 1976, 34). Despite the paper shortages of World War I, from 1867 through 1917 all submissions to Macmillan increased more than 500 percent.

Men wrote 68 percent of the 2,861 manuscripts in the years we sampled.[8]

---

7. Generalizing from Macmillan's records to submissions at other firms is difficult. Aware that Macmillan specialized in nonfiction, men may have been more likely to submit their fiction elsewhere. As we will see in chapter 5, compared to men, women were less integrated into the literary world and collectively may have been less cognizant of the stratification of firms within the publishing industry. Some women may have submitted novels to Macmillan without realizing their chance for acceptance might have been better had they sent their manuscripts to a house specializing in fiction.

There is also another possibility; ambitious for their novels or more canny about publishing, men may have submitted fiction manuscripts to Macmillan in hope of acceptance but with plans for submission to another and lesser firm, such as Tinsley or Newby, if they received a rejection. For instance, Thomas Hardy used Tinsley as a last resort three times. Insecure or defensive about the quality of their work, Victorian women may have been more likely to view a rejection letter as validation of their lack of skill and so less likely than men to seek another publisher.

8. Grouped as we initially calculated statistics, those years were November, 1866 through 1868, 1877 and 1878, 1887, 1897, 1907, and 1917. Appendix A explains the selection

Women submitted 30 percent. The gender of the remaining 2 percent of aspiring authors could not be determined. In every one of the periods studied, the men's share of all submissions hovered around 68 percent and the women's around 30 percent.

This pattern of submission by gender contradicts received wisdom. First, it differs significantly from both Fahnestock's (1973) and Gettmann's (1960) estimates of the proportion of books by women issued by Bentley in the nineteenth century. A possible explanation for this discrepancy may be that Bentley, unlike Macmillan, specialized in fiction. Second, nineteenth- and twentieth-century historians have argued that increased educational opportunities for women led to a rapid increase in the number of Victorian women writers (Gertrude Himmelfarb, personal communication, 1978). Their numbers did indeed increase. But so did the number of male writers. According to submissions to Macmillan, the proportion of writers who were women remained fairly constant.

As we will explain in chapter 5, the general expansion of the literary marketplace meant more job opportunities for all. And men benefited from those expanded opportunities more than women did. Although improved educational opportunities may have helped both women and men with literary aspirations, other factors helped men even more. As Gissing's *The New Grub Street* (1891) illustrates, men who could have used their educations to become clerks or other sorts of functionaries flocked to London to try their hand at literary endeavors. Some attempted journalism, some reviewing, some editing. If only a small proportion of the men who wanted a literary career submitted a manuscript to Macmillan, the numbers of books sent by men would have increased. Macmillan also probably received more than its fair share of manuscripts by aspiring male schoolteachers.

After 1850 the educational opportunities of middle-class women increased significantly. Although these women were better equipped to write books than previously, most seem to have entered occupations still associated with women. As the century progressed, educated women crammed into the field they had always preferred—teaching, which from 1861 through 1911 became a crowded field. In 1861, 110,260 teachers were employed in England and Wales; in 1911, 251,968. The percentage of teachers who were women remained constant. In 1861, 72.5 percent of these teachers were women; in 1911, 72.8 percent (Holcombe 1973, 202). Other educated women went into such new occupations as nursing, which was almost entirely composed of

---

of the sample. For simplicity's sake, we will refer to the years in this sample as "six decades" rather than "six groups of years."

women (Holcombe 1973, 204). And some accomplished women, such as Josephine Butler, turned to social activism.[9] Perhaps if such talented women as Butler had turned to novel writing, men might not have edged women out of the high-culture novel. But we cannot test this hypothesis.

We do know that from 1861 through 1911 the available data indicate relatively little growth in the percentage of women who were authors. Vicinus (1985) presents census information on the occupations of unmarried English women over the age of forty-five. In 1911, 13.7 percent of these 271,811 women practiced what the British census termed a "profession." By far the largest group among those professionals were teachers. More than 17,000 women were teachers, and more than 9,000 women were nurses and midwives, but only 385 women were authors and journalists. According to Vicinus' data, 0.1 percent of single professional women over the age of forty-five were authors and journalists. Even such a small proportion of female authors represents an increase in percentage from the early 1860s. Of the 56,784 women professionals categorized by occupation in table 3.1, only 0.002 percent (145) were authors. But, as we have seen, statistics on authors are unreliable because writers often support themselves through other occupations. And since norms had been modified women may have been more willing to identify themselves as authors in 1911 than in 1865.

Submission of novels. The invariant proportion of manuscripts submitted by women and men is fortuitous; it highlights expected shifts in the pattern of fiction and nonfiction submissions by women and men. We believe that the rise in submissions of fiction was caused by the increased importance of novels to literature rather than an increase in submissions by women. If men's manuscripts were increasingly novels, men were responding to the increased status of the genre. Thus, the fortuitous invariance we have described enhances our ability to test the application of the empty field phenomenon to the occupation of novelist.

As we discussed in chapter 1, that concept refers to processes through which men edge women out of an occupation that is already beginning to be associated with increased status and economic rewards. First the men "invade." Then they begin to redefine the importance of the field and the social meanings of work within it. Finally, they institutionalize their gains, even though women may try to reclaim the field. In the case of the English

9. The *DNB* identifies Josephine Butler (1823–1906) as a "social reformer." An active feminist, she worked to increase women's educational opportunities but is probably best remembered for her participation in campaigns against the Contagious Diseases Acts of 1864, 1866, and 1869. She also wrote nonfiction.

novel, that third period occurred during the Great War, well after the demise of the three-decker novel and Mudie's Select Library. It occurred during a period when one might have expected a decrease in the submissions of novels.

To test our reasoning, we must first discover what proportion of fiction and nonfiction manuscripts were submitted through the decades. Then we must discover what proportion of each genre were submitted by women and by men.

By and large, the pattern of submission of novels from the late 1860s through 1917 affirms the presence of the empty field phenomenon. It clearly attests to the increased importance of the genre through 1900. In the late 1860s fiction comprised 34 percent of the 248 manuscripts submitted to Macmillan; in 1877–1878, 31 percent of the 410 manuscripts; in 1887, 45 percent of 360 manuscripts; in 1897, 43 percent of 559 manuscripts; in 1907, 36 percent of 605 manuscripts; and in 1917, 26 percent of 461 manuscripts.

For conceptual and methodological clarity, we grouped these six decades into three periods. Grouping of years is desirable, because the concept of the empty field phenomenon defines stages in the transformation of an occupation: initial female prevalence, increased status and male invasion, redefinition of social meanings, institutionalization of male predominance. The first entries in the Macmillan ledgers were made after the status of the novel had already begun to increase. Thus, we identify the late 1860s and 1870s as the period of invasion, 1887 and 1897 as the period of redefinition, and 1907 and 1917 as the period of male predominance.

Grouping also enhances the reliability of the statistics. The cautious reader may have noticed that the numbers of manuscripts upon which we based the previous calculations of percentages of fiction submissions do not add up to 2,861, the total number of manuscripts submitted in the sample years. We could not determine to our own satisfaction the genre of 218 manuscripts (8 percent) and so excluded them from consideration. We did not exclude the same proportion of manuscripts for each year; the percent excluded varied from 3.5 percent in 1907 to 12 percent in both 1877–1878 and 1917.

The state of the Macmillan records explains the variation in the proportion of excluded manuscripts, for we used readers' reports to check the coding of genre. No reports were available for 1917, when the firm was understaffed because of the war, and fewer than usual were available for 1877–1878. When one examines the data in three groups, the amount of variation decreases, and inferences are more reliable.

Consider, then, how fiction submissions increased as the empty field phenomenon unfolded. In the period of invasion 32 percent of all manuscripts

Table 3.2: Percentage of Fiction Manuscripts (Mss.), by Gender of Author and Period, and Percentage of All Mss. Submitted That Were Fiction

	Period		
	Male Invasion (late 1860s, 1877, 1878) (%)	Redefinition (1887, 1897) (%)	Institution-alization (1907, 1917) (%)
Percentage of fiction			
By men	28	41	38
By men plus authors recorded by initials	34	50	49
By women	62	48	50
Total fiction mss.	(212)	(402)	(341)
Percentage of all manuscripts that were fiction	32	44	32
Total mss.	(658)	(919)	(1,066)

Note: Figures in parentheses are base Ns for the adjacent percentages. Total $N =$ 2,643 (658 in period of male invasion, 919 in period of redefinition, 1,066 in period of institutionalization). Manuscripts whose genre we could not determine have been excluded, as have been manuscripts for which we could not determine the gender of the author.

were novels; in the period of redefinition, 44 percent; in the period of institutionalization of male dominance, 32 percent.

The tides of fiction submissions to Macmillan capture the rise and decline of men's interest in writing novels. The cultural elite formulated the notion of the high-culture novel during the period of redefinition. Their emphasis on the emerging high-culture novel encouraged young men to view novel writing as a path to fame and glory. For example, George Bernard Shaw commented on Macmillan's rejection of five novels of ideas he submitted in the 1880s, when he was in his late twenties and early thirties. Shaw wrote, "I really hated those five novels, having drudged through them ... because there was nothing else I could or would do. . . . I wrote novels because everybody did so then" (quoted in Morgan 1943, 68). During the period of redefinition, Macmillan received an increased proportion of fiction submissions.

By 1902, during the period of male institutionalization, men's vogue for writing novels had passed. That year, *The Edinburgh Review* reported, "the best writers of prose fiction are now turning aside to try their hand at other forms. . . . The novel and the drama have never flourished together. . . . And no one can be blind to the fact that the drama is in England undergoing some such rehabilitation as the novel underwent in Scott's day" (1902b, 504–505). Fiction submissions to Macmillan decreased. But literary fads alone could not have accounted for this decrease in fiction submissions. The period of male institutionalization encompassed the Great War, which drew men and women away from their customary occupations. The Macmillan archives enable us to demonstrate that men's activity as novelists largely accounted for the variation in submitted manuscripts.

Men, women, and the submission of fiction. In table 3.2 we illustrate how men edged their way into novel writing. For each of the three periods that we have demarcated—invasion, redefinition, and institutionalization—we present the percentage of all manuscripts that were fiction, the percentage of all fiction written by men, and for comparative purposes the percentage written by women. For the sake of rigor, we offer calculations about men in two forms: first, the percentage of fiction submitted by people with men's names and by people whom the Macmillan ledgers identified as "B.A.," "M.A.," "doctor," "esquire," or clergyman; second, calculations including these men plus those identified only by initials (as in "J. R. Smith"). We believe it is safe to assume that at least through 1900 and probably through 1917 the group identified by initials was male.

The reasons we feel sure that these authors with initials were men highlight Victorian accuracy about gender. First, as we coded the data we discovered only one woman who used initials and was not identified as either "Miss" or "Mrs." She, the American sentimental novelist E. D. E. N. Southwood, did not use the male convention for initials; she used four initials, not two. Second, since the *BMC* frequently spells out the given names of authors, we searched it to discover the gender of a sample of authors identified by initials who had submitted work to Macmillan. Using dates and the titles of subsequently published manuscripts as our criteria for identification, we found that these authors were men, not women. Third, the clerks responsible for the ledgers treated gender in a polite Victorian manner. When they knew an author's name, they ignored pseudonyms. They always called any person with a woman's name "Miss" or "Mrs." Women using a male pseudonym were entered as women. For example, a clerk identified "Miss M. Kingsley" as the author of novels published under the pseudonym "Lucas Malet." Men using female pseudonyms were identified by their given male names.

All these calculations lead to the same conclusion: the activity of men corresponds to the flow of fiction manuscripts. To be sure, as the common wisdom suggests, more women wrote fiction during the period of redefinition, than previously, but *more* is a relative adjective. When discussing trends, women should be compared both to other women and to men. The increased submission of fiction by men is even more dramatic than the increase by women.

The ratio of all fiction submissions in the period of invasion (late 1860s, late 1870s) to those in the period of redefinition (1887, 1897) is 100:190. The ratio of women's submissions in the period of invasion to their submissions in the period of redefinition is somewhat lower— 100:147. Whether calculated for men only or for men and people called by initials, the ratio of men's submissions from one period to the next is considerably higher. It is 100: 279 both for men and for men and authors with initials. These ratios for men are so high because the men started from a lower base. And that is just the point. When fiction was valued relatively little, men submitted relatively little of it to Macmillan; once it had become valued, they submitted a great deal.

Furthermore, both women and men submitted less fiction during the period of male institutionalization. However calculated, men's submissions declined more than women's did. The ratio of women's fiction submissions in the period of redefinition to their submissions in the period of male institutionalization is 100:88. For men only, this ratio is 100:79; for both men and people identified by initials it is 100:83. In the first decades of the twentieth century, men were primarily responsible for the decreased flow of fiction manuscripts.

Finally, this pattern of increase and decrease in fiction submissions by gender appears to be even more dramatic and more suggestive of a male invasion of the occupation of novelist when one considers the pattern of nonfiction submissions, which varied little over the three periods. The percentage of nonfiction submitted by women was 15 percent in the period of invasion; 16 percent in the period of redefinition; and 17 percent in the period of male institutionalization. No matter how calculated, the percentage of nonfiction submitted by men is also remarkably stable.

Acceptance rates. To broach the beachhead is one thing, to gain it, another. For this occupational invasion to have been successful, the acceptance rate of men's manuscripts should have increased in each period. Concomitantly, women's fiction manuscripts should have received lower acceptance rates over time, and women's acceptance rates should have become lower that those of men. Was Macmillan increasingly likely to publish novels by men? Quite simply, yes. The acceptance rates of fiction by men were 1–2 percent in the period of male invasion, 5–6 percent in the period of redefinition, and 3–4 percent in the period of institutionalization (ranges are given to incorporate calculations of men's rates both including and excluding authors identified by their initials, who we believe were men). The acceptance rates of fiction by women for the same three periods were 6 percent, 5 percent, and 1 percent, respectively. A caution is in order: because Macmillan accepted so few novels, the differences between groups are very small, but they do follow the pattern we expected to find.

With one exception, the acceptance rates all followed the predicted pattern. That exception is the acceptance rates of men's fiction, which decreased from the period of redefinition to the period of institutionalization. But, however calculated, the men's acceptance rates were lowest in the initial period. Also as expected, the women's acceptance rates decreased in each period. Relative to one another, men's acceptance rates and women's acceptance rates display the expected pattern.[10]

Women did not repel the invasion. When male dominance was institutionalized, men's fiction was more likely to be accepted. Perhaps men were so successful compared to women because women had new occupational opportunities. After all, talented women were opening other empty fields in the areas of social reform and social welfare (Vicinus 1985). But women had begun to forge these occupations as early as the 1850s. They were increasingly active in these areas in the 1880s and 1890s, when women's fiction submissions to Macmillan had actually increased. To some extent, men's invasion probably succeeded because some talented women turned elsewhere. But largely men fared so well because their dominance of the high-culture novel had become institutionalized.

Thus far, our presentation of the empty field phenomenon has been quantitative. We have suggested that the increased submission of fiction indicated the rising status of the genre. We have also explored three phases of edging women out. In the period of male invasion (late 1860s and 1870s), aspiring women writers dominated fiction submissions and women had a higher fiction acceptance rate than men. In the second, redefinition of the novel, both men and women submitted more fiction, although the rate at

10. Whether one reads the statistics on men including or excluding authors identified by their initials affects interpretation of the statistics calculated for the period of redefinition. During that period, authors who we know were men had a higher rate than women; men plus authors identified by initials had the same rate as women. The first set of statistics suggests that the men's invasion succeeded more quickly than the second suggests. But both interpretations conform to our expectations.

which men submitted fiction increased much more than that of women. Relative to their rate of submission, men's acceptance rate increased and women's decreased. In the period of institutionalization, which encompasses World War I, men's submission of fiction declined. However, even though women submitted many more fiction manuscripts than men, men had a higher acceptance rate. Men had successfully invaded.

Qualitative data affirm these patterns. The previously discussed pattern of pseudonyms used by novelists submitting work to Macmillan provides circumstantial evidence. Readers' reports written by some important literary figures and saved in copybooks in the Macmillan Archives provide direct evidence. As the critics wrote these reports on submitted novels, they praised realism and denigrated romance. They also passed judgment on the inherent abilities of men and women as authors and as readers. The reports enable us to watch the process of redefinition unfold.

4
Edging
Women Out:
The High-Culture Novel

By the 1860s, when Macmillan and Company moved to London, individual publishers were no longer intent on making a profit as generalists. Rather the publishing industry had assumed its present coloration; firms sought to establish reputations as specialists, the source of good books of a certain kind (Coser, Kadushin, and Powell 1982; Powell 1985), for example, the three-decker novel (Bentley), the travelogue (John Murray), or textbooks and monographs (Macmillan).

Nonetheless, to meet expenses and to profit, firms published materials outside of their chosen specialty. By doing so, a publisher could also depict his firm as fulfilling the industry's unstated standards for a major publishing house. Sometimes to satisfy those requirements a production-oriented publisher would even choose to issue an individual book or line of books that at least initially might fail financially (ibid.).

Alexander Macmillan wanted his firm to be a major Victorian house. Despite its specialization in nonfiction, Macmillan and Company published fiction and, as soon as financially feasible, established a monthly magazine. Intent on establishing a reputation for excellence in any area his firm entered, Alexander hired the best literary advisers he could find to advise him about which manuscripts, if published, would be a credit to the firm and which would not.

Initially, Alexander and his advisers (termed *readers*) did not see eye to eye; although Alexander wished to establish a reputation for excellence, he wanted to make money too. And although Alexander respected his advisers he wanted the novels published by Macmillan and Company to express his literary tastes, not theirs. Thus at first he published some fiction that his advisers abhorred but thought would sell well. Ultimately, Macmillan and his readers adjusted to one another; the readers learned to assess manuscripts from Macmillan's point of view, and Macmillan learned that a book that his advisers despised would probably receive bad reviews and would thus diminish his firm's reputation.

In his biography of the House of Macmillan, novelist Charles Morgan (1943) stresses how much Alexander Macmillan's tastes and preferences shaped the firm's fiction lists. He adds that in the 1870s when Alexander's sons and nephews began to join the firm, Daniel's eldest son, Frederick, displayed a particular interest in fiction. As Alexander's involvement in the firm waned with age and infirmity, Frederick became responsible for the fiction lists. Though he still respected Alexander's opinion, Frederick also consulted John Morley, the house reader who had the greatest influence from November 1866, the date of his initial report (on Sophia Jex-Blake's nonfiction manuscript on women's colleges in the United States), through roughly 1900. By the end of his life in 1923 John Morley had been an editor, a critic, an author of intellectual and biographical histories, and a member of Parliament and the cabinet.

The activities of the publishers' readers became more important in midcentury but began as early as 1799, when John Aiken served as reader for Caldell and Davies. William Gifford started reading for John Murray's firm in 1808. The qualifications of these and other early publishers' readers were that they had been "bred up in the profession or trade of publishing" (Gettmann 1960, 189). One may infer that they were viewed as extensions of their employers, qualified because they were familiar with both their employers' tastes and "the problems involved in the making and selling of books" (ibid.).

By the 1850s publishers sought to hire readers who could serve as an extension of the audience. Many were authors whose own novels seem to capture the taste of the publisher for whom they read. Thus, elite publisher George Smith fed Charlotte Brontë one volume at a time of Thackeray's *Esmond* "so as to get the library reader's response" (Sutherland 1976, 109). In the 1860s the popular novelist and *Athenaeum* critic Geraldine Jewsbury read for Bentley's; poet, essayist, and novelist George Meredith for Chapman and Hall; and John Morley for Macmillan.

These literary figures were hardly the typical library reader. Most library readers were probably women. Most publishers' readers were men. Presumably, the publishers' readers assessed manuscripts on the basis of both their employers' past preferences and standards they shared with others in their literary networks. They then gave their notion of what a typical library reader's response might be. On occasion they based their recommendations on their own experiences as authors, especially their knowledge of Mudie's preferences.

After Mudie's distaste for Jewsbury's novel *Zoë*—he bought few copies because in one scene the heroine's decolletage was too bare—Jewsbury demanded revisions in manuscripts she thought Mudie might condemn on moral grounds. Meredith's recommendations to Thomas Hardy for revising his first novel, *The Poor Man and the Lady*, echo criticisms of Meredith's own earlier *The Ordeal of Richard Feverel*, which Mudie had detested (ibid., 216). Author-readers stood between authors and audience.

These critical interventions are important for several reasons. We alluded to one at the end of the last chapter: in the readers' reports submitted to Macmillan and Company, one can see how critics helped to edge women out of the high-culture novel.[1] There are at least four other reasons. First, the readers are another layer mediating between authors and their audience. As Habermas (1964) might have put it, the increasingly complex structure of publishing transforms a public in the eighteenth-century sense of educated people who know one another and personally discuss ideas and policies into a "market," a category of people whose tastes are presupposed by industrial forces and who do not necessarily know one another or get to make a choice about what will be published. The readers embody the growing rationalization—and hence the increasing internal structuring—of nineteenth-century publishing firms.

To be sure, many writers were from the same social class as some readers of their work. Also, authors read one another's books and essays and so constituted audiences even publics, for one another. Indeed, some of them had a major editorial influence on their colleagues' manuscripts. Others presented their work to friends or neighbors who might be deemed "common readers," but the business of publishing, both production and distribution, was increasingly geared toward the establishment of a market. And the concepts of market and public connote different formations of consciousness.

Second, the institutionalization of reading as an occupation fed the development of criticism as the activity of literary middlemen. These readers were de facto critics. In *The Rise and Fall of the Man of Letters*, John Gross (1970) shows how literary criticism became a source of income in nineteenth-century England, much as other cultural activities were also wrested from the domain of talented and unpaid amateurs. Such critics as Macmillan's reader John Morley and the essayists of the *Edinburgh Review*, whose opinions are considered in chapter 8, carved out the great tradition of English literature,

---

1. At other firms, the actions of women who served as readers contributed to the empty field phenomenon. As we explain below, they applied what they believed to be universal standards; universal standards are, however, usually male standards (Simmel 1984).

which eventually reified literature and deprecated excluded writers and speakers. By identifying the critic rather than the novelist as both author and authority, critics deprecated even those whose writing was included in the great tradition (see Williams 1977, 43–44). The critic was to assume the authority of interpreter of the world that is so frequently demonstrated by the articles in today's *New York Review of Books* or *Times* (of London) *Literary Supplement*. There the ostensible raison d'être of reviewing is transformed from summarizing and evaluating a book into an occasion for a critic to make comments about its topic. Here, too, the distinction between critic-authority and author-authority captured a shift in the structure of consciousness.

Third, the publisher's readers themselves reproduced the stratification of publishers' markets. That is, publishers chose or trained readers with an eye to their own particular market(s) as well as to pleasing Mudie's. Thus, Bentley, primarily a specialist in fiction thought to be consumed by women, employed novelist Geraldine Jewsbury at a set sum for every manuscript reviewed. By the 1870s Bentley was also paying five other women novelists to read manuscripts on a piecework basis. Macmillan and Company, however, generally resisted women novelists who asked to serve as readers—even when these women included bestselling authors whose work it published, such as Mrs. Oliphant.

Maintaining different economic relationships with their literary advisers, the publishers reproduced gender stratification as well as class stratification. Bentley paid Jewsbury, other women, and presumably male readers for each report whereas Macmillan had Morley on staff, though he worked at home; Meredith, who worked for Chapman and Hall, was also salaried.

Finally, the novel itself was becoming increasingly differentiated. The popular novel was becoming separate from the high-culture novel, although it is dangerous to reify those literary categories. Mrs. Oliphant's satiric *Miss Marjoribanks* (1866), for example, was considered a popular novel at the time of its publication, but Q. D. Leavis (1969) has recently termed it a minor classic—thus a high-culture novel. Nineteenth-century critics insisted that Dickens was a popular novelist; writing Dickens' entry in *DNB*, Leslie Stephen saw him as a writer for the uneducated. Today, Dickens' work is critically acclaimed.

Yet at midcentury the very existence of such a work as Matthew Arnold's *Culture and Anarchy* (1869) helped to articulate the concept of high culture. When Arnold published *Culture and Anarchy*, the term *high culture* was already in use. In 1860, complaining about a French literary critic who had called her a "rival" of Dinah Mulock, George Eliot described Mulock as "a writer who is read only by novel-readers, pure and simple, never by people of high culture" (quoted in Showalter 1975, 6).

Like Eliot, Arnold disliked "novel-readers, pure and simple." To him, they were "barbarians." Arnold also attacked the "pharisees," particularly religious evangelicals who applied narrowly moralistic standards to culture. In *Culture and Anarchy*, Arnold advocated diffusing the "best knowledge" and the "best ideas" to the middle classes in order to edify them socially, politically, and culturally, for to him the three were clearly intertwined.

Arnold is today held to be the preeminent mid-Victorian critic. *Culture and Anarchy* was published just after Morley joined the firm of Macmillan and Company. To a great extent, Morley's views resembled those of Arnold, whom he knew. Like Arnold, Morley preferred the gentle culture of the elite. But in Morley's reports issues of gender came to be conflated with issues of social class. Morley's reports demonstrate how a critic as reader helped to constitute a concept of culture—of what good literature is—and of how women were edged out.

In making judgments, publishers' readers drew on their notions about both culture and the stratified publishing industry as resources and constraints for determining the fate of manuscripts. But merely to state that the readers, like publishing itself, blend art and commerce is to miss the significance of their activities. Rather, in the selection of manuscripts cultural and economic processes are intertwined. They perpetually inform and shape one another, as seen in the reports that Morley submitted to Macmillan.

Most important, they also reveal how culture was reproduced as the stronghold of a male elite. The imprimatur of certain critics associated with particular circles revolving around elite literary journals indicated which novels were good literature and identified those who read these novels as participants in high culture. It also limited the ability of people outside those circles to claim cultural distinction simply because they read books—or even wrote them. Arnold and other enlightened critics may have written of raising the cultural level of the bourgeoisie and working class; they may have written of the light diffused by understanding; but they were to define the nature of that light and what was worthy of understanding. Educated, elite men were to prevail.

Morley and Alexander Macmillan participated in the process of relegating women to the popular-culture novel, which had supposedly been their domain, and thus of defining the high-culture novel as a male enterprise. But they would not have seen it in that way. For his time Morley was liberal about feminist ideas, and Macmillan published books by feminists and articles advocating more rights for women in *Macmillan's Magazine*. Like his friend John Stuart Mill, at whose table he was a frequent guest,[2] Morley seems to have believed that force of circumstances prevented women from offering manuscripts that were up to standard.[3] He and Macmillan, however, insisted that to be published manuscripts had to meet their supposedly universal standards. To appreciate how Macmillan's readers contributed to the relegation of women to popular culture, let us take a closer look at these advisers.

John Morley (1838–1923) stood foremost among them, at least in length of service to Macmillan and Company. Although he entered Oxford intending to enter the Anglican clergy, Morley lost his faith in the late 1850s. When "his father wrathfully cut off his allowance and obliged him to leave Oxford in haste with a pass degree only" (Hamer 1968, 1), Morley moved to London, where he supported himself as a journalist and traveled in intellectual circles. Unlike that staunch Christian Alexander Macmillan, Morley held his closest ties with positivists, Benthamites, and agnostics. Besides Mill, his friends included Leslie Stephen, whom he met while working on the *Saturday Review*, George Meredith, George Eliot, who respected a criticism he had written of one of her novels, and George Lewes, whom he replaced as editor of *Fortnightly Review* in 1865. In 1880 Morley became editor of the daily London newspaper *Pall Mall* as well. Morely left the *Fortnightly Review* in October 1882 and became editor of *Macmillan's Magazine* a year later. A solidly "second rank" man of letters in the estimation of John Gross (1970), Morley wrote intellectual biographies and books that might now be classified as works within the history of ideas.

Morley's life and activities were part and parcel of the growth of literature as an occupation. For instance, starting in the 1870s Morley edited for Macmillan a series on "English Men of Letters," which an *Athenaeum* critic correctly perceived as heralding an age of "literary middlemen" (*Athenaeum* 1878c,11). Some of these volumes written by then-famous authors concerned novelists. And so this series also affirmed that novelists could earn posthumous recognition as well as more immediate rewards. Morley knew most of the contemporary contributors personally; he virtually wooed some to join the series.

2. They met after Mill had expressed his admiration for Morley's article "New Ideas," published in *Saturday Review*.

3. In his very first months with Macmillan, Morley acted as though he believed that with adequate training, women might write good books. That year he suggested that a woman rewrite a biography whose topic he felt showed promise. He read the manuscript several times and after each reading offered extensive editorial suggestions. Mill developed his views of women's actual and potential accomplishments in his classic *The Subjection of Women*.

Morley used his literary activities to support his political career. In the 1870s and 1880s Morley was a politician associated with Chamberlain. (They split over issues associated with Irish home rule and the empire.) His political career brought him important positions, as well as the title viscount. Morley served as a Liberal Member of Parliament from 1883 to 1908 and as Irish Secretary in 1886, 1892, and 1895. With Gladstone, he shared primary responsibility for preparation of the first and second Home Rule Bills. He served in the Liberal Cabinets of 1886, 1892–1895, and 1905–1914. Despite his opposition to imperialism, Morley served as secretary of state for India from 1895 through 1910, a period when Indians were demanding political reforms. He resigned from the cabinet in July 1914 because he opposed Britain's entrance in World War I.

Morley, who was frequently acerbic, did not endear himself to those whose work he criticized. Gross (1970) hints that if Morely had been more personable—more amenable to playing literary politics by giving praise where he might not feel it due—contemporary estimates of his position in literature might have been higher. Nonetheless, Morley's forthrightness served Macmillan well.

Morley was more than sufficiently involved in the literary circles of his time to express the prevailing standards. For instance, in keeping with the dictates of his age and his own somewhat "feminine sensibilities" (Hamer 1968, 57), Morley deplored "immodesty." Some scenes, his reader's reports comment, are "too strong"—a euphemism for "too explicit." He praised faithfulness to life—"realistic" novels that were "true to nature" and displayed intellectual depth and good writing ("a practiced hand"). Morley was also familiar with the preferences of literary institutions, including Mudie's, as were such other Macmillan employees as business-manager and partner George Lillie Craik, who eventually married novelist Dinah Mulock.

Morley appreciated his employers. His views on religion were so different from those of the Macmillans that Morley was not sent any manuscripts on religious subjects, although he read in virtually every other nontechnical category. Yet, in his autobiography (1917), Morley praised Alexander Macmillan as a "statesman" and a "Minister of Letters"—high praise from a politician.

Morley is said to have had a sharp manner, but Mowbray Morris, his successor as principal reader and in 1885 as editor of the firm's magazine was a veritable curmudgeon. Particularly in his later years, he deplored innovations in fiction (as Morley also did at the turn of the century). He was, to put it kindly, ambivalent about women writers. Writing to a young friend, he damned the work of George Eliot as "second-hand culture got partly . . . from that very superficial creature she lived with . . . George Henry Lewes." He wrote to the same friend in 1886, "Imagine my sitting (at dinner last Friday) next to a girl, under twenty, who had published a novel, was learning Latin and Greek, and attending an Ambulance class! And yet she was quite a nice girl; though I had to tell her she would be much better employed in learning to sew on buttons, and make puddings" (Bolithio 1950, 194–195). But one woman who had contributed to *Macmillan's Magazine* eulogized Morris as a "great editor" who "took infinite pains over the manuscripts he accepted" (London *Times*, 28 June 1911).

After the turn of the century, Frederick Macmillan brought in a new fiction reader to replace Morley and Morris, Charles Whibley. In 1910 John W. Cousin listed Whibley in his biographical dictionary of English literature, although he did not include either Morley or Morris. Cousin identified Whibley as a "critic and reviewer" and author of five books, including *A Book of Scoundrels* and *Thackeray*. Morgan (1943) found Whibley's literary opinions to be conservative but judicious.

By that time the position of reader was even more specialized. When Morley started with the firm, he read in almost every field. George Grove, then editor of *Macmillan's Magazine* and soon to be editor of the monumental *Grove's Dictionary of Music*, gave occasional advice. Norman Lockyer, later knighted, became Macmillan's "consulting physician with regard to scientific books and schemes" (Morgan 1943). Physician Donald MacAlister, unmentioned by Morgan, is probably the "D. MacA" who crops up in the files as the reader of manuscripts on medicine and chemistry during the 1870s and 1880s.[4] Now and again, Charlotte Yonge commented on religion. But in most cases the reader was Morley. The clerk who kept the manuscript ledgers neatly penciled in the initials of occasional readers, but those initials are rare until the 1890s, when they sprinkle the appropriate column ("Mss. sent to reader"). By 1907 reviewing manuscripts had become such a specialized task that the firm's new ledgers had a separate column to record the identity of each manuscript's reader.

What the Readers Saw

Although Macmillan's formal arrangements for processing fiction and nonfiction were identical, in practice fiction and nonfiction were handled

4. MacAlister, a member of the Royal College of Surgeons and university lecturer at St. John's College, published on these topics with Macmillan.

differently—in part because of authors' training, in part because of their differential access to social networks, in part because the standards applicable to nonfiction are generally clearer than those pertinent to fiction.

The lines of Macmillan's ledgers recording the names of nonfiction authors are dotted with such titles as "M..A." and "Professor," and in the 1860s, before the degree became more common, with "B. A." as well. Although an occasional minister was acknowledged as the author of a story, academic titles did not sit besides the names of novelists. Having contacts with publishers through social networks, nonfiction writers were more likely to submit a proposal than were novelists. Very few fragments of novels are entered in the ledgers. Either aspiring novelists sent completed manuscripts or, as Sutherland (1976, 210) suggests, Macmillan accepted fiction manuscripts from "authors of reputation with some kind of *entrée* [to claim consideration], or from [his] regular stable of writers."

Except for members of Macmillan's stable, the reputations of nonfiction writers seem to have wielded more weight, for good or ill, than those of novelists. Even when they were introducing other fiction writers, novelists did not necessarily vouch for the quality of the work they were introducing. For instance, in 1875 Mrs. Oliphant wrote to Alexander Macmillan about a work by Miss Dworkin, daughter of the "late distinguished Professor Dworkin of Oxford," and praised her talents in art and music, but added that she had not seen the manuscript (26 January 1875). And Macmillan did reject manuscripts by novelists who had sold well. In contrast in 1887 reader T. Lauder Brunton said of Mrs. Atkins' offer of a book on massage, "From Mrs. Garrett Anderson's introduction, I should think that Mrs. Atkins must be a woman of high standing and likely to do well." (Mrs. Anderson was one of the first British women to become a doctor.) Similarly, in 1877 MacAlister's knowledge of a would-be author's reputation guided his rejection of a proposal to write a book on instrument making: "Bartlett is a good workman and laboratory assistant, but I don't think he is good enough to produce a first rate book."

Generally, it appears that standards for judging the quality of nonfiction were probably more concrete, better developed, and generally better known than those for fiction—much as is the case today. In table 4.1 we demonstrate the outcome of this tendency across the three periods: the readers saw a larger percentage of the fiction; nonfiction was more clearly either excellent or dreadful; and nonfiction was more likely to be accepted. (Our method of sampling the Macmillan records, described in appendix A, indicates that tests of statistical significance are inappropriate.)

In table 4.2 we consider the disposition of men's and women's fiction

Table 4.1: Disposition of Fiction and Nonfiction Manuscripts at Each Stage of Review, All Periods

		Genre	
		Fiction (%)	Nonfiction (%)
Initial screening			
Immediate acceptance		0	11
		(4)	(156)
Immediate rejection		26	46
		(244)	(670)
Sent to Reader		74	43
		(699)	(632)
	N	(947)	(1458)
After reader's report			
Acceptance		5	20
		(32)	(124)
Rejection		94	78
		(657)	(491)
Don't know		1	3
		(10)	(17)
	N	(699)	(632)
Final disposition			
Acceptance		4	19
		(36)	(280)
Rejection		95	80
		(901)	(1161)
Don't know		1	1
		(10)	(17)
	N	(947)	(1458)

Note: Figures in parentheses are base Ns for the adjacent percentages. Total N = 2,405 (947 fiction and 1,458 nonfiction). All percentages have been rounded.

in each period and draw two inferences from it. First, we infer that these data support the empty field phenomenon. During the period of invasion, women fared better than men. Whoever sorted the manuscripts, presumably one of the Macmillans, initially rejected roughly the same proportion of manuscripts by women (32 percent) and by men (31 percent).[5] During this

5. According to Sutherland (1976, 210), from 1866 through 1870, "The kinds of fiction [most authors submitted to Macmillan]... were predictably formulaic, and one can

Table 4.2: Disposition of Fiction Manuscripts, by Gender and Period

Period	Women				Men			
	Male Invasion (%)	Redefinition (%)	Institutionalization (%)	All Periods (%)	Male Invasion (%)	Redefinition (%)	Institutionalization (%)	All Periods (%)
Disposition								
Initial screening								
Immediate acceptance	1	0	0	0	0	0	1	0
Immediate rejection	32	19	40	30	31	14	27	22
Sent to reader	67	80	60	70	69	85	72	78
N	(127)	(191)	(169)	(487)	(73)	(203)	(166)	(442)
After reader's report								
Acceptance	8	5	3	5	2	5	3	4
Rejection	92	94	98	95	96	92	96	95
Don't know	0	1	0	0	2	3	1	2
N	(85)	(154)	(102)	(341)	(50)	(173)	(120)	(343)
Final disposition								
Acceptance	6	5	1	4	1	5	3	4
Rejection	94	95	99	96	97	93	96	95
Don't know	0	1	0	0	1	2	1	2
N	(127)	(191)	(169)	(487)	(73)	(203)	(166)	(442)

Note: Some columns do not add to 100 percent because of errors due to rounding. The total number of fiction mss., 929, excludes mss. for which we could not determine the gender of the author. The category of mss. submitted by men includes people recorded by their initials, as in J. R. Smith.

period he also sent the reader almost as many of the manuscripts by women (67 percent) as of those by men (69 percent). In subsequent periods men clearly fared better than women during this initial screening. We also infer that as the decades passed more talented men may have been submitting novels. In each period, whoever sorted the fiction manuscripts sent the reader a higher percentage of the fiction submitted by men than by women.

The disposition of manuscripts *after the reader handed in his report* also follows the pattern predicted by the empty field phenomenon. In the period of male invasion (late 1860s and 1870s), 8 percent of the fiction manuscripts by women that Morley reviewed were accepted; 2 percent of men's were. In the other two periods fiction by men and women that Morley read were equally likely to be accepted. Those figures are 5 percent in the period of redefinition and 3 percent in the period of institutionalization. One might speculate that these acceptance rates would be different if we knew the disposition of all the manuscripts. For instance, what if the few manuscripts of unknown disposition had all been accepted? The answer strengthens our case: in the period of invasion the women would still be favored; in the other two periods a greater proportion of the men's manuscripts would have been accepted after the filing of the reader's report.

The patterns are not complete in and of themselves. It is foolhardy to suppose that, by sorting manuscripts into piles of acceptance and rejection, well-meaning readers discriminated against women in some periods but not in others. We cannot know who accomplished which sorting. And we doubt that anyone at the firm would have thought to monitor the firm's activities, as we have done, by analyzing the patterns of submissions and acceptances according to the gender of authors. Such analyses are a product of the modern women's movement. But we also doubt that any publishing company does such a sorting now. The expenditure of time and funds would be too great; and we are sure that publishers and editors feel that their decisions are based on balanced business decisions that take into account the merit of the manuscripts, including their suitability for the firm.

According, let's take a closer look at what is known about the decision-making process at Macmillan and Company by examining the readers' reports.

---

categorize the novels from the stale reek of the titles, without having to read the works themselves." He explains: "Typically numerous are three-volume love stories, built around a conventional heroine . . . problem and sensation novels . . . historical romances . . . Trollopian chronicles . . . simple romances of high life, what in earlier times were called 'silver fork tales.' "

What the Readers Said

Especially in reviews of nonfiction, the readers concentrated on both quality and potential profit. The two concerns are necessarily interrelated. Generally, Macmillan strove to develop a profitable backlist, and Alexander was willing to carry a book for decades until it caught on if he was convinced of its intellectual merit. One of his business stratagems seems to have been investment in good nonfiction that at first might break even or even show a loss rather than turn a quick profit. At least through the period under examination his successors favored the same tack.

The most familiar example concerns Marshall's *Economics*, which Frederick Macmillan published during the Great Book War of the early 1890s. That "war" concerned terms for such wholesalers as bookclubs, which were attempting to undercut bookstores. The bookclubs wished to purchase books at a larger discount than was available to bookstores, much as Mudie's had done. Macmillan wanted the wholesale prices to be the same for small and large retailers, including bookclubs. To challenge the clubs, Frederick Macmillan issued Marshall's *Economics* at a small discount, which forced both bookclubs and bookstores to sell it at the declared retail price. *Economics* did not make a profit for decades, though today it is esteemed as a classic in its field.

Frederick Macmillan seems to have regarded his reputation as an economic asset, a view more than validated by Pierre Bourdieu's research on contemporary French publishing and the value of reputation as symbolic capital (1980). By issuing prestigious books, Macmillan announced to potential authors that his was the house to choose when mulling over where to send a manuscript. He announced to libraries and to readers (audiences) that his were important books, works to own, not to borrow. Morley's reviews of nonfiction consistently display his awareness of the Macmillans' strategy. The phrase "not suitable for your list" runs through his assessment of nonfiction. And he comments frequently that a book will bring no profit but "will be a credit to your list."

Although concerned with potential profit, Morley and subsequent readers did not advise Macmillan about the appropriate price for an author's copyright, as Geraldine Jewsbury advised Bentley on occasion. For instance, in September 1867 Jewsbury told Bentley of Mr. Fulham's *Time Will Tell*: "You know whether Mr. Fulham's former novels have succeeded; if they have, this is quite as good as any of them and you may take it if he does not want too much" (*Lists of the Publications of Richard Bentley and Son, 1829–1898*). She wrote of Annie Thomas' *Lance Urquant's Lover*: "It would perhaps be worth your while to take

77

if the lady were not likely to require a large sum for the MS!" (ibid.). Paid on a piecework basis and frequently adding to her letter reports the address of a friend with whom she would be staying so that manuscripts might find her, Jewsbury depended for her income on appearing to be indispensable. Paid on a retainer and keeping some office hours at Macmillan's, Morley may have delivered monetary estimates in the course of conversation that do not appear in his formal reports. Nonetheless, when reviewing novels Morley was concerned with profit.

Simultaneously, Morley located the realistic novel as high culture, while trying to build the reputation of his employer's list. As Morley and his successors tried to distinguish and define the high-culture novel through their in-house reviews, they insistently identified men with high culture and women with mass or popular culture, although they did not use these twentieth-century terms. They identified men with ideas capable of having an impact upon the mind—with activity and the production orientation associated with high culture. Women were identified with mass audiences, passive entertainment, and flutter—popular culture.

As we will show in chapter 8, Morley expressed ideas that were in the air at the time. But we doubt that either Alexander or Frederick Macmillan wanted Morley and their other readers to express innovative opinions about fiction. As noted in chapter 2, Alexander preferred Charles Kingsley's novels to those of William Makepeace Thackeray. He had also achieved significant profits from Kingsley's work. The reader's job was to identify novels that would be compatible with the fiction that the firm had already published. Nonetheless, while accomplishing this task Morley also informed the Macmillans about his notion of high culture—novels, mainly by men, that would cause readers to think. In his specific emphasis on the novel as the expression of ideas, Morley affirmed the emerging cultural hegemony.

Morley's imposition of that hegemony was sometimes caustic. As noted, Morley and the other readers rejected manuscripts much more often than they accepted them. Most of their comments were negative, sometimes scathing. According to Gettmann (1960, 107), "The employees at Chapman and Hall used to await the arrival of Meredith's reports with his pungent comments on poor work. Some of Miss Jewsbury's were equally incisive and sarcastic. She concluded her opinion of one novel with the statement, 'Reading it is like walking thro' a field of stiff clay on a rainy day.' "

The early reports. Whether his comments were sarcastic or merely condemnatory, literary critic John Morley made literary judgments. Countess von

Bothemer's *Strong Hands, Steadfast Hearts* was "of a very conventional stamp" (Readers' Reports, ms. 185); Miss Rhodes's *Ralph Redfern* was "a very fair novel of the second rank" (ibid., ms. 43).

Sometimes Morley's literary judgments were suffused with notions about what could be expected of men and women as authors. For instance, Morley praised H. Watherston's *Gossamer* for an ineffable presence of culture: "Fair, but I don't find it remarkable in any respect. Of course, there are signs that the writer is a man of culture and the book is readable" (ms. 6). The phrase "a woman of culture" has an awkward ring. And Morely condemned a novel by the popular Fanny Kemble as "old ladies' gossip . . . an oasis of the possible in a desert of intolerable twaddle" (ms. 2340). With this recommendation not to publish, he also announced that literary values potentially superseded profit. On other occasions, Morley combined concerns for quality and profit by invoking symbolic capital. Of R. Thyme's *Ravendale* he wrote: "It is a novel which might take, but which would be of no particular credit if it did" (ms. 49).

At least in his written reports, Morley insisted that manuscripts stand on the quality they presented, not on the quality that might be infused through editing. Although some of Geraldine Jewsbury's reports recommended specific revisions, Morley rarely did so after an unfortunate experience early in his tenure with Macmillan and Company. He had read Mrs. Campbell's *Life of Sarpi* three times, offering what were for him long reviews and suggestions for revisions. The fourth time he saw the manuscript, he commented in despair, "Mrs. Campbell has certainly succeeded in bringing the book a little further out of chaos . . . but even now it is only in the raw state. . . . The authoress's mind is made out of wood and further advice is useless' (ms. 44). Presumably, he felt his work on Mrs. Campbell's manuscripts had been a waste of his time. At best, as in the famous case of Thomas Hardy's first novel, Morley might suggest rejection but add that Macmillan should take a hard look at any future work of a promising young author. "If the man is young," Morley wrote in that often quoted report, "there is stuff and promise in him" (ms. 218).

To make his points about quality, Morley offered comparisons—what later critics were to call the "comparative method of criticism." On occasion he referred to contemporary authors, identifying a manuscript as imitative or derivative of a specific work. More important, he used comparisons to voice his notions about the sort of symbolic capital that Macmillan should be accumulating within the stratification of prestige in the past and present publishing industry. During the period of male invasion, Morley especially sneered at manuscripts that he thought belonged on the lists of past publishing houses specializing in "women's novels" or in large circulation newspapers for the new middle class—those potential "cultural pretenders." For instance, Miss Horner's *Isolina* has "too much of the ordinary Minerva Press stamp," although "of course, one has read worse books" (ms. 13). B. R. Green's *Pride* is "excellently suited for the London journal. I don't think it would do for you at all" (ms. 174). At the time, the circulation of the *London Journal* had reached six figures. Or, again, "the interest of the rest [of Mrs. Russell's "Mabel Stanhope"] is of the kind one has in a London Journal story. . . . I presume you don't want to take an ordinary three-volume novel" (ms. 22).

Such references to ordinary but popular work necessarily implied distinctions between high culture and popular culture. They suggest that in the late 1860s Morley was already engaged in redefining the novel as a potentially elite genre. The same connotation is implicit in a later comment that a book is suited for Tinsley, a firm that had built its profits on the "ordinary" three-volume circulating library novel, including many by popular midcentury authors.

In his reports Morley identified the circulating library novel with mediocrity and profit, not with quality. Of Reverend J. B. Wells's *The Wilverdeens of Summerdown*, he wrote it is "worth publishing, *not* however by you. I think it is too little above the average Circulating Library" (ms. 71). Similarly, a fragment of M. Penrose's *Miss Milbank's Management* has "very much the air of the ordinary novel of the Circulating Library" (ms. 197). Although Macmillan and Company sold novels to Mudie's, presumably Alexander did not want his publications identified as ordinary.

Part of the community working to impose culture on anarchy, Morley argued that economic considerations were unimportant in determining whether a work was of high culture. As Bourdieu (1984) points out, one must be economically secure—elite—to argue the irrelevance of finances. Yet Morley was also defining a market position for Macmillan. Jewsbury was less likely to condemn a novel for being ordinary or suited only for a circulating library. (Much of Bentley's profit came from novels purchased by circulating libraries.) She sometimes recommended a manuscript for a specific line that Bentley published, at times approving types of novels or authors that Morley disliked.

Consider Morley's comments on Miss Walker's *Martin Deane*. He damned it by comparing it to the work of Bentley authors and to romances. "The authoress has written a story which is readable enough as the stories of Mrs. Riddell and of Mrs. Wood [Bentley books that sold well] are readable . . . worth printing by anyone who wanted a romance in his list, not otherwise" (ms. 197). Jewsbury had recommended Mrs. Wood's highly successful *East Lynne* without hesitation, although she had criticized its grammar. Even though Bentley had rejected Mrs. Riddell's early novels, he published much work by both Wood and Riddell.

Bentley profited mightily from Mudie's Select Library. But in contrasting Macmillan with Bentley, Morley was not condemning all circulating libraries. In these reviews from the period of invasion, Morley was not singling out Mudie's for condemnation. Rather, he condemned the ordinary circulating library novel (perhaps the ordinary novel to be found at Mudie's) and the ordinary circulating library—the library associated only with the novel—but not the Select Library that Charles Mudie was then building.

In the periods of redefinition and institutionalization, subsequent Macmillan readers, presumably Mowbray Morris, Charles Whibley, and on occasion Morley, mentioned circulating libraries and their novels, but the tone of their references changed. Rather than condemning novels bound for ordinary libraries, from the late 1880s on they wrote of the ordinary novel suited only for Mudie's Library. The queens of the circulating library, many published by Bentley, supposedly reigned during the period of redefinition. The three-decker novel disappeared at the end of that period and was an object of disdain to literati by the period of institutionalization—although such well-known authors of three-deckers as Thackeray, Hardy, and Meredith were then praised as "modern."

The contrast between Morley's reactions and Bentley's publications does not mean that Morley and Macmillan were concerned with quality whereas Jewsbury and Bentley cared only for profit. Rather, Morley was actively engaged in excluding the romance—that form cultivated by women—from acceptable culture.[6] For instance, Morley simultaneously praised and dismissed Rosamund Harvey's "romance pure and simple." He found it "full of ability of the story-telling kind . . . exceptionally coherent and well-written. The plot is excellently kept and its secrets excellently kept back. The characters are well-drawn. The dialogue . . . unusually good and careful. But remember, all these virtues are in a field that is not of the highest" (ms. 236). A contemporary

---

6. Williams (1976) notes that this is the period in English history when the terms *culture* and *cultivation* were assuming relatively discrete meanings. Thus, in an earlier era a member of the literary elite might have been described as either "cultivated" or "cultured." The term cultivate continued to have some of its original agricultural associations, still found in such contemporary phrases as "to cultivate a friendship." By the end of the nineteenth century, the term cultured had lost its agricultural overtones; applied to authors, the term cultivated seemed stilted. We mean to imply that Morley acted as though he believed women might till the field of romance without achieving status within literary culture.

analogy is Doris Lessing's *Shikasta* series, which is science fiction. Lessing is a major writer; Harvey clearly was not. Associated with high culture, Lessing was sufficiently defensive about writing science fiction to introduce the series with a preface to the first volume as though to justify her work in that literary category.

Finally, during the periods of invasion and redefinition, Morley affirmed his concern for culture and for "men of culture" in his references to readers. In his reports, readers came in several varieties: ordinary, ladies, gossipers, and people with taste. Morley slighted all but the last group, whom he supposedly represented. Differentiating among readers in terms of both potential sales and implied taste, he measured them against the preferences of the cultural elite and found most of them wanting.

Again some examples. "Creditability" was not enough to warrant publication of Emily Ponsby's *Lord Latimer*. Morley warned, "I fear that the majority of ordinary readers would find the story too tame for lack of action and variety, yet... it is a creditable piece of work" (ms. 4). After his first four months with the firm, Morley wrote of E. G. Nisbett's *My Brides*: "If you want a novel, it strikes me [as] more in your line than I have yet seen. But mind, it is very, very simple, emphatically a novel for ladies" (ms. 37). Reverend Tyrwhitt's novel about Oxford—which was eventually published by another firm—had limited economic and critical appeal: although it had "the virtues of gossip for those who like gossip," it would "languidly interest a good many people belonging to university circles for a short season" (ms. 2309).

But taste—that is, good taste, the taste of those with cultural capital—resided in "the virtuous part of the public" (ms. 225), with which Morley identified. For them, as for Morley, books were to have an impact upon the mind. Thus, Morley criticized Miss Dillwyn's two-volume novel, submitted in 1887: "Like all Miss Dillwyn's writing, the book before me is brisk, fresh, smart, and humouristic; yet somehow, it doesn't have enough of these qualities to make a mark on one's mind" (ms. 5313).

Morley was very concerned about the mark on one's mind that supposedly constituted the promise of culture. His comments on reader's reports indicate that he saw it as a masculine virtue. By assigning a gender to this virtue, Morley affirmed that the high-culture novel was imbued with the supposed virtues of culturally elite men. Like his liberal friend John Stuart Mill, Morley may have felt that women could be taught to develop their minds but that they had not yet accomplished such a task.

Morley's disdain for the average middle-class woman must have been strong, for occasionally he treated a woman author, her manuscript, and her potential (presumably female) readers as though they were one and the same. Take Morley's comment on Miss E. Eyre's *Gabrielle and her Guardian*: "There is a real idea at the center of this story. . . . the treatment of it is very fair . . . but it is not masculine and robust. . . . There is a fluttering of petticoats and billing and cooing among women. . . . it is like five o'clock tea in three volumes" (ms. 196). His comment on *Heathercourt Rectory* by best-selling children's author Mrs. Molesworth similarly identified the novel with its readers. "Few men would get through it and the ladies who read it would hardly think the better of their own minds if they liked it strongly" (ms. 2482). During the decade in which Morley wrote these reviews, *Macmillan's Magazine* ran articles that favored improved education for women as well as women's entry into both politics and the professions.

Morley and Macmillan did not damn the taste of the average woman merely because they were men. To be sure, when men define their standards as universal standards, they infuse them with male concerns. "Man's *position of power* does not only assure his relative superiority over women, but it assures that his standards become generalized as generically human standards that are to govern the behavior of men and women alike" (Simmel quoted in Coser 1977, emphasis in original; cf. Simmel 1984).

Some women had enough power to participate in the creation of high culture. But these women also identified male standards as universal standards. Thus, Geraldine Jewsbury associated light entertainment with books addressed to women readers. As was typical of her generation of women novelists (Showalter 1977), she approved of strong professional women while holding to traditional Victorian notions about the separation of private (female) and public (male) spheres. Consider the following juxtaposition in her recommendation to reject a book in the late 1860s: "There's ability in the author, *but* the novel is not an entertaining one. I do not think any lady reader would be found to go thro' the first half of the first volume of plot" (*Lists of the Publications of Richard Bentley and Son, 1829–1898*). In the Macmillan readers' reports that we read, we could not find any reviews that damned men for being slight. Men who read or wrote what might have been termed "slight novels" were dismissed as "young" and so as still capable of developing approved literary tastes.

Almost all the reviews we have quoted have been from the period of invasion. As we have seen, in these years Morley was already redefining the novel by stressing realism and insistently distinguishing it from the earlier romances associated with women. Why, then, call the 1880s and 1890s the "period of redefinition"? First, the modern one-volume novel emerged in the 1890s. Because mid- and late nineteenth-century literary criticism perpetually reassessed the novel, we judge it best to reserve the term *redefinition* for the years immediately before and after the emergence of the modern one-volume novel.

Second, those rare occasions when a Macmillan overruled Morley or Morris suggest that during the 1860s and 1870s the novel was still emerging as high culture. When Alexander Macmillan overruled Morley in this period, he did so because he was not willing to accept the economic consequences of Morley's rejection of romances and other potentially profitable fiction. Although he did not use the term, we suspect that Alexander found Morley somewhat too "advanced" in his views. When Frederick Macmillan overruled Morley and Morris in the 1890s, it was because they were too old-fashioned. Let us review those decisions involving the readers' assessment.

Four of the eight accepted works of fiction submitted over the transom in 1867, 1868, 1877, and 1878 were romances. We infer that Alexander Macmillan disliked the economic implications of Morley's negative reports on Edith Milner's *The Rose of Raby*, Miss Rowsell's *Through the Twilight*, Mary Allan-Olnery's *La Comtesse Estelle,* and Miss Walker's *The Connells of Connell Castle* (all published pseudonymously by Macmillan, some with title changes). Morley was advising rejection of novels he expected to enable a profit. Potential sales were certainly a factor in the case of Walker's "melodramatic romance," which Morley had described as having a "mysterious complex plot—with blood and madness and dead man's bones . . . ought to be published and would sell—but certainly not your style of publication" (ms. 65). That description does not fit Morgan's characterization of Macmillan's personal taste. Assessment of the market must also have been a factor in Macmillan's acceptance of Hugh Harrie's novel in 1888. The reader's report states, "It is a story of the moment and the occasion. It describes the ignoble nature of wire-pulling at elections. . . . Of course, the book is not of the highest class. It will not live six months. But considering its actuality I should think it might have some small run and be worth the risking" (ms. 5391). In fiction as in nonfiction, Macmillan preferred to publish a book that would last a long time and so to reap the benefits of an active backlist; he preferred to amass symbolic capital in the hope that it would eventually be converted to economic capital. Before the new standards had taken firm hold, however, Macmillan was not always averse to turning a quick profit by publishing what would soon be viewed as popular culture.

Consider Frederick Macmillan's acceptance of Maurice Hewlett's *The Forest Lovers*, published in 1898. The manuscript came to his attention through Mrs. W. K. Clifford, a writer who held at homes for other writers on Sunday afternoons. Frederick sent it to Mowbray Morris, whose review was "lukewarm" (Morgan 1943, 148). According to Morgan, "Frederick Macmillan did not accept this as final. Mrs. Clifford had said with moderate emphasis that it was a good book and with extreme emphasis that it would be greatly popular. It was sent, therefore, to the court of appeal—John Morley."

For decades Morley had served the firm well. By the 1890s his literary judgments were conservative; he confused aspects of an emerging modernism with the romantic prerealism he had attacked at the beginning of his long career. But Morley's judgments had been reliable in the past, and even today, through either loyalty or respect, publishing houses frequently draw on long-standing advisers (see Powell 1985). Morley's review displayed his continuing denigration of romance. He wrote:

> A romance . . . not without quality, but marked by intense *artificiality* in every way. The style is clearly fashioned on Meredith, but not everyone can bend the bow of Ulysses; it has not the depth, richness or flash of G. M.; in other words, it has the affectation without the thought. . . . I find it readable enough in a *very* lazy moment; I mean, if I were in a lazy mood, I think the book would hold me in an easy way. But I cannot believe it will go very far with the public. . . . Of anything like true excellence either of invention or of writing I confess I find but moderate supply. (Morgan 1943, 150)

Frederick had decided to reject the book when he met Mrs. Clifford at a party. When she learned of his decision, she told him he was "throwing away a small fortune; she had never felt more certain about the popularity of any book, but she was aware that others must have said as much to him before and she asked only one thing: that he would not return the manuscript until he had read it himself" (ibid., 149–150.) Frederick read the book and accepted it without enthusiasm. He advised Hewlett in his letter of acceptance, "We are disposed to undertake the risk of publishing the book although we shall be more sorry than surprised if the circulating library public find it too fantastic for its taste" (ibid., 150).

Again, the economic motive prompted a Macmillan to overrule the house readers, though he seems to have concurred in Morley's assessment of the manuscript. But now those readers were promoting the standards of the past. Frederick's reference to circulating libraries also invoked a bygone era, for Mudie's no longer purchased three-volume novels. By the turn of the century, Morgan tells us, both Morley and Morris were old-fashioned (ibid, 218–219).

The later reports. Reports by Morley's successors, especially Mowbray Morris, do not significantly depart from the patterns we have described. Here is

Morgan's assessment of the readers after Charles Whibley replaced Mowbray Morris after Morris' death in 1911.

> Morley on his own true territory—history, politics, biography, literary criticism—was an advisor of the first rank, but he had a resistance to new developments in imaginative writing. He seems to have felt in his heart that fiction was not worth his moral and intellectual powder and shot.... Outwardly, Whibley also was on the safe side, but whereas Morley's conservatism was a by-product of radical righteousness, Whibley's had fire and light in it which enabled him to see and know himself, to mark and evaluate his prejudices, and to prevent the fictions of aesthetic taste from being obscured by moral indignations. (ibid., 219)

As for Morris, Morgan politely hints that he was considerably more closed-minded than John Morley. Morgan (1943) notes that Charles Whibley's taste was more modern than either Morley's or Morris', and he suggests that Macmillan's fiction list deteriorated in the 1890s, when both men were still influential.

Nonetheless, the differences that did emerge in the 1890s are worth noting. First, Macmillan's literary advisers condemned novels that they judged fit only for Mudie's Select Library (which discontinued three-deckers in 1894) rather than for other "ordinary" circulating libraries. Twenty years before, Morley had debunked only Mudie's "ordinary novels." Second, the readers implicitly ranked the literary qualities of various fiction lists then issued by Macmillan; for by the 1890s Macmillan published a Colonial Library. The readers treated the colonies with the same cultural contempt that they extended to women; some fiction was only for the Colonial Library, not for England. For instance, in 1907 an unknown reader (who sounds like Mowbray Morris) wrote of a novel by the established author Charles Gleig, "any comments are perhaps superfluous. We are pretty well agreed, I think, that for your Colonial Library ... it is the author's name, and not his work, that really matters. As I share your ignorance of Mr. Gleig and all his work, that seems to end it" (ms. 17592).

Third, fiction by women was denigrated in a more complicated way. Although Morley had mocked slight and feminine writing, in the 1890s and later an unidentified reader (possible Mowbray Morris) advised the firm that the quality of work by women writers had deteriorated. Once there had been women writers worth publishing, but no more. Contemporary women writers did not suit. Past quality was invoked to dismiss present performance.

More straightforward denigration of women also occurred. Take the reader's comment about *Morland* by Helen Baylics, which he read in 1907: "The author's ignorance of human nature equals her ignorance of society and her (it is impossible to believe that any man invented such a feebly impossible sequence of circumstances or such wooden bullies . . .) ignorance of the English language" (ms. 17893). That same reader generally despised women's intellectual ability, writing of Miss E. F. Buckley's *Greek Mythology*: "The plain truth is that this is not woman's work, and a woman has neither the knowledge nor the literary tact necessary for it" (ms. 17907).

Unfortunately, because the offices of the firm were drastically understaffed during World War I, readers' reports on the manuscripts submitted in 1917 were never copied into a book, so we cannot know whether reports written after Mowbray Morris' death also deprecate women. And, more generally, we cannot know exactly how women were treated after men's hegemony was institutionalized. Perhaps some were the golden exceptions to the rule, though the percentage of fiction by women accepted during the period of institutionalization would not make one think so. (It was a scant 1 percent compared to men's 3 percent.) For now, we simply conclude that the readers' reports prepared for Macmillan and Company articulated distinctions between high-culture and popular-culture novels. Although the readers may not have intended to do so, their reports helped to keep women writers in the position that had traditionally been available to them—authors of popular culture. Thus, in the later decades women did not seem suitable authors for Macmillan.

Were the Readers Right?

To say that Macmillan's readers felt that women wrote inferior work is one thing. To assess their opinion on novels that have disappeared is another. Manuscripts that were never published have vanished in family attics. Manuscripts that were eventually published may have been rewritten before they appeared in print, even if they were issued a year or two after their rejection by Macmillan. There is no way to read what John Morley and Mowbray Morris read to learn whether their evaluations were sensible.

Adapting the techniques used by sociologists of science, we devised a way around this problem.[7] We formulated two series of questions about the publication records of novelists from which inferences might be drawn. The

---

7. Sociologists of science derive indicators of the quality of publications by devising an index composed of the amount an author has published and the number of times the author's work is cited by other scientists. These measures are controversial. For a look at the controversy about applying these measures to women scientists, see Cole 1979; and for criticism, see Tuchman 1980; White 1982; Reskin 1980.

first set provides a loose indication of the quality of rejected manuscripts: Were any of the rejected manuscripts ever published? If so, were they published by one of the seven Victorian houses whose novels, according to Sutherland, are still read today? The second set provides a loose indication of the quality of rejected authors: What was the literary career of the author before this rejected manuscript was submitted? For example, was this the first work of a soon-to-be-great novelist? Or was it submitted by someone who, as far as is known, never published a book in Great Britain?

We answered both sets of questions by looking up in the *BMC* a systematic sample of the authors whose fiction was rejected in the late 1870s, 1897, and 1907. We then coded the number of their fiction and nonfiction books held by the British Library, which since the nineteenth century has served as a repository of all British publications. Our procedure yielded indicators of minimum quality, *if* one accepts the assumption that an eventually published manuscript is of higher quality than a never-published manuscript. (To accept this assumption, one must also assume that a novel was not substantially rewritten between the time Macmillan rejected it and the book's eventual publication. And one must assume that the quality of the novel rather than the author's contacts prompted its eventual publication.) We call the quality of eventually accepted novels "minimal" because a published book is not necessarily a good book. We must suppose that every reader has had the experience of finishing a book and wondering how it ever got to be published.

Although we found it much harder to locate women than men in the *BMC*, overall, we located virtually the same percentage of male and female authors of rejected novels (table 4.3). Our difficulty arose from Macmillan's practice of listing in the ledgers the first name or initials of rejected men, as in "James R. Smith" or "J. R. Smith" or even "J. R. Smith, M. A.," but frequently calling women merely "Miss Smith." The additional information provided for men enabled us to locate the right man, but all too often we could not tell whether the Miss Smith listed in the *BMC* was Macmillan's rejected author.

We infer from table 4.3 that women whose manuscripts Macmillan rejected were at least as likely to publish books as were men who received rejection notices. Put somewhat differently, women were not edged out of the field of writing all sorts of novels rather primarily the high-culture novel. Overall 40 percent of the sampled women and 42 percent of the sampled men whose novels Macmillan had rejected published at least one book and so are listed in the *BMC*. However, we cannot infer the consequences of the empty field phenomenon for women's publication activities in each period.

Table 4.3: Percentages of Authors of Rejected Novels Listed in the *BMC*, by Gender and Year of Submission

| | Year | | | |
	1877–1878	1897	1917	All Years
Women	34	50	33	40
	(77)	(109)	(72)	(258)
Men				
(includes authors	62	43	44	42
identified by initials)	(40)	(113)	(43)	(196)
All authors	35	46	37	41
	(117)	(222)	(115)	(454)

Note: Figures in parentheses are base Ns for the adjacent percentages. Total N = 454 manuscripts sampled in the specified years. Each author is counted once per manuscript. Thus, if an author submitted two manuscripts, each of which fell into our sample, he or she has been counted twice.

As suggested by table 4.3, our ability to locate male and female authors does not seem to be directly correlated with rejection rates. In the period of invasion, Macmillan accepted a higher proportion of novels submitted by women than by men, but novels by men were more likely to be published eventually. If minimum quality were the sole indicator of acceptance or rejection, we should have been able to find a higher percentage of women. Similarly, in the period of redefinition, when novels by men and women had comparable rejection rates, we located a higher percentage of female authors of rejected novels than of male authors. The period of male institutionalization is the only period when the pattern corresponds with our expectations. Novels by men had a higher acceptance rate than those by women, and we located a higher percentage of men than women. Either our indicator is flawed, or we are working with too few periods to discern a pattern, or there is no pattern to be found.

We do, however, find a pattern in the data concerning the *previous* publication records of authors of rejected fiction manuscripts (table 4.4). Because we had a harder time locating women, these data also understate women's accomplishments. As Sutherland (1976, 210) had surmised, most of the authors were novices. We infer that Macmillan was most hospitable to women novelists during the period of male invasion, when women were much less likely than men to have previously published either fiction or nonfiction but had their highest acceptance rate. Conversely, we infer that Macmillan

Table 4.4: Publication Records of a Subsample of Authors of Rejected Manuscripts, by Gender and Year of Submission

	Women				Men			
	Year				Year			
	1877–78 (%)	1897 (%)	1917 (%)	All Years (%)	1877–78 (%)	1897 (%)	1917 (%)	All Years (%)
Past publication records								
Never published fiction before submitting to Macmillan	84	66	76	74	75	73	79	75
Never published either fiction or nonfiction before submitting to Macmillan	82	62	72	71	65	66	74	68
Eventual publication records								
Never published any fiction	65	46	67	57	60	58	53	57
Never published a book	64	44	64	55	60	54	51	54
Probably published this novel after Macmillan rejected it	18	22	14	19	8	18	21	16
N	(77)	(109)	(72)	(258)	(40)	(113)	(43)	(196)

Note: An author was counted each time he or she submitted a rejected manuscript. For instance, an author who submitted two manuscripts was counted twice, if both manuscripts fell in the sample. The category of men includes authors identified by their initials in the ledgers. Authors who fell into the subsample but were not listed in the *BMC* are included in our calculations.

was most favorable to male novelists during the period of male institution-alization. In those decades the men and women who had submitted rejected novels were equally likely to be novices, but men had a higher acceptance rate. (Seventy-six percent of the women whose novels were rejected and 79 percent of the comparable men had not published a novel before they had submitted their manuscript to Macmillan.)

The men whose novels Macmillan had rejected did have one advantage over the women whose work was rejected. In each period and especially during the period of male invasion, before submitting a novel to Macmillan the men were more likely than women were to have published at least one book. During the period of male invasion, 10 percent of the rejected men but only 2 percent of the women had previously published a book of nonfiction. We infer that these men were slightly more likely than the women to be nonfiction authors trying their hand at a novel.

Subsequently, the men and women who had written rejected novels were equally likely to publish at least one novel or nonfiction book. There are some variations by period. But we cannot infer that at some time in the future the men played a more important role in literature than the women did or vice versa.[8]

Finally, the subsequent history of rejected manuscripts supports the inference that the empty field phenomenon applied to the occupation of novelist. In the period of male invasion and in the period of redefinition, a higher percentage of women's rejected manuscripts than of men's were sub-sequently published. In the period of male institutionalization, a higher per-centage of men's rejected manuscripts were eventually published.

Very few of the rejected manuscripts were subsequently issued by one of the seven firms that Sutherland (1976) claims published novels that are still read today. All told, 9 of 454 manuscripts rejected by Macmillan were published by other leading firms. Two of those manuscripts were by men and had been rejected during the period of redefinition. Of the 7 by women, 3 had been rejected during the period of invasion and 4 in the period of redefinition.

No measure can ever be definitive, and our measures are certainly flawed. Thus, we cannot claim that they confirm the presence of the empty field phenomenon—but they seem to do so. In each period the women and men

---

8. We also reviewed the subsequent publication records of authors of novels rejected by Macmillan. The means and standard deviations for both women and men are virtually identical. Both this finding and table 4.4 uphold Sutherland's (1976, 210) supposition that few of the novices who submitted novels to Macmillan were to become published authors.

who submitted novels that Macmillan rejected were likely to be novices. During the period of male invasion, when we claim that the novel was still identified with women, women were more likely eventually to publish their rejected novels. During the period of institutionalization, when we claim that the high-culture novel had become identified with men, men were more likely to eventually publish their rejected novel.

Taken together, Macmillan's records indicate that although women continued to publish novels they were edged out of the high-culture novel. The politics of culture were also the politics of gender. As we will see in the next chapter, other data also confirm the operation of the empty field phenomenon.

5
Who Gained
from Industrialization?

n a world containing ideal data, we could learn more about the empty field phenomenon by examining the lives of the women and men who submitted manuscripts to Macmillan and Company. Information about their lives would help us to assess how well equipped the women writers were to take advantage of any opportunities that came their way. Did these women come from the same social classes as their male counterparts? Were they as well educated as the men? Did they have equal access to relevant intellectual and social networks? Did they edit journals, magazines, newspapers, or other sorts of periodicals? Knowing more about their lives, we might also learn more about how they and their work were assessed in their own time.

But based as they are on limited information about the authors who submitted manuscripts the analyses presented in previous chapters could consider neither the lives and careers of authors nor how their work was assessed by their contemporaries. Not only are the rejected manuscripts unavailable, but in many instances it was impossible to locate even the names of the rejected authors in the *BMC*.

But we can learn more about how the empty field phenomenon operated by examining another group of authors—those whose dreams of being a famous novelist succeeded and who were even lauded after their death. Indeed, it is theoretically pertinent to do so, for in previous chapters we stressed that the women whose novels Macmillan rejected were as likely as their male counterparts to publish their manuscripts eventually. Women were not edged out of all fiction writing; they were edged out of writing high-culture novels. Although some novels by such women as Jane Austen and George Eliot are today recognized as high culture, as men defined the characteristics of the high-culture novel, they also defined it as a male preserve. By looking at the very successful, we can learn whether women and men were praised for the same sorts of accomplishments, whether they shared pathways to fame, and whether they brought similar qualifications and experiences to the pathways they followed. We can identify some of the social structural processes through which men became identified with the high-culture novel.

To understand the effect of the empty field phenomenon on the careers of successful nineteenth-century authors, we examine the lives of some prominent authors who published before 1840, the year we have used to mark the emergence of the Victorian literary system, and some who began publishing after that year. In this way we can situate our discussion of Macmillan's activities in their larger historical context. In an attempt to see the literary world as those authors did—to adopt as much as possible nineteenth-century notions of the life of the man of letters—in this chapter and next we draw on data gleaned through a systematic content analysis of the listings of a sample of authors in the twenty-three volumes of that grand nineteenth-century compendium the *DNB*, issued between 1885 and 1911.

For reasons explained below, the authors in our *DNB* sample were born between 1750 and 1865. Since the Macmillan ledgers began in 1866, we assume that many of the novelists who submitted manuscripts to Macmillan were contemporaries of the *DNB* authors who began publishing after 1840. Other novelists, especially those who submitted work to Macmillan during the period of male institutionalization (1907 and 1917), were probably born after 1865. Our assumption does not require a great leap of faith: the names of some of the *DNB* authors who began publishing after 1840 appear in the ledgers that record submissions to Macmillan and Company from 1866 through 1897.

We will demonstrate that the changing British literary milieu, particularly new opportunities for authors produced by changes in the publishing system, probably served men more than women and male novelists more than female novelists. Before doing so, however, we will describe just why the *DNB* is an ideal source of data—how it captures Victorian notions of the appropriate career of the appropriate "man of letters" and so facilitates an understanding of how Victorian cultural entrepreneurs treated male and female authors—and how our use of the *DNB* departs from earlier attempts to study systematically the lives of a sample of English writers.

The Dictionary of National Biography (*DNB*)

There is a fortuitous and marvelous cohesiveness about the first twenty-three volumes of the *DNB* that lent it standing during the Victorian and Edwardian eras. The first twenty-one volumes and the first two supplements were edited by accomplished and respected late-Victorian men of letters, Leslie Stephen and Sidney Lee, conceived and issued by a respected publisher, George Smith of the elite Smith, Elder and Company, and heralded at the time as a major accomplishment in the history of English letters. Information about writers in the *DNB* can be used to study the opportunities available to Victorian women novelists precisely because it was issued during the period when the field of letters was consolidating in England, much as art academies and museums were consolidating in the United States (see DiMaggio 1982).

The *DNB* was intended to be "exhaustive," "authoritative," and a "munificent contribution to the literature of England." According to Stephen, "We intended . . . to supply a useful manual for all serious students of British history and literature. We were to achieve that end by bringing together as concisely as possible all that was so far known about *every person who might conceivably be interesting to such students. . . .* We were to treat all manner of people . . . and not only men of mark, but everyone about whom the question might arise in the course of general reading, Who was he?" (Stephen 1903, 568, emphasis added). Stephen referred to the "smaller articles" as "perhaps the most valuable part of the book" (ibid., 572) because "it is the second-rate people" about whom not much is easily known and "who really become generally accessible through the dictionary alone—that provide the really useful reading. . . . Nobody need look at Addison or Byron or Milton in a dictionary [though they are extensively treated in the *DNB*]. He can find fuller and better notices in every library" (Stephen 1898, 22). The editors of the *DNB* consciously sought to capture the notions of men of mark and second-rate people characteristic of the late nineteenth century.

The procedures used to select entries affirm the desire of these cultural entrepreneurs to be all-inclusive. The editorial staff included a compiler of lists that "comprised all names that had hitherto been treated in independent works of biography, in general dictionaries, in collections of lives . . . and in obituary notices in the leading journals and periodicals," as well as those located through scholarship "which had hitherto escaped biographical notice" (Lee 1963–1964, lxiii). Starting in 1883, drafts of those lists were published twice a year in the *Athenaeum* so that readers could offer "suggestions or corrections."

The editors were confident that they had succeeded in including the names of everyone who qualified for recognition. They believed that their procedures for selecting individuals discriminated quality. Indeed, they explicitly eschewed the notion that quality might lie in the eye of the beholder. Consider this assessment of the dictionary by Sidney Lee, who served as Stephen's subeditor from 1883, his co-editor from 1890 to 1891, and his successor from 1891 to 1912, and so edited the first two supplements. After calculating the ratio of entries to the number of adults believed to have lived in England in each century, Lee thought that the "causes of the rise, fall, or stagnation of the ratio of distinction" might reflect the impact of historical circumstances on the "opportunities" for people to meet the requirements of the "Dictionary's level of distinction" (ibid., lxix). Lee recognized that more materials were available on the nineteenth century and that this availability may have influenced the greater proportional inclusion of nineteenth-century women and men. But, as was also true of Leslie Stephen (and later of F. R. Leavis), Lee clearly believed it possible to discriminate among absolute levels of distinction. He did not view fame as a social construction.

In general, Lee's and Stephen's classification of authors assumed that distinguished authors transcended their social origins; less distinguished authors supposedly did not. These notions were implicit in the selection of biographers of the 260 women and 267 men authors whose entries we analyzed. Those who wrote about lesser authors were chosen more on the basis of their expertise about social origin than about literary specialty. Inasmuch as this pattern of hierarchical evaluation of quality and social origin holds, Stephen and Lee were naming writers to their versions of a great national tradition (first rank) and lesser regional or subcultural traditions (second or third rank).

These coding schemes were implicit in the specialties of the biographers of the authors whose entries we analyzed. Almost half of these entries (48 percent) were written by ten people. These ten people, arranged by the specialties with which Lee himself identified them, and the number of men and women portrayed by each are listed in table 5.1. That system of specialties stressed quality, social origin, and social characteristics; for the classificatory system was based on literary excellence, time period, place of origin, religion, gender, and occupation. These ten authors portrayed 154 women and 100 men. Women outnumber men because 67 women are placed in the category "minor women writers"; the editors did not devise a category for "minor male writers."

The assignment of specialties was not random. Four of the ten biographers listed in table 5.1 were either core staff of the *DNB* or close family of that staff. Leslie Stephen was the first editor. Starting with the volume on people whose names began with *B* and continuing through subsequent letters of the alphabet, Thompson Cooper was compiler of the lists of those for whom biographies were to be prepared (Lee 1963–1964, lxiii). From 1891 Thomas Seccombe was subeditor. Elizabeth Lee was the sister of the unmarried Sidney Lee and ran his household.

Table 5.1: The Principal Biographers and Their Specialties, by Gender
of Authors Portrayed

Biographers and their specialties	Men Portrayed (N)	Women Portrayed (N)
Excellence		
Sir Leslie Stephen ("the great names in literature and philosophy")	7	8
Social Characteristics, Time Period		
Thomas Seccombe ("chiefly literature of the last three centuries")	9	8
Dr. Richard Garnett, C. B. ("men of letters of the nineteenth century")	15	23
George Clement Boase ("men of varied kinds of distinction in the nineteenth century")	15	16
Time and Place		
William Courtney ("Cornishmen and literary workers of the eighteenth century")	13	3
Place		
Thomas Bayne ("Scots")	12	9
Charles William Sutton ("various authors of Lancashire birth")	8	7
Religion		
Thompson Cooper ("Roman Catholic divines and writers")	10	6
Gender		
Elizabeth Lee ("minor women writers")	1	67
Occupation		
John Knight ("actors")	10	7
Total	100	154

The pattern of information included in the *DNB* and the structure of presentation also captured how people in the nineteenth century thought about men and women. Consider the missing information. After leaving the *DNB* Leslie Stephen had recalled, "I used rigidly to excise the sentence, 'Nothing is known of his birth or parentage,' which tended to appear in half the lives, because where nothing is known it seems simpler that nothing should be said" (1898, 22). Thus, we interpret missing information as an indication of what was not known about an author's life, and what was not

Table 5.2: Distribution of Information Missing from *DNB* Biographies,
by Gender and Year of Birth

	Women Authors		Men Authors	
	1750–1814 (%)	1815–1864 (%)	1750–1814 (%)	1815–1864 (%)
Missing Information				
Family of Origin				
Author's parent(s) in entry's first sentence	23	19	38	18
Occupation of author's father	21	13	32	18
Socio-economic status of mother before marriage	74	71	81	71
Family of Procreation				
Marriage	8	7	36	25
Job of first spouse	15	14	86	83
Socio-economic status of first spouse	73	65	77	67
Any Children	56	52	55	52
Friends				
Whether author had influential friends	32	57	31	26
N	(154)	(91)	(175)	(87)

known of a life may be indicative of what was not considered important enough to be remembered. The pattern of inclusion and exclusion for each gender announced the editors' acceptance of the nineteenth-century belief that a woman's social class is dependent upon a man's (for example, Basch 1974). The *DNB* more often gave information about the parents of women than about those of men, about fathers than mothers, and about the husbands of women authors than about the wives of male authors (table 5.2; see appendix A for a discussion of the issue of statistical significance). Thus, the *DNB* editors actively reproduced Victorian beliefs about gender and class hierarchies. The arrangement of male and female biographies assumed that women's status was determined by men and that families were more important to women than to men. The biographies of women authors chronologically integrated information about their marriages and their children into the text. Those of men generally contained a brief sentence about marriage and children in the next-to-last paragraph, just before mention of the burial site and extant portraits of the author (when known).

The biographies of Matilda Anne Mackarness and her father, James Robinson Planché, provide apt examples of the differential treatment of marriage in the lives of women and men. Despite the length of Elizabeth Lee's biography of Matilda Anne Mackarness—84 lines, less than one-third her father's 285 lines—Mackarness's biography integrated her personal and professional lives; her father's did not. Not until the last paragraph of Planché's biography was his family of procreation mentioned. "On 26 April 1821 he married Elizabeth St. George" (*DNB* 15: 1283). The thirteen sentences in the body of Mackarness's biography chronologically present her birth (1826), first publication (1845), marriage (1852), widowhood (1868), subsequent residence with her father, and death (1881) (*DNB* 12: 561).

Also, women's biographies stressed sociability; the man's biography that did so was rare. Whereas the next-to-last paragraph in a man's biography was about his family, that in a woman's biography often noted her charm and graciousness, particularly as a hostess for men. Accordingly, one reads that Lady Bury "was always distinguished by her passion for belles lettres and was accustomed to do the honors of Scotland to the literary celebrities of the day." One learns of Clementina Sterling Graham that "mingling freely with all classes of society, she knew how to bring them together," for they "met at her house, which would have been called a salon . . . but it had none of the exclusiveness of a clique."

These very biases of the *DNB* make it an ideal source for examining the opportunities and limitations placed on Victorian women authors, for the men of letters who assembled the *DNB* expressed the ideas of their times as they assigned, wrote, and edited evaluations of writers. Those ideas necessarily included which genres were appropriate for women and which for men. And so, deliberately or inadvertently, they expressed the processes associated with the empty field phenomenon.

The sample and periodization. We wanted our sample to be as comparable *as possible* to our sample of authors who had submitted manuscripts to Macmillan and Company. Some of the authors in the Macmillan sample earned their livelihood through writing; others, especially the men, practiced another occupation as well. Thus, we did not limit our *DNB* sample to those whom the *DNB* identified as author, essayist, novelist, poet, or dramatist. As one might expect from the scant number of books published by most people in the Macmillan sample, however, more of the *DNB* authors than of the Macmillan aspirants earned their livelihood as authors.

We selected as our sample (1) all 267 women born between 1750 and 1865 who had a separate entry in the *DNB* and who, according to the *DNB*, had published during their lifetimes at least one piece of imaginative literature (poem, short story, novel) or had written a play that was performed somewhere and (2) a random sample of 267 men who met those same conditions. To choose the sample of men, we counted the number of pages in the *DNB*, divided by 267, and from a random start selected the first man meeting our criteria whose entry we encountered in the selected spans of pages.[1] (For a more extended discussion of our sampling procedure, see appendix A.)

We supplemented formal content analyses of these entries with a count of the books of fiction, nonfiction, and poetry that each author had published, as listed in the *BMC*. We also used the *BMC* to code whether any memoirs, biographies, and critical commentaries of an author's work had been issued and if so how many, whether an author's books had been translated into other languages, whether an author had compiled an anthology, the dates of his or her first and last publications, and any hiatus between books lasting more than five years.

Ours is not the first attempt to examine systematically the lives and careers of nineteenth-century authors. At least two literary critics acting as historians have carried out systematic studies of authors' backgrounds and careers, and a sociologist has published another. Each introduced a scheme for periodization that made assumptions about how authors' childhood so-cialization articulated with literary systems. Each is unsuitable for our purposes, for those assumptions prevent systematic assessments of novelists' opportun-ities to publish and so of our central proposition that the Victorian occupation of novelist was governed by the empty field phenomenon.

In his now classic *The Long Revolution* (1961, 254–270), Raymond Williams discussed the social origins of nearly 350 authors born between 1470 and 1920. He claimed that especially during the late nineteenth century "outsiders," including women and regional writers, introduced innovations in English literature. One hundred thirty-five of the authors whose origins and educations Williams examined were born between 1730 and 1880. The authors on whom he based his generalization made

---

1. These criteria excluded some well-known authors. For instance, we did not include Emily Brontë in our sample because she is listed under the entry of her sister Charlotte. We do not know how representative our sample of men is because our sampling method prevented us from learning anything about the other male writers listed in the *DNB*. We do know that some very famous authors, such as Charles Dickens, are not in our sample. Because of missing information, every member of the sample was not included in every analysis.

up the universe of authors listed in the index of the *Oxford Introduction to English Literature*. Even though, as befits his hypotheses, Williams was particularly sensitive to the class and regional origins of authors in different periods, he assumed that education and socialization before the age of ten had an awesome impact upon what adult authors wrote. He did not consider how subsequent socialization and either class-based or gender-based opportunities may have influenced writers' accomplishments.

Williams divided his sample into "convenient" 50-year periods that nonetheless capture such accepted literary divisions as the age of romantic literature (1780–1830). (Williams noted, however, that this period encompassed "second-generation Romantics" and the early and mid Victorians.) He then placed in each period men and women born between the ten years preceding the start and the ten years preceding the end of each literary period. For instance, those whom he classified as "second-generation Romantics and early and mid-Victorians" were born between 1770 and 1820.

Williams made several assumptions that do not necessarily affect the validity of his conclusions but certainly prevent us from replicating his methods. One assumption implicit in his periodization was that childhood socialization had a greater impact upon literary output than did the conditions encountered by authors as they first began to publish. Although Williams stressed that the number of books published each year began to burgeon in the 1830s, an author born in 1772 (as was Samuel Taylor Coleridge) encountered rather different literary standards than an author born between 1810 and 1820 (the last decade of the period). Realist novelists born in that decade include Dickens, Trollope, Thackeray, Eliot, and Gaskell.

A second and related assumption was that literary periods coincide with changing conditions for writers and publishers. That is, Williams' periodization assumes that all authors born between 1770 and 1820 encountered the same or similar conditions when they sought to publish their work. This assumption matters because, as we will see in chapter 7, publishers frequently demanded manuscript changes to meet their notions of the preferences of changing distribution systems. In the Victorian era publishers preferred to issue three-volume novels because Mudie's Select Library preferred to purchase three-volume novels, and so authors struggled to fit their novels into that form (Sutherland 1976).

This assumption does not hold for the authors born between 1770 and 1820. Those born at the beginning of the period faced a series of options—dealing with booksellers, publishing by subscription, making a contract with one publisher or with several publishers who together might underwrite publication costs. But with the exception of Dickens, who reintroduced eighteenth-century methods of distribution for some of his novels, those born between 1810 and 1820 generally signed separate contracts for separate books, sometimes with separate publishers, much as is done today. These publishers had to meet the demands of Charles Mudie before he would purchase books for his circulating library.

A third assumption implicit in Williams' periodization is that childhood socialization had the same meaning for men and for women. At first glance, this assumption appears sound. Even though psychologists discuss gender differences in early socialization, no one has ever demonstrated that differential gender socialization has an impact on the accomplishments of male and female writers. Common sense suggests, however, that the different expectations about their proper life course engendered in middle-class boys and girls throughout the eighteenth century and most of the nineteenth century must have had consequences for their literary activity. Women were given inferior educations and were taught that they should not write for self-expression and might only write for money if severely pressed for funds. As we have seen, many women claimed to turn to writing only when financial circumstances pressed them to do so. Accordingly, it is probable that women's orientation toward writing differed from that of men. Not only may they have written on different topics and exhibited different skills, as Victorian critics claim, but their decision to write for publication may have come later—after the death or financial failure of a father or husband (see Showalter 1977). What writing meant to women as wage earners may have been different from what it meant to men, who from earliest childhood knew they were expected to earn money to support a family. Gender socialization may also have affected men's and women's ability to deal shrewdly with publishers and to negotiate significant payment for their work.

Richard Altick's (1962) study of authors was intended to refute Williams' generalizations about the importance of outsiders to literary innovation by examining the lives of less famous writers. He compiled from the *Cambridge Bibliography of English Literature, Volume III* and Millet's *Contemporary British Literature* a list of 1,100 authors active in the nineteenth and twentieth centuries, 849 of whom were classified as nineteenth-century writers. Altick's article did not consider socialization. It emphasized popularity, for Altick's methods were designed to address the question, whose work was popular during which period?

Altick categorized the authors whose lives he analyzed according to when their work was published. He named three periods for the nineteenth century: 1800–1835, 1835–1870, and 1870–1900. An author placed in the first thirty-five-year span might have been born in 1765 or in 1805, to choose two arbitrary dates. As far as we know, Altick's three nineteenth-century periods are also arbitrary; they do not correspond to periods in either the history of publishing or the history of literacy, both of which Altick had developed elsewhere (1957). Nor do they coincide with periods commonly used to discuss the changing opportunities for authors (see Collins 1928; cf. Gross 1970).

Sociologist Diana Laurenson (1969) used yet another set of categories. She wanted to examine differences between what she called "institutionalized" and "individualized" authors, terms corresponding roughly to writers of popular culture and high culture. She examined data on 170 writers, one of every five authors listed in either the *DNB* or *Everyman's Dictionary of Literary Biography* who were born or died between 1860 and 1900. For her, living during a time of literary transformation, regardless of one's age, seemed sufficient to produce some kind of influence on literary output or quality. The nonuniformity of the nature and degree of that impact is necessarily problematic.

Since we are concerned with literary periods, the development of publishing, and opportunities for women writers, we sought to devise a classificatory system that could distinguish three phenomena: socialization, including educational opportunities; the supposedly greater association of women with the novel; and changes in the publishing system. Because 1840 has been said to mark the rising prestige of the novel and because the major elements of the nineteenth-century system of publishing and distributing books were in place by 1840, we chose 1840 as an admittedly reified line to divide periods. Like Williams (1961), we then calculated backward to set a date marking the birth of people who would be classified in each period. We chose 1814/1815 as the line between "early" and "late" authors because people born in 1815 would be twenty-five years old in 1840. Their education presumably behind them, their careers chosen if not set, their marriage prospects assessed if not accomplished, these twenty-five-year-olds would then be confronting a changing literary system. Presumably both men and women who were twenty-five years old would have a sense of their past and their possible future.

As expected, the boundaries between the groups were not firm. The 1840s are a transitional decade. Thirteen percent of the early authors (born 1750–1814) first published in the 1840s, as did 19 percent of the late authors (born 1815–1865).[2] But most early authors (83 percent) published their first

2. We found the date in which 236 of the women and 243 of the men in our sample first published a book. We did not locate the dates of book publication for the other authors because sometimes the *BMC* omits that information. Additionally, some of the sampled authors never published a book; our procedures specified that someone who had published merely

Table 5.3: Year First Book Was Published, by Gender and Period

	Early Women (%)	Late Women (%)	Early Men (%)	Late Men (%)	All Authors (%)
First book before 1840	79	2	86	11	56
First book during the 1840s	14	24	13	13	15
First book 1850 to 1900	7	74	1	76	29
	100	100	100	100	100
N	(149)	(87)	(160)	(83)	(479)

Note: This table presents data about authors for whom relevant information was available. Five early women, 4 late women, 15 early men, and 4 late men were excluded.

book before 1840, and most late authors (94 percent) began to publish books after 1840.

The boundaries are not rigid (table 5.3): women were likely to begin their publishing careers somewhat later than men, but these differences are not significant.[3] In general the boundaries that we chose to mark periods do

one poem in a newspaper would be included among the sampled authors. Our sample also includes playwrights who had at least one of their works performed; many plays are staged but never published.

3. We do not report tests of significance, which are intended to estimate the probability that one can generalize from a sample to the population from which it is drawn. (For instance, if a particular statistic is significant at the 0.01 level, there is a high probability that one can generalize from the sample to the population.)

But it is not clear what universe our *DNB* sample is drawn from. Our computations include all women in the *DNB* who met our criteria and for whom the relevant data were available. The men are a sample for whom the relevant information was available. One can use statistical tests to compare these two groups, but tests of statistical significance seem foolish. To what population would tests of significance refer?

Nonetheless, those who find this sort of information useful might wish to know some statistics about the division of the sample into the four groups used in subsequent analyses. Chi square tests indicate that the 1814/1815 birth boundary does distinguish between (1) women who first published before or after 1840 (X^2 = 124.6, 1 degree of freedom, significance = 0.000), (2) men first publishing before or after 1840 (X^2 = 126.9, 1 degree of freedom, significance = 0.000), (3) and everyone in the sample publishing before or after 1840 (X^2 = 253.8, 1 degree of freedom, significance = 0.000). Women as a group were likely to publish their first book later than men. Early women were about as likely to publish their differentiate authors' involvement with the novel, as subsequent analyses will confirm. They yield a sample of 154 early women, 91 late women, 175 early men, and 87 late men.

Consequences of our sampling procedure. Our sampling procedure made women seem more professionally active than men. Because of the limitations on their career opportunities, the women in our sample were more likely to be mainly authors than were the men, who often practiced another occupation as well. A man who was a famous barrister and published one poem might be caught in our sample. Using our procedure,[4] we could not have selected a comparable woman; a woman could not have become any sort of barrister, let alone a famous one, and a woman who published only one poem would never have been listed in the *DNB*. By our criteria those earning their livelihood as authors included 55 percent of the early women, 68 percent of the late women, 18 percent of the early men, and 44 percent of the late men. Men displayed the greatest increase in identification as "only author" after the centralization of publishing. Because the women in our sample were more likely to have been "only authors" than the men were, the following analyses stress men's increased advantages *relative* to women.

Industrialization and the Profession of Writing

In England changes in the "profession" of author went hand in hand with the rationalization of publishing. In chapter 2 we noted that contemporary novelists and other authors are technically not professionals in that they do

---

first book before 1840 as early men were (x^2 = 3.2, 1 degree of freedom, significance = 0.07). Late women were somewhat more likely to begin publishing after 1840 than were late men (x^2 = 5.1, 1 degree of freedom, significance = 0.02).

4. We coded an individual's occupation as an author if the first sentence of that individual's *DNB* entry described him or her as: an author, writer, or miscellaneous writer, a novelist, a dramatist, a poet, a journalist, an editor, a critic, a children's or religious writer, a man or woman of letters, a biographer, a hymn or song writer, a philosophical writer, a writer on art, a translator, or an essayist. Even the song writers in our sample published at least one work of imaginative literature. To qualify as an author, the individual could not be identified as a member of a nonliterary occupation in the first sentence of his or her *DNB* entry. Thus, we did not code as an author an individual identified as "physician and biographer."

Although there is much variation in the number of books the sampled authors published (statistically indicated by standard deviations [S.D.]), on the whole women published more. The mean number of books published by each group is: early women, 15.4 (S.D., 18.3); late women, 26.4 (S.D., 33.5); early men, 13.9 (S.D., 18.2); late men, 19.8 (S.D., 22.3). Women also had a more regular publication pattern.

not have a unique license and mandate, they do not have specialized training, and they cannot control entrance to and expulsion from their occupation. Authors' claim to professional status was even weaker in the eighteenth and early nineteenth centuries, when the organizational context of their work prevented professional status. Authors "scribbled" at home and sold their product to (frequently unethical) commercial entrepreneurs—booksellers.

As we have seen, as the nineteenth century progressed, authors' status improved. Increased literacy brought more readers, who demanded more reading material and of different kinds. Concomitantly, publishing houses increasingly differentiated themselves from the older stationers and booksellers, drew on new printing and paper technologies, issued more books and periodicals, and specialized. All this publishing activity created more opportunities for authors to earn both income and honor; a demand for books necessarily created a demand for authors. Popular authors—those whom the reading public favored and preferred—could expect larger sums for their work.

Income might translate into honor. Known to an ever larger middle-class reading public, more novelists could become cultural heroes, a status that had been reserved for Sir Walter Scott early in the nineteenth century. The popularity of Charles Dickens, mobbed by adoring fans as he walked the streets of London, was based on the awesome circulation of his novels. Although other authors were not as lionized, the fervor of literary controversies about such matters as the identities of Currer Bell (Charlotte Brontë) and George Eliot fed upon the familiarity of the large middle-class reading public with Bell's *Jane Eyre* and Eliot's *Adam Bede*.

In the nineteenth century the processes associated with industrial rationalization frequently meant geographic centralization. As other industries had done, publishing had become centralized, and this had consequences for British intellectual life—and for authors. At the beginning of the nineteenth century intellectual circles flourished in such major sites of learning as Oxford, Cambridge, and Edinburgh, which were also the homes of important publishing houses. But even the small (by twentieth-century standards) city of Norwich boasted intense intellectual activity because it was or had been the home of major late eighteenth-century and early nineteenth-century figures, such as essayist Harriet Martineau, poet and novelist Amelia Opie, biologist Sir James Edward Smith, and German literature expert William Taylor.[5]

5. Their biographies, autobiographies, and memoirs and those of other Norwich residents were collectively reviewed by C. Rachel Jones in the *Edinburgh Review* (1879), together with the catalogue of an exhibition of the principal "Artists of the Norwich School."

Neither Norwich nor any other small city boasted an equally active and productive intellectual and creative life in the mid-nineteenth century. For the centralization of intellectual life increasingly mandated the migration of intellectuals, including authors, to London.

This movement was part of a larger redistribution of the population caused by the industrialization of England. Farm laborers migrated to the growing cities of the North. But London, England's commercial and civic center, expanded even more rapidly. In the first half of the nineteenth century, its population quadrupled as London attracted not only an ever larger industrial proletariat but also the sons of the nation's expanding middle class who sought success in commercial and governmental bureaucracies (Supple 1978).

The increased importance of London offered advantages to publishing houses in London, including readier access to potential authors and markets, to the pulse of national life, and to financing. Publishers could hope that London financiers were more enlightened than, for instance, the Cambridge pharmacist who as the Macmillans' silent partner in 1843 opposed some of their original projects. And some firms, such as Blackwood and Sons, established two offices: one in the city of their initial foundation (in this case Edinburgh), the other in the new center of the publishing industry, London. Indeed, the year Blackwood's London office opened, 1840, suggests that by that decade publishing was centralizing; there is no other sound reason for an eminently successful Scots firm to move to the preeminent English city. Hundreds of large and small firms flourished in London.

By moving to London, the site of so much publishing activity, intellectual workers could hope to further their careers by using family contacts and school friendships to enter the appropriate social and intellectual networks and through these networks to gain eventual employment on the many new journals, newspapers, and magazines started after 1832.[6] For instance, author Edmund Yates was introduced to literary circles and literary life by his author-uncle (*DNB*); John Morley made his way through old school ties (Hamer 1968); and Daniel Macmillan, in his first effort to enter the London publishing world, stayed with another young man from his hometown who had migrated earlier and who also sponsored him for potential jobs (Morgan 1943).

We have stressed the migration of young men, but young women came, too. For instance, after the death of her bankrupt but once wealthy father in Ireland the young, impoverished, and as yet unmarried Mrs. J. H. Riddell, eventually a successful and popular novelist, moved to London with her mother

---

6. Powell (1985) notes a similar phenomenon today; academics located in New York have better odds of getting published than scholars at more elite universities in the hinterlands.

and walked from one publishing house to another, seeking a firm that would accept her first novel (Bleiler 1977).

In the mid-nineteenth century London was not the only center of British intellectual life. One can hardly dismiss Oxford, Cambridge, and Edinburgh, seats of education, scholarship, and controversy. But friendships that formed at college saw their social and economic utility realized in London. Nor can one dismiss the specter of the individual author scribbling away in a village or northern urban center and eventually mailing a prized manuscript to a London publisher. Many well-known nineteenth-century novelists entered London literary circles only after their first book was published. Of those whom F. R. Leavis considered when he compiled his list of authors in *The Great Tradition* (1969), Elizabeth Gaskell, the Brontës, and Shorthouse come quickly to mind. But having entered London literary and intellectual circles with the publication of a praised book, the out-of-town authors might take advantage of their new contacts to forge new publishing contracts with those whom they had met.

Authors' residence and publishers. Data in the *DNB* affirm the increased importance of London as an intellectual center. They affirm, too, that late men were the authors most likely to take advantage of what London had to offer.

Consider the question of birthplace and residence as an adult. We have data about these items for 88 percent of the sampled authors. Of these, 20 percent of the early authors and 20 percent of the late authors were born in London. Yet late authors were much more likely to spend at least five years in London. Fifty-six percent of them, but only 31 percent of early authors, did so.

Of the late authors, men were more likely than women to spend five years in London (63 versus 49 percent). Men were more likely to move there (fig. 5.1). Presumably, men made independent decisions about residence, but most women's geographic mobility was tied to the preferences of their husbands and fathers. Fifty-seven percent of late men born elsewhere moved to London; only 40 percent of late women born elsewhere did so.[7] Thus, late men were the authors most likely to be in a geographic position to participate

---

7. Today economic and sociological studies argue that, because family responsibilities give women less geographic mobility than men, women may forego promotions requiring a geographic transfer, or assuming they will not move, their bosses may not ask them to do so. Such studies assume that a family will relocate for a husband's promotion but not for a wife's career advancement. That assumption may be flawed. In *Men and Women of the Corporation* (1977) Rosabeth Moss Kantor describes familial and occupational conditions that discourage men from accepting geographic transfers.

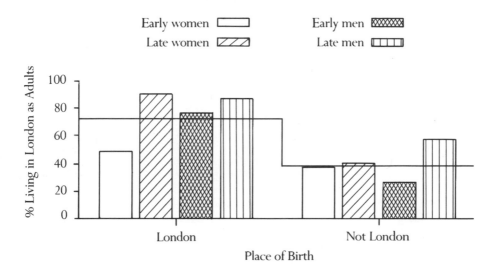

Figure 5.1
Percentage of Authors Living in London at Least Five Years as Adults,
by Specified Variables

in intellectual networks and so to convert social contacts into professional opportunities.

But were authors able to convert residence in London into publication by a London publisher? Authors who spent at least five adult years in London after the centralization of the publishing industry were those most likely to publish their first books with a London firm (fig. 5.2).[8] For men, moving to London seems to have been a key to publishing their first book with a London firm, especially after 1840. For women of both periods, residence in London as an adult seems irrelevant to obtaining a London publisher—though the authors most likely to have a London publisher were women living in London before publishing had centralized and therefore before having a London pub-

8. Although two-thirds of all the authors published a first book with a London firm, even more of them published the majority of their books with a London publisher. Since initial success may lead to contracts with a more prestigious publisher, this pattern makes sense. Two findings about the authors for whom we have information are worth reporting. Living in London was a decided advantage to early women; all of them published most of their books with a London firm. It seemed to be a necessity for all men. For instance, 95 percent of the late men who lived in London for at least five years published with a London firm; but only 57 percent of the late men who did not spend five years in London published with a London house.

Figure 5.2
Percentage of Authors Publishing Their First Book with a London Firm,
by Residence in London

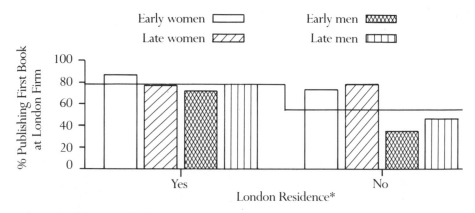

*London residents lived there at least five years as adults.

lisher was prestigious.[9] In the specific sense that men's likelihood of having a London publisher increased relative to women's likelihood of doing so, men gained more than women from the centralization of the publishing industry.

Editing. We have argued that the increased literacy associated with industrialization brought more opportunities to earn money through literature. One sphere in which opportunities occurred was editing. When job opportunities expanded for literary workers the authors in the *DNB* sample became more likely to engage in literary activities that yielded money. Again we infer from our data that after 1840 men gained more from these expanded opportunities than women did.

One expanded arena was editing books. That activity included a variety of projects, such as compiling original essays or selections of previously published poetry, selecting and sometimes revising other people's letters and memoirs, preparing almanacs and directories, and supervising a series of books

9. We believe that the women's greater likelihood of publishing their first books with a London firm is also an artifact of who is listed in the *DNB*. Analyses to be presented in subsequent chapters suggest that women novelists (and more of the women than the men in our sample were novelists) had to accomplish more than men to receive a listing. The greater likelihood that women would publish their first book with a London firm may represent the overachievement necessary for them to receive recognition in the form of an entry in the *DNB*.

on a specified theme. Thus, the *BMC* identified one "edited" book by a member of our *DNB* sample as "Poetry for Children, consisting of short pieces to be committed to memory, selected by Lucy Aiken." (It went through seven printings and was ultimately revised for another publisher.) The *BMC* described another book by a member of this sample as "Henry Burke's Dramatic Almanac; cf. Henry Burke's Theatrical Director for the year 1860 edited by J. A. Herauld, (poet and dramatist)." Among authors associated with Macmillan, Charlotte Yonge and Elizabeth Sewell compiled historical selections on religious topics, and John Morley supervised the touted series "English Men of Letters."

Another expanded area was editing the increasing number of periodicals. Although some edited books went through multiple printings and editions, editing periodicals would have provided a more stable income. We assume that those who edited periodicals in the mid- and late nineteenth century belonged to a more elite group than editors of books. To edit a periodical, one must have been appointed, and such appointments were frequently made through networks of friends. For instance, friendships influenced Morley's assignment to the editorship of *Fortnightly Review*. And when searching for an editor of "Macmillan's Magazine" Alexander Macmillan turned to elite men whom he knew through his extensive contacts in literary networks (Morgan 1943). Authors maintained more of the initiative in compiling anthologies. Although a publisher might think of a commercially viable anthology and then use his contacts to locate an editor, more frequently an author compiling an anthology selected materials and then obtained a publisher, tasks facilitated by having the appropriate contacts.

Few of the members of our sample edited periodicals—only 13 percent of all of the early authors and 24 percent of all of the late authors. Most of that increase resulted from the activities of men, presumably because of "old boy networks." (The percentages of all men and women in each period who edited periodicals are as follows: early women, 12 percent; late women, 15 percent; early men, 15 percent; late men, 33 percent.)

As expected, more members of the sample (46 percent of them) edited at least one book. This pattern of activity is slightly different from the pattern of editing periodicals. Women were more likely to edit books before the centralization of publishing in London, when 47 percent of them did so; men were more likely to edit books after it, when 55 percent of the late men engaged in this activity. (Forty percent of late women and 45 percent of early men also edited at least one book.) We infer that in both of these arenas, men gained more economically than women did from what John Gross (1970) wrote of as the rise of the "English man of letters."

In both sorts of editing, living in London again assisted authors. Late authors who lived in London at least five years as adults were more likely than other authors to edit periodicals (panel A of fig. 5.3). And of those spending at least five years in London, late men were the most likely group to do so. Late men and early women living in London were the groups most likely to edit books (panel B of fig. 5.3).

Professional participation. Nineteenth-century sources reviewed in Chapter 7 hint that women received less money than men for comparable work. But for both men and women the more literary work one did, the more likely it was that one could support oneself. As opportunities expanded, men's rate of participation in literature increased—at least in their apparent activity as professionals. Our criterion for professional participation was either (1) publishing at least eight books or (2) publishing five books and either editing books or periodicals or translating books.[10] We estimated that by engaging in at least this amount of professional activity an author could support himself or herself for a while. Although in general late authors were more likely to meet these criteria, men's increased activity accounts for most of the increase. (The relevant percentages of authors meeting our criteria for high professional participation are as follows: early women, 70 percent; late women, 76 percent; early men, 49 percent; late men, 64 percent.) Again, living in London was a decided advantage. Eighty-five percent of late women living in London met our criteria for professional participation, as did 75 percent of late men (fig. 5.4). But men living in London showed the greatest increase in professional participation after publishing had centralized.

Some may feel that the data contradict our argument: The percentages of all women, of late women, and of late women living in London who met our criteria are higher than the percentages for comparable men. We believe these findings are artifacts of the sampling procedure: As explained above, our sample includes more women than men whom the *DNB* identified as some sort of author but not as a member of another occupation. Because of their limited opportunities, women were less likely to hold other jobs, were more likely to write a lot, and so were more likely to meet the first of our criteria for professional participation, publishing at least eight books.

Because of their geographic mobility men were more likely than women to enjoy the benefits deriving from the centralization of the publishing industry in London. But they may also have gained more because they had the education

10. We selected these criteria after reviewing the distribution of the activities of our sample.

Figure 5.3
Percentage of Authors Who Edited Periodicals or Books,
by Residence in London

Early women ☐   Early men ◇◇◇◇

Late women ▨   Late men ⊞

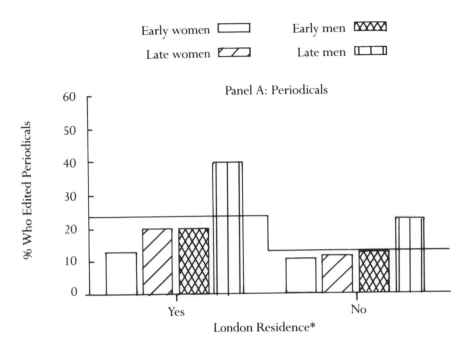

Panel A: Periodicals

% Who Edited Periodicals

60
50
40
30
20
10
0

Yes   No

London Residence*

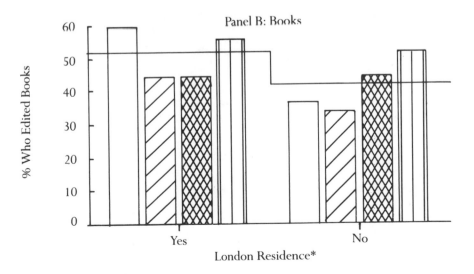

Panel B: Books

% Who Edited Books

60
50
40
30
20
10
0

Yes   No

London Residence*

*London residents lived there at least five years as adults.

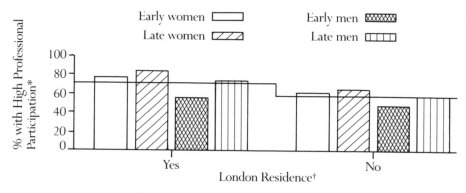

Figure 5.4
Percentage of Authors Having High Professional Participation,
by Adult Residence in London

†London residents lived there at least five years as adults.
*See text for definition of high professional participation.

with which to gain more. Women were more likely than men to come from upper-middle-class and upper-class families; their fathers were more likely to be concentrated in the classic liberal professions of medicine, law, and the clergy (See chapter 6). But their formal education was scanty compared to that of men.

Authors' education. As the historical literature repeatedly attests (Vicinus 1985; Burstyn 1980), Victorian women simply did not have as many educational opportunities as did their brothers, husbands, male cousins, and neighbors. Colleges for women did not open until the second half of the century, and then most of them did not teach women the same skills that were taught to men. Publicly financed schools for women were not instituted until well into the nineteenth century.

As one might expect, most of the female authors in our sample had scarcely any formal education (table 5.4). Even late women were less likely to have had formal education than early men were. The amount of formal education that an author received cannot account for the accomplishments of our four groups of authors, for if education were the crucial factor in determining whether an author succeeded, all men in the sample would have consistently achieved more than all women. But, as demonstrated in this chapter, in some cases early women achieved more than early men.

If we assume that able women continued to attempt literary careers, what then accounts for the greater accomplishments of late men, including

Table 5.4: Highest Level of Education Achieved, by Gender and Period

	Early Women (%)	Late Women (%)	Early Men (%)	Late Men (%)
Institutional				
Elite university	0	1	42	40
Nonelite university	0	4	9	17
Elite boading school	0	0	3	6
Nonelite boarding school	11	17	6	13
Local school	4	3	9	7
Subtotal	15	25	70*	83
Noninstitutional education				
Private tutor	6	6	3	2
Taught at home	9	14	2	1
Self-taught	4	4	3	0
Subtotal	19*	24	8	3
Not mentioned	66	51	23	14
Total	100	100	101*	100

*Error due to rounding.

their records as editors? Formal schooling helped to provide networks of friends upon whom they could draw for assistance. Not only were men able to enter literary networks once they lived in London, but they had access to influential individuals presumably known through family contacts or school ties.

There are two ways to see how much more likely successful men were to take advantage of family contacts and school ties. One is to examine the advantage enjoyed by writers whose parents, grandparents, uncles, aunts, siblings, or cousins were involved in the arts.[11] Presumably, if these kin were authors, editors, journalists, musicians, actors, or artists, they might have provided valuable introductions to a young relative with literary ambitions and so have smoothed the way. (We assume that many artists, musicians, and authors were acquainted with one another. For instance, the early nineteenth-century poet Amelia Opie had met her husband, artist John Opie, at

11. Epstein (1981) states that male judges and attorneys prefer to work with women attorneys whose parents or husbands are also in law. She suggests that, to these men, the involvement of women's parents and spouses may indicate that the women share men's suppositions about appropriate conduct. Their families render these women "safe."

a London gathering.) Another is to examine the sorts of influential people with whom selected authors in our sample maintained friendships.

Past research on artists (see Tuchman 1974b) has emphasized the crucial intercession of grandfathers and fathers who were artists and who nurtured the talent of a third generation by both providing early training and facilitating careers. Such assistance has been particularly vital to women. Until the twentieth century, most women artists were members of families of artists. Presumably, without familial intercession their talents would have languished, or without the encouragement provided by a father or brother they might have chosen more conventional lives. Until the twentieth century, many, but not most, male artists also belonged to families of artists; their families sponsored them for membership in guilds and academies. But men who lacked these important family ties also succeeded as artists. Art historians (for example, Nochlin 1971) add that help from fathers and grandfathers has been critical to men, such as Pablo Picasso and Alexander Calder. They suggest that for men of exceptional talent membership in a family of artists brought recognition of precocious ability, very early and excellent training, and career assistance. They infer that women artists historically may have required a leg up to gain even minimal recognition. Familial assistance may have helped men reach headier heights.

Families also provided a leg up for many of the women in the *DNB* sample (table 5.5). In each period women were more likely than men to have a parent, grandparent, aunt, uncle, sibling, or cousin involved in the arts. But once an author, a woman did not necessarily benefit from familial involvement in the arts. Among women familial involvement was not associated with meeting our criteria for professional participation. But men whose families were involved in the arts were slightly more likely than women to meet our criteria for professional participation. Furthermore, among the authors most likely to have taken advantage of available literary opportunities—those living at least five years in London and also meeting our criteria for professional participation—almost exactly the same proportion of women and men had relatives involved in cultural milieus. For women especially, family help may have simply made a literary career possible but may not have been sufficient to bring great fame.

Although some women had families in the arts, few could draw on influential friendships to enter critical networks. To see how much more likely men were to enter varied networks, consider the sorts of influential friends the *DNB* identified for a highly select population, the 152 women and men who lived in London for at least five years as adults and also met our criteria for professional participation. (We have the necessary information for all but

Table 5.5: Percentage of Specified Authors with Involvement of Family
Members in Cultural Milieus, by Four Groups

	Early Women (%)	Late Women (%)	Early Men (%)	Late Men (%)
All authors	40	44	28	35
	(149)	(86)	(158)	(83)
Authors who met criteria for professional participation	39	33	42	38
	(99)	(69)	(88)	(61)
Authors who met criteria for professional participation and lived in London at least 5 years	34	35	34	33
	(41)	(34)	(35)	(36)

Note: Figures in parentheses are base Ns for the adjacent percentages. All base Ns
    include only those authors for whom the relevant data were available. The
    entire sample includes 154 early women, 91 late women, 175 early men, and
    87 late men.

five of them.) According to previous analyses, they might be identified as the
group most likely to make vital contacts.

We classified their influential friends using the following categories:
literary; political, religious, or intellectual; artistic; musical or theatrical;
qualifying for at least two of these categories (varied); or simply not mentioned. Recall that Sir Leslie Stephen had stated "I used rigidly to excise
the sentence, 'Nothing is known of his birth or parentage,' . . . because where
nothing is known it seems simpler that nothing should be said" (Stephen
1898, 22). In this instance, the "not mentioned" category may be taken to
mean both "nothing is known" and "his friends were not worth knowing";
for the names of authors' friends mentioned in the *DNB* are almost always
members of elites.

Accordingly, the patterns of selected friendships are particularly revealing
(table 5.6). They indicate that as a group, late men were active in more
networks. First, the early women and the early men were more specialized
than the late women and men; they were more likely to have friendships
with other literary people. Second, the late men had the most varied friendships; they were the authors whose *DNB* listings were most likely to include
friends from two or more of our categories. Third, late women were least

117

Table 5.6: Percentage of Authors Who Met our Criteria for Professional Participation, Lived in London at Least Five Years as Adults, and Had Specified Sorts of Friends, by Gender and Period

	Early Women (%)	Late Women (%)	Early Men (%)	Late Men (%)	All Authors (%)
Literary friends	41	32	40	33	37
Varied	26	3	23	31	21
Not mentioned	29	47	20	25	30
Other*	4	18	17	11	12
	100	100	100	100	100
N	(42)	(34)	(35)	(36)	(147)

Note: This table presents data about the relatively few authors for whom information was available. The entire sample includes 154 early women, 91 late women, 175 early men, and 87 late men.

*Includes (1) friends in political, religious, intellectual, and academic spheres; (2) friends in other arts; and (3) friends in the commercial end of the literary world, such as publishers.

likely to have had influential friends mentioned—although their deaths were sufficiently recent for their friends' names to be known.

What does this add up to? Men could convert both family and school ties into friendships with influential people. It seems safe to assume that some of their old school pals grew up to be influential people. Friendships gave them an edge, perhaps more than family ties. Although women were more likely than men to have help from their families, they were less likely to have influential friends. They led more restricted social lives. Women may not have been able to convert their ties into the sorts of help that ultimately brought greater recognition to men.[12]

We can imagine a discussion among a select group of men trying to choose an editor for an established journal. One might say to another, "How about Leslie Stephen? He knows everyone." (In this context, the term "everyone" means "everyone we care about.") Of course this conversation would never have been held. Because elite British men shared assumptions about the qualifications for literary posts, they would not have spelled out the need

12. In chapter 6 we consider how much family ties might have helped authors to attain fame. For technical reasons, however, we cannot weigh the importance of family ties against the importance of friends.

for an editor to know the people that they knew; they would merely have assumed it.

Nor would such elite men have needed to articulate their shared assumption that an editor, a coworker, or a responsible subordinate should be a man. Throughout the nineteenth century the doctrine of separate spheres with its insistent distinction between the (male) public and the (female) private realms hardened (Poovey 1984). Women might work for money or face seclusion in the home. Although realizing that their public activity would probably prevent marriage or remarriage, throughout the century more "redundant" single and widowed middle-class women entered the labor force (Vicinus 1985). Mostly, they were employed at such women's jobs as teaching, nursing, or performing clerical tasks defined as suitable for women (see Holcombe 1973; Zimmeck 1986). The doctrine of separate spheres stressed that if, against all probability and even late in life, a middle-class author married she should stop writing, as Macmillan partner and business manager George Lillie Craik had wished his wife Dinah Mulock to do (Showalter 1975). If she supported her husband with her pen, an author might give her husband undue credit for her own accomplishments, as did the ghost-story writer Mrs. Riddell (Black 1893).

Especially after publishing centralized, those culture brokers who accepted manuscripts and made potentially remunerative appointments to literary posts must have preferred the work of men, for they vested men with more symbolic capital than women, even as they protected their own class interests.

As publishing centralized and authors gained somewhat more control of their activities, men gained more than women. But did men also successfully invade fiction writing? Did the empty field phenomenon prevail?

6

The Invasion,
or How Women Wrote
More for Less

rom our foray through the *DNB* we have inferred that whatever their chosen genres male authors gained more from the expansion of literary opportunities than women did. Men increasingly published their first book with a London firm, edited both books and periodicals, met our criteria for professional participation, were identified as "authors," and published without a break of six years or more. To be sure, women's participation in these activities grew, too, but not as much as men's. And women wrote more. But did they write more novels? Did men invade the high-culture novel? Were men's novels appreciated more than women's were? Analyses of the entries for our sampled authors in the *DNB* and the *BMC* indicate that men did invade and that women worked harder and harder to get less.

In the discussion of periodization in chapter 5, we assumed that socialization and shared experiences may lead to a proclivity to engage in certain kinds of activities, but that to reach fulfillment proclivities must meet suitable opportunities. Thus, although authors may wish to publish novels, they cannot do so unless publishers wish to produce their books. One can get some sense of the increased market for fiction manuscripts by examining how many novels were published by the early and late authors, women and men. We address this question in several ways. We examine which *DNB* authors published at least one novel, other genres in which *DNB* authors published at least one work, which authors published many novels, and which groups of authors specialized in which genres.

As the novel became the dominant Victorian genre, published authors were more likely to have at least one novel to their credit (table 6.1). All authors who began publishing after 1840—that is late men and late women—were more likely to publish at least one novel than were those who began

Table 6.1: Percentage of Authors Who Published at least One Novel,
by Period, Gender, and Date of First Published Book

	Early Women (%)	Early Men (%)	Late Women (%)	Late Men (%)	All Authors (%)
Published a book before 1840	75 (117)	38 (138)	* (2)	* (9)	55 (266)
Published a book after 1840	81 (32)	32 (22)	91 (85)	63 (74)	74 (213)
All authors	76 (149)	37 (160)	97 (87)	63 (83)	63 (479)

Note: Figures in parentheses are base Ns for the adjacent percentages. All base Ns include only those authors for whom the relevant data were available. The entire sample includes 154 early women, 91 late women, 175 early men, and 87 late men.
*Too few cases for the statistics in this cell to be meaningful.

publishing before then. The activity of men accounts for most of the increased likelihood of authors' publishing at least one novel after 1840. The percentage of late men (63 percent) publishing at least one novel was almost twice that of the comparable group of early men (37 percent). Both early women (76 percent) and late women (97 percent) were more likely to publish novels than men born in either period. But the percentage of women publishing at least one novel did not increase appreciably from one period to the next.

At first glance, the finding that both early and late women were more likely than their male peers to publish at least one novel seems to go against the notion that men edged women out of the occupation of novel writing. But we do not accept a literal interpretation of the finding. Since, as literary critics are quick to remind us, novels differ in quality, many of the women authors may have been writing the romances that John Morley had so disdained as he reviewed manuscripts for Macmillan. Since Macmillan published romances despite Morley's recommendations, this possibility has some merit. But if more women and men spent time and effort preparing novels, they must have engaged less in other sorts of writing. Were women and men equally likely to abandon other genres to write novels? Do the patterns of authors' literary production affirm the female dominance of the novel apparently displayed in table 6.1?

To address these issues, we examine the distribution of authors' books across genres. Were the genres in which authors wrote associated with shifts in reading preferences and so in publishing preferences? Then we tackle the problem of differentiating on the basis of quality among the novels published by the authors sampled from the *DNB*. Finally, we ask how, if at all, men's participation as cultural entrepreneurs may have influenced definitions of quality.

Who Published How Much of What?

Gender and genre. As more and more people became literate and came to prefer novels to other genres, the novel became a more profitable arena for writers. Some literary critics (for example, Lukács 1964) have claimed that the nineteenth-century novel was a "bourgeois genre" because it appealed to bourgeois readers and was financed through capitalist market mechanisms. By these criteria, poetry might be defined as an aristocratic genre. Traditionally, it had been financed through patrons or sinecures, such as that granted to John Milton, and historically, its readers had been members of the elite. One might expect that in an age of bourgeois readers the rise in the status of the novel occurred somewhat at the expense of poetry; for poetry required educated readers and so might be less profitable to publishers.

To be sure, many novelists also published poems. For women novelists in particular, the publication of poetry represented a form of validation, especially since even the best of them, such as George Eliot, felt insecure about their ignorance of the Greek and Latin considered so essential to men's education (Showalter, personal communication). Yet even though many late authors who wrote novels also wrote poetry, they tended to concentrate on the bourgeois form.

Three separate analyses confirm that the increased publication of novels was associated with decreased publication of poetry. First, a greater percentage of late authors (90 percent of the women, 62 percent of the men) than of early authors (77 percent of the women, 32 percent of the men) published at least one novel, whereas a smaller percentage of late authors than early authors published at least one book of poetry (early women, 60 percent; early men, 76 percent; late women, 44 percent; and late men, 56 percent). The proportion who published at least one book of nonfiction remained roughly the same (early women, 66 percent; early men, 77 percent; late women, 67 percent; and late men, 88 percent); men accounted for most of the differences from one period to the next.

Second, a greater percentage of late authors than early authors published nine novels or more, whereas a smaller percentage of late authors published an amount of poetry comparable to that of early authors. We calculated the ratios of the number of late men and women publishing at least nine books in specified genres to early women and men with comparable publishing records, setting the number of early women and of early men who had published at least nine books in a specified genre to equal 100. For women, the ratios were 193, 108, 88, and 104 for fiction, poetry, nonfiction, and all genres, respectively. For men, the comparable ratios were 428, 55, 131, and 132, respectively. The number of men publishing many novels increased quite markedly especially when compared to the women, even as fewer men published a comparable amount of poetry. Compared to women, men also increasingly published nonfiction.

Third, there was a shift in the genre in which authors published most of their books. Writing one novel or even nine novels is decidedly different from being an author who specializes in writing novels—a novelist. Accordingly, we distinguished between those who wrote novels and those who were novelists. If over half of an author's books as listed in the *BMC* belonged to a particular genre, we classified that author as a specialist in that genre. Using this method, we deemed some authors to be novelists, poets, dramatists, or nonfiction specialists and the rest to be generalists (no genre). For instance, between 1871 and his death in 1928 Thomas Hardy published thirty-two books: eighteen books of fiction (including four collections of his short stories), nine books of poetry, a book of essays, and four plays. (We are counting Hardy's three-part play *The Dynasts*, published by Macmillan in 1903, 1906, and 1908, as three separate publications.) By our criterion, Hardy was a novelist because most of his publications (56 percent) were fiction.

The category of late women includes more specialists than any other (table 6.2). To us, this connotes the exclusion of women from that developing generalist role "the English man of letters," a probability reviewed in chapter 5. As specialists, more women were novelists; more men, nonfiction writers. We infer that some men wrote novels as a fling. Although 62 percent of the late men wrote at least one novel and as many as 21 percent of the late men wrote nine or more novels, only 19 percent of them qualified as novelists. Late men turned to the novel at the expense of poetry; a quarter of the early authors mainly published poetry whereas few late authors did.

But where were all these new novelists coming from? Were they earning

Table 6.2: Distribution of Authors by Literary Specialty,
by Gender and Period

		Early Women (%)	Late Women (%)	Early Men (%)	Late Men (%)	All Authors (%)
Novelists		37	63	4	19	28
Poets		21	10	29	9	19
Nonfiction authors		20	15	43	49	32
Dramatists		2	1	4	5	3
No genre		21	11	19	18	18
		101*	100	100	100	100
	N	(151)	(89)	(161)	(84)	(485)

Note: Figures in parentheses are base Ns for the adjacent percentages. All base Ns include only those authors for whom the relevant data were available. The entire sample includes 154 early women, 91 late women, 175 early men, and 87 late men.
*Error due to rounding.

their livelihood as authors? To answer these questions, we examined the dominant genres of writers who met our criteria for professional participation (professionals) and those who did not (hobbyists). In each period, professionals and hobbyists did indeed concentrate on different genres. Professional writers were more likely than hobbyists to write novels and nonfiction; hobbyists, to write poetry (table 6.3).

In table 6.3 we provide some evidence of men's invasion of the novel. In the late period three times as many male professionals were novelists as in the early period, and fourteen times as many were hobbyists. To be sure, these very high rates of change result from the fact that few early men wrote novels. But another finding suggests that the very low base of early male novelists is not the pertinent issue. For among male professionals the publication of poetry decreased markedly. Fifteen percent of the early male professionals published poetry whereas 6 percent of the late male professionals did so.

Findings such as these do not distinguish among novels on the basis of quality. The distinction between a great novel and pulp is of some importance because we have claimed that throughout the nineteenth century and especially after 1840 the cultural elite was defining high culture and popular culture. And we have also claimed that men captured the more esteemed area while women remained authors of popular fiction.

Table 6.3: Distribution of Professional and Hobbyist Authors among Specialties, by Gender, Period, and Genre

	Early Women (%)	Late Women (%)	Early Men (%)	Late Men (%)	All Authors (%)
Professionals					
Novelists	41	69	7	21	34
Poets	15	7	15	6	12
Nonfiction authors	24	13	59	55	37
Dramatists and no genre	<u>30</u>	<u>11</u>	<u>19</u>	<u>18</u>	<u>17</u>
	100	100	100	100	100
N	(101)	(71)	(70)	(62)	(325)
Hobbyists					
Novelists	30	40	1	14	16
Poets	32	22	46	18	35
Nonfiction authors	10	22	23	32	20
Dramatists and no genre	<u>28</u>	<u>16</u>	<u>30</u>	<u>36</u>	<u>29</u>
	100	100	100	100	100
N	(50)	(18)	(91)	(22)	(160)
Total (Professionals and Hobbyists)	(151)	(89)	(161)	(84)	(485)

Note: All base *N*s include only those authors for whom relevant data were available. Three early women, 2 late women, 14 early men, and 3 late men were excluded.

Circumstantial evidence suggests a complex pattern of sorting authors and books into those of high culture and popular culture. To use a modern analogy, even though the job of surgeon is a male preserve some surgeons are female. In the Victorian era, men did not simply abandon the popular novel, nor were all women excluded from the high-culture novel. Male and female authors, however, received different sorts of recognition for their novels. Before reviewing the data, let us consider the problem of assessing the quality of literary work.

The Problem of Quality

As we have suggested, no clear line divides the high culture novel and the popular novel. A work considered popular culture in one period may be considered high culture in the next. Furthermore, in Victorian times some novels qualified simultaneously as high culture and popular culture: they received critical acclaim *and* sold very well. Thackeray's novels are a case in point. The Victorian critics considered Thackeray to be one of their greatest novelists, and his work went through many editions.

Literary critics and sociologists have sought ways to analyze the varying assessments of quality that a work may receive. One method, common to both approaches, is to emphasize the building of reputations. (In literary criticism this approach is termed *reception theory*.) Thus, Jane Tompkins (1985) traces how Hawthorne, considered a sentimental novelist in his own time, was declared a modern novelist after his death. She convincingly argues that through "loose ties" with the Boston literary elite Hawthorne was praised in literary journals that were to become increasingly influential as the years passed. The second generation of critics associated with that journal continued to praise Hawthorne, but increasingly they singled out works that were not widely read in Hawthorne's day and ignored much of his work that earlier fans had adored. Recreating Hawthorne's oeuvre by redefining which of his works were "important," they created a "modern Hawthorne."

Sociologists have taken a similar tack. They do not try to determine whether specific works by specific authors have invariant quality—that is, speak to the human condition as it has been revealed in different social and literary periods. Rather, they ask, as reception theorists do, how authors (or artists) attained recognition as "great." (Emphasizing the sociocultural context of literary judgments, this sociological approach is a form of cultural relativism.) The question "how did authors become famous?" matters because fame matters to the social organization of literature.

Because it has immediate exchange value in the literary market, a good reputation is, to use Pierre Bourdieu's phrase (1984), a kind of "symbolic capital." That is, the more fame one has, the more one might be expected to accumulate more fame, much as economic capital helps one to amass more economic capital. Working in the sociology of science, Robert K. Merton (1968) has dubbed this tendency the Matthew Effect from the gospel maxim "Unto every one that hath shall be given, and he shall have abundance; but from him that hath not shall be taken away even that which he hath." In writing, the more fame an author has, the more easily he or she might be expected to sell new work to a publisher, to receive reviews and other forms of recognition, and to convert this recognition into the sales of books to readers. For example, during the late Victorian period the relatively unknown Frances Hoey and the well-known and popular Edmund Yates supposedly agreed to attribute five of Hoey's novels to Yates in order to increase sales.

In his *Autobiography* Trollope (1980) provides another example of how fame brings money. After becoming an established novelist, Trollope decided to assess the complaints of unknown novelists that they could not sell their work. Altering his style appropriately, he convinced his publisher, Blackwood, to issue two of his novels under a pseudonym to see whether he could build a second reputation. Blackwood agreed in the belief that the works of an "experienced author would make their way even without the writer's name," but "declined a [pseudonymous] third attempt." According to the novelist, "Another ten years of unpaid flogging labor might have built up a second reputation. But this at any rate did seem clear to me, that with all the increased advantages which practice in my art must have given me, I could not induce English readers to read what I gave them, unless I gave it with my name" (quoted in Becker 1982, 24). Indeed, Trollope emphasized, just as a woman might send to Fortnum and Mason's for a pie because that firm had established a solid reputation for selling good pies over the years, so the average reader prefers the books of authors with solid reputations.

According to Bourdieu (1980), even if an author's book does not sell well, the more an author is acclaimed by the dominant high-culture critics, the greater the likelihood that the author's future work will be published by a firm that invests in the present to build a strong backlist in the future. Acclaim increases the likelihood that an author's work will be published by a firm dedicated to selling it well after the current season's bestseller list has faded into memory (cf. Coser, Kadushin, and Powell 1982).

Fame begets fame in other ways, too. Germaine Greer (1979) reminds us of how this process operates in the case of works by artists who have died. Desiring to own, sell, or be associated with famous artists' works, dealers, curators, and critics may attribute the works of lesser artists to their more famous contemporaries. According to Greer, since women have historically been classified as less important, over the centuries the best work in the oeuvres of women may have been attributed to more famous artists—men.

The organization of social life may also decrease women's fame. In "Artistic Reputations: The Case of the Disappearing Lady Etchers in Britain," Gladys Engel Lang and Kurt Lang (1982) examined the social practices that perpetuated the names and work of male etchers while eradicating the reputations of women whose etchings were of comparable quality. They found that after the male etchers died their widows or children organized retrospective exhibitions of their work or published a catalog raisonné of their work. But when the women etchers died their work died, too. No one celebrated their oeuvres. Lang and Lang give examples of male and female etchers who had been married to one another; as is demographically probable, the wife often outlived her husband. Typically, the widow or their children arranged public memorials for the man, but after the woman's death her work was ignored.

Sometimes an author may manipulate social structures to achieve fame or to achieve the sort of fame desired. Robert Kapsis (1985; cf. Lamont 1985) offers an example of this phenomenon in his work on the film director Alfred Hitchcock. Annoyed that he was regarded as a director of "mere genre movies" (as a popular director) rather than as a director of high-culture films (as an artist) Hitchcock sought to take control of a flattering biography that François Truffaut proposed to prepare. He wished to insure that it was sufficiently adulatory. Hitchcock then used a portion of Truffaut's biography and Peter Bogdanovitch's admiration for his work to participate in Bogdanovitch's arrangements for a Hitchcock retrospective at New York's Museum of Modern Art. Before the retrospective opened, Hitchcock made sure that New York film critics had seen Truffaut's heady praise of his films. He anticipated that, knowing that a respected European director of high culture films regarded him as a hero, New York critics would be disposed to recognize him as an inspirational artist as well. Hitchcock's ploy worked. Of course, Hitchcock was in a position to take advantage of these opportunities to promote himself as not all directors, artists, or novelists are. Again the Matthew Effect (Merton 1968) operates; the more one has, the more one gets.

Recognizing that judgments of quality vary and result from social practices within art worlds, we turn to the social production of fame to learn more about the social processes associated with the empty field phenomenon. How did the social backgrounds of authors and the quantity of their work contribute to their fame in the late Victorian and Edwardian eras? Precisely because the *DNB* contributed to the formation of the literary canon, it provides ideal data. Knowing the degree of fame enjoyed by male and female novelists as seen through the lens of the *DNB*, we may ask such questions as, After 1840, were men who became novelists more likely to become famous than women? Were men and women rewarded equally for comparable achievements?

Fame and the empty field phenomenon. To answer these questions, we used information in the *DNB* and in the *BMC* to construct an index of fame, which varies from zero to four points. Reasoning that friendships, alliances, and contacts with influential people might influence the degree of fame that an author achieved, we gave one point to each author whom the *DNB* described as knowing at least five influential people. We then sought to adapt a measure commonly used in the sociology of science, in which a scientist's reputation in the academic community is assessed by counting citations to her or his work in either the *Science Citation Index* or the *Social Science Citation Index*. If the *DNB*'s entry about an author was longer than most author's entries, over 150 lines, the author received one point. We assumed that the translation of at least one work into another language indicates recognition, as does the existence of biographies and critical commentaries. Noting that the *DNB*'s listing of authors' publications frequently missed items, we turned to the *BMC* for additional information. If the *BMC* indicated that at least one of an author's works had been translated into another language, the author received one point. An author also received one point if five books or more about either the author or her or his works had been published.[1] The twenty authors who scored 4 and the thirty-seven authors who received a score of 3 are indicated in appendix A.

Inspection of the names and scores reveals that the index made sensible discriminations. No major writer in the sample scored lower than 3. (By "major" we mean generally considered important by literary critics. Such major writers as Wilkie Collins, Charles Dickens, and William Makepeace Thackeray were not in the sample.) Because of its limited range and the peculiarities in its construction, this "fame index" is of only heuristic value. Nonetheless, by using the index to study the four groups of authors we illuminate aspects of the empty field phenomenon.

We have seen that the centralization of publishing and the profession-alization of literature benefited men more than women. Examination of scores on the heuristic fame index reveals that after 1840 the empty field phenomenon applied to literature. As literature became an increasingly prestigious activity, men increasingly basked in the public eye. The fifty-seven most famous people include more early women than early men but more late men than late women. Those who received 3 or 4 on the fame index included 13 percent of all the early women, 8 percent of the early men, 8 percent of the late women, and 18 percent of the late men. With the rise of the English man of letters, the mean fame of men increased while that of women decreased (fig. 6.1). But men and women achieved fame differently.

1. The inclusiveness of the four items varied, as follows: 26 percent of the sample had at least one book translated, 25 percent of the sample had a *DNB* entry of over 150 lines, 23 percent of the sample had contacts with at least five influential people, and 9 percent of the sample authors had at least five books written about them or their work.

The index has the sort of distribution one would expect: 54 percent of the sample scored 0, 24 percent scored 1, 11 percent scored 2, 7 percent scored 3, and 4 percent scored 4. Reliability tests indicate that the scale itself is internally consistent with individual item correlations ranking from a low of 0.34 to a high of 0.6 and alpha equal to 0.65.

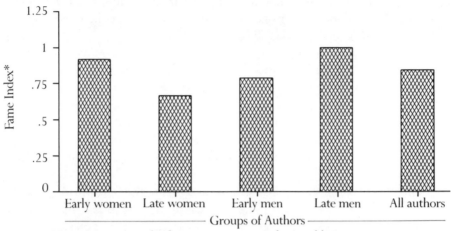

Figure 6.1
Mean Fame of Authors, by Gender and Period

*For more statistical information, see appendix B, table B.1

The Achievement of Fame

For women, especially late women, publication of a book was very likely to mean publication of a novel (fig. 6.2). Not so for men. Men wrote novels, and novels largely account for the increased literary productivity from one period to the next. But writing novels did not necessarily contribute to fame. Publications in the traditionally male bastions of poetry, plays, and nonfiction were more likely to do so.

Our statement that the genre in which authors wrote contributed to the likelihood of their achieving fame is based on a series of regression analyses, a statistical method that makes it possible to determine the form and strength of relationships among variables. We used regression analysis to ask a series of questions: How did the number of books that an author wrote in various genres contribute to that author's fame? Did the socioeconomic status of an author's father assist an author?[2] Did help from a family member involved in

2. Father's status, calculated from the Treiman index (Treiman 1977), was used as a stand-in for social class and such other background factors as education, for we assumed that fathers with higher status were likely to dedicate more resources to their children's education. The Treiman index offers scores for men's socioeconomic status that are supposedly valid historically and cross-nationally. We had attempted to devise our own measurements of class so that we could discuss class rather than socioeconomic status, but we ran into

Figure 6.2
Means of Specified Variables, by Gender and Period

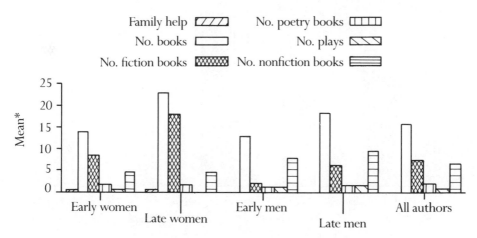

*For more statistical information, see appendix B, table B.2.

cultural milieus ease an author's way?[3] By asking about what we have called "family help," we supposed that the accomplishments of one family member might enhance the reputation of another, as appears to be the case with the writing Stracheys and Mitfords in the twentieth century and the Kingsleys in the nineteenth century.

Trying to isolate those for whom our variables were most likely to bring fame, we asked these questions sequentially of all sample members who belonged to a series of groups and for whom relevant data were available: all authors, early women, late women, early men, late men, and specialists in the novel, poetry, and nonfiction.

Did the number of books that an author wrote in certain genres influence the amount of fame that he or she received? Yes. When we ran a regression equation that included this information, we were able to predict fame better

two serious problems: We could not devise a measure that captured the shift in the composition of social classes in the nineteenth century, and so many of the authors were drawn from the same or neighboring classes that our scale had minimal variation.

3. We coded family help as a dummy variable, 1 indicating that an author's grandparent, parent, uncle, aunt, sibling, or cousin had been involved in cultural milieus as an author, journalist, editor, artist, musicians, or actor. In chapter 5, we discussed the variable we constructed to indicate the possibility of family help.

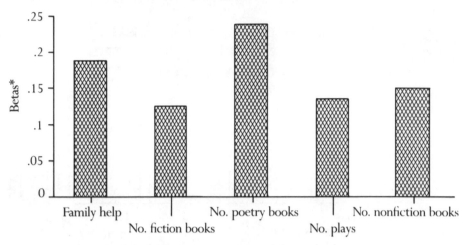

Figure 6.3
Variables Predicting Fame of All Authors

*For more statistical information, see appendix B, table B.2.

than using a variant of this equation that substituted the total number of books an author had published for the number of books published in each of the four genres.[4] As expected, help from family members active in the arts had a more powerful impact on fame than all but one of the genre variables (fig. 6.3). Indeed the aristocratic genre, poetry, made the most important contribution to the degree of fame achieved by all of our authors.[5] Of the four genres we considered, the new bourgeois genre, the novel, made the least contribution. Father's socioeconomic status, period, and gender did not significantly contribute to achieving fame.

But perhaps the simultaneous consideration of all authors masked some pertinent group differences. To assess this possibility, we asked, Did men and women, early and late authors attain fame differently? Was family help more likely to contribute to the fame of women than of men? Did the number of books published in each of these four genres contribute *in the same way* to the achievement of fame by writers in the four groups? To answer these questions, we ran additional sets of regression analyses, one for each of our four groups. In each of the first set, we tried to predict fame using the genre variables as well as family help and father's socioeconomic status. In the

4. The adjusted R^2 for the first equation was 16 percent and for the second, 12 percent.
    5. The beta of poetry is 0.242 and that of family help is 0.188.

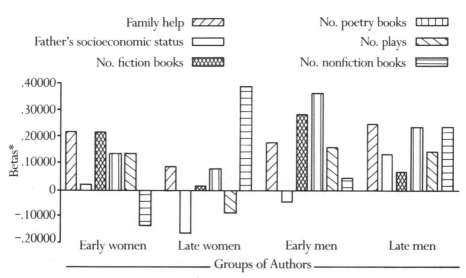

Figure 6.4
Varibles Contributing to Fame of Authors, by Gender and Period

*For more statistical information, see appendix B, table B.3.

second, we substituted the number of books an author had published for the four genre variables (fig. 6.4).

Our expectations were fulfilled. The analyses using the number of books an author had published did not predict fame as well as the analyses using the number of books published in each of the four genres.[6] Additionally, simultaneous consideration of all the authors had indeed concealed significant group differences. With the exception of the equation for early women, these regression analyses predicted the degree of authors' fame much better than our previous analyses had. But these data also presented a puzzle: Why did the analyses explain so poorly the degree of fame garnered by early women, the very authors who contributed most heavily to the development of the novel? We will address this issue later.

As we expected, more routes to fame were available to men. First, late women were the only group that did not convert family help into fame; family help assisted both early women and early and late men. Second, from one period to the next men's and women's ability to use literary activity as

6. The adjusted R^2 for the four groups in this second set of equations were: early women, 0.058; late women, 0.056; early men, 0.195; late men, 0.216. With the exception of the equation for early women, we have explained a surprising amount of the variance.

a vehicle for upward mobility shifted (as indicated by the signs of the beta values for father's socioeconomic status).[7] Early women could take advantage of their father's social status; late women were less likely to do so.[8] Early men were not likely to achieve upward mobility through literary activity; late men were. The more status the fathers of late men had, the more fame late men got. Once there, they could use their status to advantage.[9]

Men had more routes to fame in other ways as well. Nineteenth-century literati participated in the rise of the English man of letters (Gross 1970). Our data confirm Gross' argument that the man of letters wrote nonfiction. Writing nonfiction enhanced the likelihood that all late authors would achieve fame. But as was shown in figure 6.2 late men were more likely to publish nonfiction than late women. And late women's opportunities to achieve fame appear to have been restricted to nonfiction, as it was the only genre that contributed to the degree of fame they achieved. Thus, late women's best chance to achieve fame was by publishing in a genre that they seemed to find relatively unappealing. In contrast, late men were likely to increase their degree of fame by publishing either poetry or nonfiction.

Early men also had somewhat different paths to fame than early women. Early men were significantly likely to achieve fame if they published poetry; novels mattered somewhat; plays less; nonfiction was irrelevant to their achievement of fame. Publishing novels contributed most to early women's

7. We have based our statements about the contribution of father's socioeconomic status to fame on results that are not statistically significant but our reasons for claiming that late men did better than early men make sense.

8. Indeed, late women from the most well-to-do families of origin, those most likely to have had an adequate education, achieved less fame than late women from families with supposedly fewer economic and social resources. It is as though there were a cap on these women's achievements.

Studies have frequently noted that women in a given profession are drawn from a slightly higher class background than their male colleagues and yet receive less recognition than men do, as though women needed more qualifications to gain entrance to the profession but could not then convert those qualifications into recognition for accomplishment. An early study noting this phenomenon is Jessie Bernard's *Academic Women* (1964). The pattern is more complex when one takes race and ethnicity into account.

9. Early men came from wealthier families than late men (the mean socioeconomic status of the fathers of early men is higher than that of late men's fathers, and the standard deviation for the fathers of early men is lower). We infer that either many early men were dilettantes (men from wealthy backgrounds who wrote for their own pleasure but did not strive to hone their craft) or that it was more socially acceptable for late men to go into literature.

fame, publishing poetry and plays provided somewhat less recognition, and writing nonfiction *detracted* from appreciation of their accomplishments.[10]

These findings do not affirm the operation of the empty field phenomenon or indicate that publishing novels contributed differently to the fame of women and men. Rather, for both early women and early men, the more novels one wrote, the more likely one was to score well on the fame index. The findings also indicate that the novel did not contribute much to the fame of the late authors. If anything, the findings indicate that as time passed the novel was devalued. Was it?

Was the Novel Devalued?

The emphasis on nonfiction for late authors reveals the values of the men who wrote and assembled the *DNB*. Today, newspapers' obituary pages overrepresent reporters and editors because of the high value that reporters place on themselves and their own work (Tuchman 1974a). So too, we suspect, the men of letters who edited the *DNB* particularly valued essays and literary criticism, as well as religious and historical studies. Six of the biographers listed in table 5.1 and editor Sidney Lee have entries in the *DNB*. Their biographers discussed them as "men of letters"—"nonfiction writers," to use our more neutral term, or "intellectuals," in twentieth-century parlance.

Ultimately, the values held by these men of letters expressed both class and gender distinctions. By the time the *DNB* was being assembled, rising literacy had created an increased number of middle-class and working-class readers who preferred the novel to other kinds of literature (Altick 1957). From the vantage point of the late Victorian and Edwardian cultural elite, as the numbers of readers with low status swelled, the popular novel commanded relatively low prestige, especially when compared with the emerging high-status (art) novel and with nonfiction.

We can infer how the editors of the *DNB* viewed fiction by examining more closely the fame acquired and the number of novels written by diverse groups of authors. Reading the *DNB* biographies, we noticed that some of the early women, such as Jane Austen, wrote a few valued novels whereas most of the late women, such as Mrs. Molesworth, wrote many popular works. (In Mrs. Molesworth's case many of these were children's books.)

10. For early men the relevant betas are poetry, 0.379; novels, 0.292; plays, 0.168. For early women the relevant betas are novels, 0.221; poetry, 0.147; plays, 0.150; and nonfiction, −0.131.

Perhaps the *DNB* editors devalued fiction relative to nonfiction because after 1840 so many popular novelists wrote so much of such dubious quality, as the *DNB* editors judged quality. That possibility seems sensible. Maintaining the constant pace that accompanies voluminous production was difficult. At least that is the implication of some critical judgments of Mrs. Oliphant, a prolific writer whose early novels are today thought to be her best work (see Walbank 1950).

Furthermore, many early women novelists who wrote relatively little have received more recognition than those who wrote more. Those early novelists who scored 3 or 4 on the fame index include such women as Fanny Burney (*Evelina*), Maria Edgeworth (*Castle Rackrent*), Elizabeth Gaskell (*Mary Barton*), and Ann Radcliffe, who "invented" the Gothic novel; and the men, George Bulwer-Lytton (*Pelham*) and Charles Lever (*Charles O'Malley*).[11] With the exception of Maria Edgeworth, these very famous women wrote relatively little, especially when compared with the most famous late novelists. That so many superb early women novelists published relatively little accounts for the failure of our regression equations to predict the degree of fame they achieved. These early women may have seemed important to the compilers of the *DNB* because the novel was to develop a high-culture form and so its early exemplars achieved a degree of retroactive renown.

Of course, most people who wrote relatively few novels did not write superb books. But the demonstration of this truism is interesting because of what it tells us about early women. For the moment, suppose that the less famous novelists, women like Mrs. Molesworth, gained entry to the *DNB* because they wrote so much that was widely read that the compilers of the *DNB* could not ignore them. We believe that the editors included many women, especially early women, because they could not ignore their achievements.

How can we test this interpretation? Can we learn whether some early women who wrote relatively little gained little fame, whether some early women who wrote relatively little gained much fame, and whether the remaining early women who wrote more achieved middling fame? A more complex form of regression analysis, curvilinear regression, permits us to assess this possibility. If our interpretation is correct, curvilinear regression analyses would increase our ability to explain the degree of fame early women achieved but would not do so as much for authors in the other three groups.

---

11. Although he fell into our sample, we do not mention George Meredith here. According to his listing in the *BMC*, he wrote in so many genres that we did not classify him as a novelist.

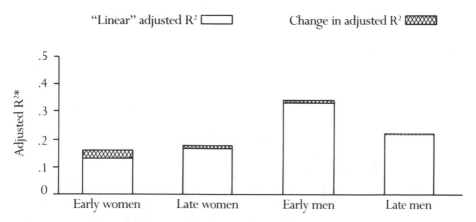

Figure 6.5
Change in Adjusted R^2 When Fiction Is Curvilinear

"Linear" adjusted R^2 ▭   Change in adjusted R^2 ▨

*For more statistical information, see appendix B, tables B.4 and B.5.

Accordingly, we performed curvilinear regression analyses for the four groups of authors. The results essentially confirmed our expectations (fig. 6.5). The new equations improved our ability to predict the fame of early women. They did not alter our ability to predict the fame of the other three groups of authors.[12]

What does this mean? Up to a point, the more novels an early woman wrote, the more likely she was to achieve some degree of fame.[13] After that

12. In each of the four curvilinear regression analyses, we substituted the square root of the number of novels published for the equivalent variable used in the previous analyses. The new equations improved our ability to predict the fame of early women. They did not appreciably alter our ability to predict the fame of the other three groups of authors; the change in adjusted R^2 is more negligible for early men and remains the same for both late women and late men.

Because analyses using the square root of the number of books of fiction published either slightly improve our results or have no impact on them, we used this variable in most other analyses reported later in this chapter. We checked our results against regression analyses defining the variable fiction as the number of novels published. Since both definitions of the variable for fiction yielded similar results, we have favored consistent definition of this variable.

13. In economics, the resulting curve is termed a backward leaning supply curve. It is usually read as meaning that after a certain point the supply of workers decreases, for they can earn more elsewhere. In the context of our argument, however, it makes no sense to say that after a certain point the supply of writers decreases. Rather, we argue, after a

point, early women garnered fame because their accomplishments could not be ignored, given the developing interpretation of British literary genres. But *late women wrote more and more to achieve less and less.* Late women scored lowest on the fame index, but they wrote appreciably more books and appreciably more novels than did authors in the other three groups.

If our reasoning is correct, our argument should also apply to how novelists garnered fame. Did women and men novelists achieve fame differently? Unfortunately, to demonstrate that we are right is difficult because too few men were novelists for separate regression analyses of the four groups to yield meaningful results.[14] Almost all of the 130 novelists were women (43 percent were early women; 41 percent, late women; 5 percent, early men; and 11 percent, late men).

How to proceed? We executed separate regression analyses of the three groups of specialists with sufficient cases to yield meaningful results: novelists, poets, and nonfiction writers. Most of the 94 poets were early authors (33 percent were early women; 10 percent, late women; 49 percent, early men; and 8 percent, late men). Most of the 151 nonfiction authors were men (18 percent were early women; 9 percent, late women; 46 percent, early men; and 27 percent, late men).

These analyses affirmed the importance of fiction to garnering fame (figs. 6.6 and 6.7). Writing novels contributed significantly not only to the fame of novelists but to the fame of poets and nonfiction authors as well. But writing nonfiction or poetry did not significantly influence the fame of novelists.[15]

Did their gender give men an advantage in achieving fame? Relatively speaking, being a man helped novelists more than poets or nonfiction writers. Gender contributed more to the fame of male novelists than the number of novels published. Being a man helped poets achieve fame, although how much poetry they had published mattered even more. And gender did not contribute to the fame of nonfiction writers.[16]

---

certain point the amount of recognition elite men were willing to bestow on women writers decreased.

14. For technical reasons, regression analysis demands a certain number of cases for each variable in the equation. The number of cases of early or late male novelists in our sample is insufficient to perform regression analyses for these groups.

15. Another finding also tends to support the contribution of novel writing to fame; the mean fame of novelists was somewhat larger than that of either poets or nonfiction authors but the standard deviations of all three groups are too large to impute significance.

16. For novelists, the beta of gender is 0.184 and that of the novel is 0.175. For poets, the beta of gender is 0.273 and that of poetry is 0.404.

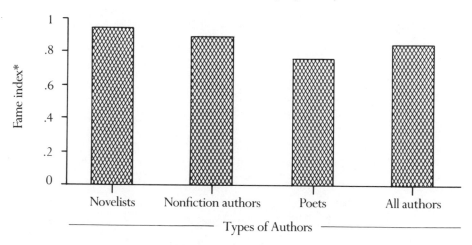

Figure 6.6
Mean Fame of Authors, by Specialty

*For more statistical information, see appendix B, table B.7.

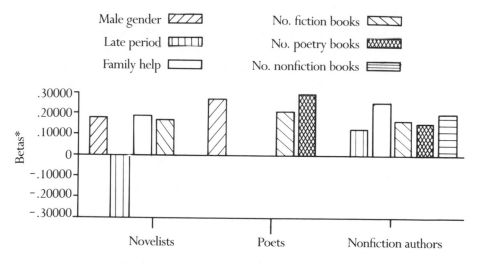

Figure 6.7
Significant Contributions of Variables to Authors' Fame,
by Authors' Specialty

*For more statistical information, see appendix B, table B.6.

Figure 6.8
Specified Variables Predicting Fame of All Authors

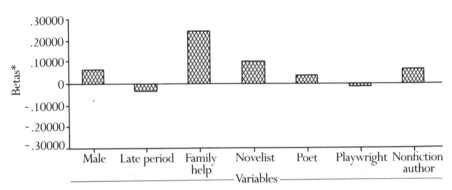

*For more statistical information, see appendix B, tables B.8 and B.9. "Yes" coded as 1, "no" as 0.

These tests seem to confirm that men successfully invaded the empty field of novel writing by writing high-culture novels. An additional regression analysis offers some substantiation. By weighing the impact of gender, period, family help, and an author's specialty on an author's fame, it asked whether late male novelists were more likely to achieve fame than other groups.

Our expectations were partially confirmed. We expected an author's period to matter; it did not. As our theory predicted, however, a male novelist with family help was more likely to achieve fame than any other writer (fig. 6.8). Family help was so important to becoming famous that, to use the Victorian term, a "poetess" with familial ties to others in the arts might achieve more fame than a male novelist lacking similar familial ties.[17]

Since family help was not evenly distributed across the sample, we are faced with a seeming paradox. On the one hand, a higher percentage of late women had access to family help than did authors in any other group (44 percent of late women, 40 percent of early women, 35 percent of late men, and 28 percent of early men). Furthermore, of all the variables that we have considered, family help most affected the fame of novelists—and a whopping 63 percent of the late women were novelists, a considerably higher percentage than in any other group (table 6.2). On the other hand, although family help contributed significantly to the fame of early women and all men, it did not significantly affect the fame of late women (fig. 6.4).

17. The betas indicate that the "poetess" with family help would score 0.251 on the fame index, the male novelist, 0.178.

Why did family help assist all novelists except late women? To answer this question, we ran a regression analysis comparable to the others reported in this chapter for the 56 late women novelists. Help from family members in the arts did not contribute significantly to their fame; writing nonfiction did.[18] Accordingly, we infer that our expectations have been upheld. Since late women could convert neither family help nor the number of novels they wrote to fame, we infer that the members of the cultural elite who wrote and edited the *DNB* devalued the work of late women novelists.

Late women were edged out of the high culture novel. Writing fiction was more likely to contribute to the fame of late men than to that of late women. The fiction that late men wrote received cultural validation; novels by late women did not. Presumably, many of the late men wrote high-culture novels whereas late women were more likely to publish popular novels. Men and women achieved fame differently.

What else may we conclude? The status of the English man of letters did indeed increase. But since the regression analyses consistently suggest that late women who wrote novels could also garner fame by writing nonfiction we are faced with a final question. Could both late women and late men convert status achieved through writing nonfiction into the sort of symbolic capital that enabled some authors to have a say in distinguishing the high-culture novel from the popular novel? Did both late women and late men contribute equally to the politics of culture or have an equal opportunity to do so?

Probably not. Victorian men of letters achieved some hegemony over the novel because their work was not confined to letters. Many men of letters assumed positions of public importance. Some served in the House of Commons. Although he did not publish fiction, John Morley is nonetheless an apt example. As previously noted, he edited several prestigious journals. He edited literary series. He wrote important books in the history of ideas. He also was a member of several Liberal cabinets, served as secretary of state for India, and eventually was named viscount in recognition of his political services.

There are other indications that men who met our criteria for professional participation were more likely than women to have formed friendships and alliances that they could use to exercise literary sway. Professionals with influential friends in literary circles include 31 percent of the late men and 25

---

18. These results obtained whether we entered fiction as the number of novels published plus one or as the square root of that sum. The beta for father's socioeconomic status was also significant. (Its sign was negative.) When we excluded the two outliers, the beta for nonfiction was not significant, and it was slightly lower than the beta for poetry.

percent of the late women. Twenty-four percent of the late men but only 6 percent of the late women had friends in several influential networks. The *DNB* omits information about the friendships of more than half (58 percent) of the late women who met our criteria but only 29 percent of the late men. But, as we saw in chapter 5, what the compilers of the *DNB* chose to omit was itself telling. For biographers of the late women to learn the names of the friends of these recently deceased women would have been relatively easy.

Again there are several possibilities: Perhaps late men could hold sway over fiction because the late men and late women who wrote nonfiction concentrated on different topics. Perhaps the late men tackled topics more likely to bring acclaim. We did not code the sorts of nonfiction written by the authors listed in the *DNB*. We did, however, code this information for authors who submitted nonfiction to Macmillan between 1866 and 1887. These data demonstrate that the category "nonfiction" is a catchall. In the past (and today), men and women have tended to write about very different topics. Men dominated the sorts of nonfiction that mattered most to Victorians.

Macmillan and Nonfiction

Throughout the sixty-year period we examined, women submitted roughly 15 percent of the nonfiction manuscripts that Macmillan received, and the firm accepted roughly 10 percent of those submissions. In the years for which we coded the sorts of nonfiction submitted and accepted (1866–1868, 1877–1878, and 1887), men were more likely to have written and to have had accepted the sorts of nonfiction identified with the Victorian man of letters.

A caveat is in order: What we have thus far termed "nonfiction submitted to Macmillan" is more properly termed "not novels, not poetry," for the category includes short stories, children's books, and English translations of foreign literature. Short stories and some children's books are clearly fiction. Relying heavily on the readers' reports on the manuscripts submitted between 1866 and 1887, we coded the content into fourteen subcategories including biography; philosophy; history; politics, public policy and commentary; natural sciences; and physical sciences and mathematics. Unfortunately, the following information about the genres in which men and women submitted manuscripts must be taken with several grains of salt.[19]

19. Since fewer "not novels, not poetry" manuscripts than manuscripts of novels were

However, even within these "salty limits," we found that submissions of "not novels, not poetry" were heavily gender-typed. The percentages of women and men who submitted manuscripts in the fourteen subcategories between 1866 and 1887 are shown in table 6.4. (The years are considered together because in any decade some subcategories have too few cases to permit generalizations.) The manuscripts are categorized as either "high prestige" (the sorts of publications written by men of letters), "men's specialties," "mixed specialties" (content that might be written by either a woman or a man), and "women's specialties." The specialties in which men were most concentrated reveal how gender-typed these submissions were. Women submitted some manuscripts in the fields valued by men of letters, but generally they stuck to their own specialties, much as men did. Not one man submitted a manuscript about the position of women in society.

This gender-typing influenced both the initial acceptance rates of manuscripts submitted by women and men (before manuscripts were sent to a reader) and their ultimate acceptance rates (table 6.5). Women were less likely than men to have their manuscripts accepted before a reader was called in, and they were less likely to have their manuscripts ultimately accepted—unless they were writing books about women's issues or for children. Conversely, men were most likely to submit in their "own" fields, and their manuscripts in those fields fared best. Indeed, the men's initial acceptance rates decreased in a rank order from men's specialties to women's specialties with one tie, and their ultimate acceptance rates follow rank order as well with one exception.

The patterns for women are less clear. Their submissions follow rank order; their acceptance rates do not. Women fared relatively well in the high-prestige specialties, in which their final acceptance rate (19 percent) was about the same as their rate in male specialties (17 percent). There were, though, some peculiarities in the acceptance of their work in the high-prestige and mixed specialties. The readers may even have felt that most women were incapable of writing in some nonfiction fields, as a reader quoted in chapter 4 had indeed argued in 1897. For if manuscripts that women submitted in

---

sent to a reader, our coding of these subcategories is not as reliable as our coding of novels. Overall, we felt confident about 90 percent of our ascriptions of subcategories, but these vary greatly from a low of 50 percent for fields in which women specialized, such as children's books and discussions of women's issues, to a high of 90 percent in such men's specialties as natural sciences, mathematics, social sciences, and geology.

Table 6.4: Percentage of Submitted Manuscripts by Men and of Accepted Manuscripts by Men in Four Nonfiction Categories, 1866–1887

	Nonfiction Categories*				
	Men's Specialties (%)	High Prestige (%)	Mixed Specialties (%)	Women's Specialties (%)	All Categories (%)
Mss. submitted	95 (111)	87 (235)	79 (161)	52 (21)	85 (528)
Mss. accepted	98 (49)	89 (55)	94 (34)	33 (6)	91 (144)

Note: Figures in parentheses are base *N*s for the adjacent percentages. 528 mss. were submitted in these four categories of nonfiction, and 144 were accepted. Of 111 mss. submitted in men's specialties, 95 percent were by men; of 49 mss. accepted in men's specialties, 98 percent were by men.

*The topics considered in these categories are: (1) Male Specialties—natural sciences, physical sciences, mathematics; classics; social science, geography, economics; (2) High Prestige Specialties—biography; philosophy; history; politics, public policy, commentary; religion; literary criticism; (3) Mixed Specialties—biography; travel and exotic places; texts and reference books; (4) Female Categories—women's topics; and children's books. All topics are mainly submitted by men, and there is some overlap between categories, for men submitted 73 percent of the biographies (listed under High Prestige) and 78 percent of the children's books (listed under Women's Specialties). The percentage of men in the topics listed under Male Specialties varied from 92 to 96 percent; under High Prestige, 73 to 94 percent, with the low figure belonging to biographies; Mixed Specialties, from 79 percent to 81 percent; and Female Specialties, from 0 to 78 percent.

Table 6.5: Percentage of Nonfiction Manuscripts Initially and Ultimately Accepted, 1866–1887, by Gender

| | Men's Specialties (%) | Specialties | | | All Categories (%) |
		High Prestige (%)	Mixed Specialties (%)	Women's Specialties (%)	
Women					
Immediately accepted	17	7	6	20	8
Ultimately accepted	17	19	6	40	16
N	(6)	(31)	(33)	(10)	(80)
Men					
Immediately accepted	32	16	16	0	19
Ultimately accepted	46	24	25	18	29
N	(105)	(204)	(128)	(11)	(448)
Women and men					
Immediately accepted	32	15	14	10	18
Ultimately accepted	44	23	21	29	27
N	(111)	(235)	(161)	(21)	(528)

Note: Figures in parentheses are base Ns for the adjacent percentages. In these four categories of nonfiction, 528 mss. were submitted, and 144 were ultimately accepted, 131 written by men and 13 by women.

145

Table 6.6: Selected Statistics about Authors of Rejected Nonfiction
Manuscripts for 1877–1878, 1897, 1917

		Women (%)	Men (%)	All Authors (%)
Percentage located in *BMC*		50	59	55
	N	(103)	(130)	(233)
Percentage who had previously published a nonfiction book		33	65	52
Percentage who had previously published a book		48	65	58
Percentage who eventually published a nonfiction book		85	96	91
Percentage who eventually published a book		92	96	95
Percentage who published this book		41	40	41
	N	(52)	(76)	(128)

Note: Calculations include books that had been published elswhere before submission
to Macmillan, such as books published in the United States or the colonies.

the high prestige and mixed specialties were not accepted immediately, they
were not ultimately accepted either.[20] It seems safe to say that men dominated
the nonfiction most pertinent to amassing symbolic capital. Nearly all of the
nonfiction manuscripts that Macmillan accepted were written by men.

Finally, men's higher acceptance rate across all categories of nonfiction
probably does not indicate higher quality. Despite the great difficulties we
experienced in locating women in the *BMC*, women and men whose nonfiction
was rejected were almost as likely to have a listing there and almost as likely
to publish their rejected manuscripts with other firms. Selected information
about the fate of rejected nonfiction manuscripts and about their authors is
presented in table 6.6. Women's manuscripts fared surprisingly well, for the
men whose nonfiction manuscripts were rejected were more experienced
authors of nonfiction. More men had previously published nonfiction; more
women had previously published fiction.

After their rejection by Macmillan, the men published more nonfiction

20. We have encountered two other cases of this close association between immediate
and eventual rejection: fiction submitted by men during the period of invasion and fiction
submitted by women during the period of male institutionalization. In those instances, we
argued, this close association indicated presuppositions about who should be writing novels.

than the women, displaying again their dominance of nonfiction. The women, in contrast, had more success publishing novels. Among the authors of rejected nonfiction located in the *BMC*, the women eventually published almost six times as many novels as the men, whereas the men eventually published almost twice as much nonfiction as the women. Nonfiction was maintained as a preserve of serious male authors.

Men successfully broached the walls of fiction—when they cared to do so. Both the men and the women whose fiction Macmillan accepted tended to be hobbyists. By the end of their careers they had not published at least eight books and so had not met the critieria for professional participation applied earlier to the authors in the *DNB* sample.

What hobbyists write may be indicative of what the general reader values. Not in professional milieus and potentially influenced by their friends, who were likely also to have been general readers, they might have "taken a stab" at writing in the genre that they and other general readers most enjoyed reading. Or as aspiring authors not yet integrated into the literary world, they might have felt that the novel had high prestige. The publishing records of the male and female hobbyists in the Macmillan sample are very much alike. The mean number of books published by both groups is 2, and both books were likely to have been novels.

These interpretations of the activity of the aspiring authors in the Macmillan sample seem appropriate, for their publishing records differ from those of the hobbyists and professionals in the *DNB* sample, authors who presumably were familiar with the values of the literary world. The *DNB* hobbyists were more likely than the professionals to specialize in poetry (see table 6.3). And we saw that writing poetry increased the probability of achieving fame for all authors except late women (fig. 6.4). Among the professionals the late men tended to specialize in nonfiction, as befitted Victorian men of letters (table 6.3).

Yet, even though men in the Macmillan sample were concentrated in nonfiction, the professionals among them published novels, too. The standard deviation for the number of novels published by authors whose nonfiction Macmillan had rejected (11.0) is higher than the means (2.4). This pattern indicates that several women and several men published many novels, but most published none or few.

Nonfiction was associated with positions enabling authors to exercise cultural power, to participate in the establishment of cultural standards, and even to help develop the literary canon. To assume that men could therefore convert their dominance of nonfiction into power over fiction seems reasonable. Among the fields that they virtually monopolized were areas favored by men of letters, including literary criticism, biography, and social commentary. And, we have shown, men had more contacts with influential people and more contacts with the sorts of people who mattered to *men* of letters.

Finally, our consideration of writers listed in the *DNB* revealed that women were concentrated in fiction, were recognized when their accomplishments could not be ignored, tended to work harder than men for the relatively scant recognition that most of them received, and submitted their manuscripts in a literary world dominated by men. As time passed, men increasingly wrote fiction—although a larger proportion of the women listed in the *DNB* were novelists. Nonetheless, male novelists, especially the early male novelists, seemed to have garnered a greater degree of fame than women—and for less published work.

Using inferences to follow a logical trail, we have presented a complex argument. Evidence gathered from the Macmillan Archives suggested that men had edged women out of the novel. Using data gathered from the *DNB*, we affirmed the application of the empty field phenomenon to women. We showed that men increasingly wrote novels, became novelists, and garnered more fame for their fiction than women. We inferred that men were more likely than women to be recognized as high culture novelists. Furthermore, individual men could use their power as cultural brokers to help themselves and other men to attain success.

As we will see in chapter 7, men were likely to receive more money for their novels than women were. In chapter 8 we will demonstrate that late-nineteenth-century men continued the eighteenth-century practice of applying different critical standards to novels by men and women, frequently implying that fiction by women was not a serious cultural endeavor.

7

Macmillan's Contracts
with Novelists

Fame pays. In Victorian days, as now, novelists whose books sold well could expect to receive better contractual terms than colleagues whose novels rarely moved from the library or bookstore shelf.

Did gender pay, too? Were men likely to get contracts that were more remunerative than those of women? These questions matter in two ways. First, if men's cultural dominance was converted into more generous contracts than those granted women, their cultural capital had economic consequences. Second, differential pay has frequently been associated with shifts in the gender composition of occupations.

More often than not, social status and pay are linked. White-collar-women's jobs are lower in social status than white-collar-men's jobs, and they pay less. When the occupation of secretary became less skilled and thus more open to women, the work began to pay less and to have less status. So did the jobs of (factory-based) bakers and (computerized) typesetters, which are today increasingly held by women. Conversely, when men have taken over women's fields, the status and income associated with many tasks have increased. When doctors (mainly men) superseded midwives (mainly women), they received more for supervising births than midwives had.

Some early commentators on the Victorian novel seem to think that men earned more for their novels than women did. In 1907 George Saintsbury commented that in the nineteenth century writing novels had "become the method by which 'the professional man or woman of letters' earned 'his plentiful or her scanty income'" (Griest 1970, 4). Earlier we noted that as editor of *Household Words* Charles Dickens paid Charles Lever more than Elizabeth Gaskell for a manuscript of equivalent length (Sutherland 1976). But a critic's assertion and a scholar's example do not prove that publishers paid women and men on different scales.

To address the issue of differential pay for male and female novelists, we now consider Macmillan's contracts with successful Victorian novelists. Victorians did not regard those whose contracts we will discuss as novelists of the first rank, but they were widely read and well known. Some of them were women and some, men. All but the American F. Marion Crawford were listed in the *DNB*. Appendix C lists the novelists whose contracts and correspondence with Macmillan we examined.

Most of these novelists were at least middle class, and some were wealthy by Victorian standards. Several who insisted on maintaining life-styles beyond their income, however, were perpetually pressed for money and credit. Mrs. Oliphant, F. Marion Crawford, and Henry Kingsley were among those always in need of funds. Charlotte Yonge needed money in her later life. Each needed money for different reasons. Margaret Oliphant was supporting her brother's children as well as her own and putting them through an elite education. Charlotte Yonge gave her early profits to charity. After the death of her parents and other family setbacks, she had a reduced income. Henry Kingsley was estranged from his family and spent his expectations before they were realized. F. Marion Crawford, born in Rome of American parents, lived lavishly in an expatriate community in Italy and liked to travel.

Because they earned a fair amount, these novelists were atypical. Most authors earned little by writing. Since they had few occupational alternatives, women were more likely to be among those struggling to get by. The *DNB* sample included several women who wrote more than a hundred books each, presumably because they needed the money. (Mrs. Oliphant was one of these authors.) When G. H. Thring in his manuscript on the Society for Authors discussed once-successful novelists who needed financial help in the 1890s, his examples were all women. The *DNB* was more likely to state that early women received a civil pension in old age than to report state support for early men.[1] Even the acclaimed Fanny Burney, who wrote her last novels to support herself and her emigré husband and to educate their son, retired to a civil pension.

We stress women's weaker financial position because Macmillan's contracts with novelists do not indicate overt gender discrimination. Macmillan's records demonstrate that authors who most needed money had the least negotiating power with Macmillan (and presumably with other publishers).

---

1. Our content analysis of biographies in the *DNB* revealed that 8 percent of early women were assisted by civil pensions, as were 5 percent of the early men; eight percent of both the late women and the late men received a civil pension.

We therefore infer that most women novelists were in a weaker position during contractual negotiations than most men.

Other evidence supports our inference. In the 1880s, when the Society of Authors was founded to improve and to guard authors' financial rights, women were excluded from membership. Control of remuneration is a central aspect of professionalism. The initial exclusion of women suggests that the society's male members did not view them as professionals.

Mid-nineteenth-century authors did not sign the same kind of contracts with publishers as later authors did; the provisions of standard contracts changed throughout the century. One aim of the society was to introduce what was for England a new type of contract between authors and publishers, the royalty system. (American publishers had used the royalty system since the 1830s.) Authors' claims to increased professionalism was one factor involved in their eventual success. Another was changes in publishers' notions of their own authors' financial rights. A third was changes in the distribution system for novels. We will stress this third factor because it helps to explain the difference between British and American contracts. Circulating libraries did not dominate the distribution of books in the United States. Although some books were serialized in magazines as was also done in England, most readers obtained books in stores where they were sold at a nominal fee compared to prices in British bookstores.[2]

The standard contract is particularly important because: (1) it is a structural, binding, and impersonal agreement; (2) when members of an occupation cannot exercise the sort of monopoly enjoyed by such classic professionals as doctors and lawyers, their claim to professionalism may rest on the ability to determine what kind of work they will do and how they will be paid for doing it; and (3) professionalization may be impeded when the provisions of these standard contracts are heavily influenced by an institution that is not a party to them.

In the case of the nineteenth-century novel, that third party was a distributor, Mudie's Select Library, which in some years was the largest purchaser of novels in the world. The power of Mudie's was akin to the

2. Douglas (1978) reviews the economics of nineteenth-century American publishing. Since American and British publishers first reached agreement on international copyright in 1891, for most of the century many American firms pirated British books and sold them at a very low price. For instance, "In 1843 *A Christmas Carol* sold for 6¢ in the United States and the equivalent of $2.50 in England" (Griswold 1981, 748). See Griswold (1981) for a discussion of the impact of copyright agreements on the works of American authors.

power wielded today by such immense American jobbers as Ingrams and Baker & Taylor and such huge American bookstore chains as Waldenbooks and B. Dalton. These jobbers and chains may have an impact on which books trade publishers issue, much as American television networks influence which programs production companies initiate. Certainly Mudie's affected more than contracts. It also affected the form and content of the products it distributed.[3] Charles Mudie demanded three-volume novels and preferred them to be suitable for family reading.

The impact of Mudie's Select Library on authors' contracts was not inevitable. Rather, the relationship between publishers and distributors that dominated British publishing from 1840 through 1880 developed from the eventual interdependence of a series of institutions each of which grew independently from conditions associated with industrial capitalism. Retrospectively, however, the Victorian system does seem inevitable, much as whatever system grows out of contemporary publishers' explorations of electronic publishing will seem inevitable fifty years from now. That seeming inevitability stems from the simultaneous development of Mudie's Select Library and the British publishing industry.

Mudie's Select Library

Mudie's Select Library seems a logical outgrowth of early practices. As Griest stresses in her history of Mudie's Library (1970), two strains gave impetus to the circulating libraries of the nineteenth century. First, in the early eighteenth century bookshops provided stools for customers to use while reading. Somewhat later, they extended this practice to permit customers to take books outside the shop.[4]

3. In recent studies of contemporary entertainment, Gitlin (1983), Cantor (1981), and Hirsch (1978) have stressed the power of distribution systems over the social production of popular culture. As Gitlin explains, when such distribution systems as the television networks, taken together, have a virtual monopoly they may dictate to production companies such basic and peripheral aspects of their wares as plot and casting, cinematic style, and even set decoration.

Cantor (1981) adds that distribution systems may also influence whether "media workers" can claim classical professional status. In her examples, the television networks set the degree of autonomy experienced by "production workers." Indeed, networks control such essential elements of professionalism as entry to and departure from the occupations of actor, writer, director, and producer. The power of the networks' blacklist during the McCarthy era is a extreme case in point, though it merely represents an extension of the networks' routine activities.

4. This section draws heavily on Griest (1970). The earliest lender was probably

Second, during this same period reading clubs flourished. Requirements for club membership anticipated those Charles Mudie used a century later: "Anyone who could pay the entrance fee of a guinea, plus a shilling a quarter, was eligible for membership" (Griest 1970, 8). But reading clubs were self-governing. Thus, when one of the earliest bookstore-libraries failed in 1745, the library's members kept the books and established a club, a "non-commercial organization to be run by a committee elected by the subscribers."

When circulating libraries were housed in bookstores, the retailers-libraries had an interest in keeping the price of books low to discourage book borrowing. When the libraries and the bookstores parted company, however, lenders and retailers had competing interests. Low book prices helped book sales. High prices helped libraries and, especially when the publishers gave extra discounts to libraries that bought novels in bulk, endangered booksellers' profits. This practice made it difficult for booksellers to price their books competitively. By 1810, according to Griest, "The increase in average novel prices from 2s a volume in 1780 to a high of 7s in 1810 reflect[ed] the growing importance of the influence of the circulating libraries over publishers" (ibid.).

Material conditions and the phenomenal sales of Walter Scott's *Kenilworth* (1821) further bolstered book prices and so libraries. The retail price of *Kenilworth*, 30s, helped to establish 30s 6p as the subsequent standard price of a novel. By 1833 the practice of borrowing novels from libraries was so well established that Smith, Elder failed in its attempt to buck the libraries by issuing original novels in a "Library of Romance" for 6s a volume. After only four months and four volumes, Smith, Elder bowed to pressure from the libraries and brought out three-volume novels at the high prices that libraries demanded.

That format governed fiction. Indeed, from roughly 1800 on circulating libraries were synonymous with fiction. Some publishers encouraged this identification of circulating libraries with fiction. William Lane, the owner of the Minerva Press, which specialized in romances, established his own circulating libraries, which mainly stocked fiction. Mudie's Select Library at first succeeded because it seemed to break the identification of libraries with novels.

Charles Edward Mudie's personal attributes also contributed to that break with the past and to the success of his library. Long lived, he started lending books in 1842, when he was 22 years old and the novel was coming into its own. He guided the library's policies through the 1880s, when the

---

Allan Ramsay of Edinburgh, though the term *circulating library* was introduced in London between 1740 and 1742 by Rev. Samuel Fancourt's book-lending establishments.

literary sensibilities of a new generation of upper-middle-class subscribers diverged from the tastes that Charles Edward Mudie had shared with their parents and grandparents. Additionally, Mudie's astute business policies undercut his early competition and gave him weapons to impel most publishers to meet his expectations.

When Mudie first lent books from his Bloomsbury stationary and newspaper shop, he featured volumes from his own collection, "books of a progressive kind, including American transcendental works" (Griest 1970, 17). Those borrowing these books were mainly students at the nearby, newly founded University of London, who viewed Mudie's selections as compatible with their tastes, "radical in politics and . . . liberal in religion" (Francis Espinasse, quoted in ibid., 19).

To emphasize his library's cultural distinction, Mudie termed it "select." He stocked "poetry, history, biography, travel and adventure, scientific and religious works, the English and even the American reviews, as well as fiction . . . , a marked change from the earlier [libraries] whose shelves were loaded with volumes from, or similar to those from, the Minerva Press" (ibid., 18). From the first, Mudie's Library was select in another sense as well. Viewing the volumes that other libraries stocked as morally dubious, he carefully excluded some books for moral reasons. Mudie's reading preferences never changed. His refusal or inability to change his literary tastes ultimately contributed to his library's demise, but in 1842 his policies were considered enlightened.

Stocking the right books does not inevitably lead to financial success. Mudie's business policies encouraged subscribers too. When Mudie first lent books he drastically undercut the competition, which charged from five to ten guineas a year. He charged a guinea a year, and the price never changed. Mudie bought in larger quantities than his competitors to ensure the availability of works he felt should be popular. He also widely advertised the arrival of new volumes and earned additional money by selling used volumes. And Mudie's Select Library was bolstered by economic circumstances; the depression of 1847 discouraged the purchase of such luxuries as books.

By 1852 Mudie no longer catered to students. The carriages of polite society clattered to Mudie's new building at the corner of New Oxford and Museum Streets. They carried subscribers confident that Mudie's bulk-purchase policy would enable them to find the books they wanted at an attractive price. Before long, Mudie's Select Library was sending books wherever British readers were to be found.

Mudie's success was so great that in 1864 he reorganized his library into a limited liability company. He owned half the stock; the other half was owned by publishers, including John Murray and Richard Bentley, from whom the library purchased hundreds of books, especially novels. Thus, the publishers catering to the emerging upper-middle class had a double interest in conforming to Mudie's dictates. When their novels met Charles Edward Mudie's standards, he purchased hundreds of copies and so guaranteed the publisher a profit. When Mudie's Select Library made a profit, those publishers who were shareholders made a second profit.

As for Charles Edward Mudie, he drew profits from lending books, from stock in his own firm, and from selling used copies. His library was so successful that in 1858 W. H. Smith invited Mudie to start circulating libraries at the railroad bookstalls that Smith had established. Mudie's refusal ultimately contributed to his stagnation and downfall; for the new mode of Victorian transportation, the train, transformed middle-class Victorian reading habits. Smith's railroad bookstalls were to flourish much as today's airport bookstores do, by selling to commuters and other travelers. But mid-nineteenth-century London had more train stations than it now has airports, and the stations were more conveniently located than the airports are. Unlike today's airport bookstores, railroad bookstalls could also hope to serve those who lived or worked nearby.

Reading habits and the three-decker. It is easier to read on a train than in a horsedrawn carriage, but trains are not conducive to the perusal of a massive three-decker. By library-supported convention, the three-decker had set a leisurely pace; it was frequently read aloud by an assembled family. Charlotte Yonge's *Heir of Redclyffe* depicts the custom. The family might pause between passages or chapters to discuss the characters, ideas, and moralities offered in their communal reading, much as earlier Puritan families had analyzed the religious works they read together after dinner. Trains do not encourage leisurely or collective reading.

W. H. Smith's railroad bookstalls carried some three-deckers. But the bookstalls' success announced that reading had assumed a different place in social life. Changed living conditions, including increased literacy, had brought changed reading conditions and so different sorts of novels.

By the mid-1880s Mudie's Select Library no longer turned a profit on the three-decker. A market for its used books no longer existed. By the mid-1880s his cellars were full of used books that no one wanted to buy. They were potential mulch, for readers who wanted to own copies of their favorite three-deckers purchased them in inexpensive reprints. In the 1850s Mudie had enough power to prevent the publishers whose books he stocked from reissuing three-deckers as reprints for six months to a year after their initial publication in the library hardback format. But he could not prevent the eventual publication of popular titles in cheap editions. By the 1880s publishers frequently issued the hardback and paperback formats in the same year.

When Charles Edward Mudie died at a ripe age in the 1890s, his son and heir informed the newly formed Publishers Association that Mudie's Select Library would no longer purchase three-decker novels. And in 1894 Mudie's merged with the library and railroad stalls of W. H. Smith.

We date the breakup of Mudie's hegemony over publishers to the 1880s. Before that decade the novel had become the prototypical genre of the age. (As we have seen, literary historians claim that the process of achieving that status lasted from 1840 through 1880.) In the 1890s, when publishers sold books mainly through bookstores, authors increasingly offered publishers one-volume fiction manuscripts. Book clubs, such as the one organized by the London *Times*, tried to replace Mudie's as a key distributor and to challenge bookstores by buying novels at a discount as Mudie's had done. Led by Frederick Macmillan, the Publishers Association resisted such attempts at discounting and ultimately won. Publishers and only publishers were to set uniform wholesale prices. No third party was to hold sway over them, as Mudie's Select Library had done.[5] As we shall see, publishers' financial independence from a massive distributor enabled them to increase their hold on authors.

In the 1890s the Publishers Association identified their interests as bolstering bookstores. Most bookstores were small independents threatened by clubs that could offer discounts; when owners of small bookstores tried to undercut each other's prices to increase sales, they faced decreasing profit margins. Many publishers sympathized with their plight; the families of some publishers, including Frederick Macmillan's father and uncle, had once been

---

5. To today's publishers, the actions of the Publishers Association make little sense. A director of a British firm concurred with an American senior editor, who explained, "All [book] clubs operate by offering members prices lower than list; they can do this only if they get a special discount. This lowers the publisher's take per copy—but the clubs buy in bulk, so the publisher isn't hurt. Also . . . most clubs except the very biggest [Book of the Month and Literary Guild] buy their copies from the publisher, which means that his unit cost is greatly improved; therefore the publisher makes more money on the copies he sells through bookstores." She continued, "The issue of clubs (and chains and big jobbers) is still with us; together they've forced the trade discount up to 50 percent, including full return privileges. But the objection comes mostly from the bookstores, especially the small independents; for the publishers, the system has compensations. One drawback [for publishers] is that some clubs, especially the specialized ones, sell in the publisher's own market and thus *reduce* the publisher's revenue" (Gladys Topkis, letter to Gaye Tuchman, 12 November 1986).

small independents. Furthermore, having used circulating libraries, most readers were not accustomed to buying books, especially not at their list price. Members of the Publishers Association assumed that the decline of circulating libraries would encourage these readers to obtain books through book clubs. Because small independent bookstores would be unable to compete with the clubs, the publishers feared that the book clubs would establish the kind of power over them that Mudie's Select Library had so recently enjoyed.

But to concentrate on the demise of Mudie's Select Library is to get ahead of the story of the changing publishers' contract. In the 1850s, when Alexander Macmillan published his first novel, Mudie's reigned. To profit from novels, publishers had to issue fiction that satisfied Charles Mudie's class-based taste. Aware of the virtual collapse of the publishing industry in the economic crisis of the 1820s and realizing that books were among the first items that consumers abandoned in times of financial stress, publishers conformed to Mudie's requirements. Mudie's preferences affected the content of the novels. Equally crucial, the distribution system he had perfected directly and indirectly influenced author's contracts. From 1864 through 1880, publishers who owned stock in Mudie's Select Library had even greater incentive to try to satisfy Mudie's tastes.

Mudie's initial decision to promote a novel—to stock many copies, to advertise it extensively, to display it prominently—had a direct affect on a novel's popularity. Later, in order to price the used volumes it sold, Mudie estimated his subscribers' desire to read a novel, the very consumer demand he had helped create. Some publishers visited the library to learn the price for used volumes of an author's previous book. They then treated the resale price as an indicator of the author's current popularity and used this information to determine the terms they offered for that author's next novel. (Today some publishers use bestseller lists or reports of paperback advances in this way.) Other effects of Mudie's Library on authors' contracts were more complex.

Publishers' Profits and Authors' Contracts

At midcentury, publishers' inability to buck Mudie's Select Library encouraged a standard operating procedure. A publisher who wanted to publish fiction was obliged to issue several three-decker novels a year of the sort that Mudie favored. As we saw in chapter 2, Mudie's favor virtually ensured a profit for the publisher—an adequate but relatively small amount on each novel. This practice had literary consequences, particularly for authors.

First, it encouraged the growth of the novel as publishers sought fiction to buy (Becker 1982). Since Mudie's bought large quantities of popular novels, publishers could expect some of the fiction they issued to yield considerable profit. Aspiring authors increasingly tried their hand at this developing genre. The novel became the dominant form of imaginative literature.

Second, the more novels published, the greater the likelihood that some would be of memorable quality, by either nineteenth- or twentieth-century standards. A large pool of authors constituted a "critical mass" that necessarily contained some people of great talent and skill. Those talented authors whose work sold well might have more power when negotiating contracts for future work.

Third, since there was a large pool of aspirants, each one of them was potentially replaceable. Behind every marginally successful novelist stood another hopeful writer waiting to take his or her place. The interchangeability of marginally successful novelists meant that for much of the nineteenth century most novelists could not dare to challenge the standard contracts offered by publishers. They could not claim the right to determine how they would be paid for their work. Dependent on Mudie's Select Library for a profit, but seemingly confident that it would purchase large quantities of certain kinds of books, publishers set contracts. Although the specific terms of contracts changed over time, for much of the nineteenth century the obligations and responsibilities set forth in contracts were standard. The very notion of a standard publishing contract implies that individual authors have little power, especially if publishers are more interested in maintaining their relationship with their key distributor (Mudie's) than with most authors. A publisher needed to appeal to Mudie's tastes and to formulate contracts that would neither drive away successful authors nor discourage aspirants.

In theory, a contract is a binding agreement between equals under the law. Supposedly individuals enter into contracts as equals because each has a say about the nature of the exchange governed by the contract.[6] But a worker—in our case, an author—may be so constrained economically that he or she cannot refuse a job. If so, the employer is free to set the terms of the contract, and the worker (or author) must agree. By concentrating on the final moment of exchange represented by a handshake, signature, or

---

6. Hartsock (1983) points out that contemporary microeconomic theory and sociology's exchange theory adopt that notion of fictitious equality. Both theories presuppose that a laborer may choose not to work for a specific employer or, to use Peter Blau's classic example (cited by Hartsock), that a woman may refuse a date with a specific man. Note that both examples presuppose inequality inasmuch as the employee and woman do not initiate the exchanges.

exchange of goods for money, we ignore the power exercised by the individuals as they negotiated their agreement. For much of the nineteenth century, when authors and publishers executed agreements, publishers were the powerful party.[7]

Publishers' powers. There were six kinds of contracts in the nineteenth century: subscription (as many as two hundred people underwriting the costs of publishing a book in return for a copy); commission (with the author assuming responsibility for costs); profit-sharing; outright purchase of copyright for a lump sum; purchase of copyright for a limited and specified period of time (a lease) or for a specified number of copies; and payment of a royalty. By 1840 publishers rarely issued contracts involving either subscription or commission. While stressing that contracts were "standard," they slowly shifted from one sort of contract to another as each successive type appeared a better (or even necessary) vehicle for keeping authors in line but still facilitated bulk sales to Mudie's.

Consider how, in 1863, Alexander Macmillan explained the practice of publishing on commission to Charlotte Yonge, a prolific and popular author. (Many of her novels went through multiple editions; some, especially *Heir of Redclyffe* are still read today.) When Yonge's former publisher, John Parker, went out of business and Macmillan purchased his backlist, Yonge wrote to Macmillan explaining that Parker had published her work on commission, so she owned most of the plates necessary to reprint her books. Yonge asked Macmillan how he handled publishing on commission, and his answer stressed the *standard* agreement: "The terms for publishing on commission are I believe uniform among publishers. The whole of publication expenses, such as printing, paper, binding, and advertising are charged to the author; and a commission of 10 percent on the sales is charged [credited] to the publisher, when he renders accounts" (letter to Yonge, 9 October 1863).

This contract clearly favors the publisher, for the author takes all the risk. Although these terms were supposedly "uniform among publishers," by the 1860s most publishers did not favor publishing on commission, because the contract virtually invited authors to argue about how the publisher had kept the record of expenditures and sales and whether the authors had received the correct payment. An author's ire could have consequences for the publisher. If the book had been sufficiently successful to warrant a second edition, an angry author who owned the plates might take it to another publisher.

7. Coser (1978) emphasizes that this is still the case today. Told that a publisher is offering its standard terms, an author must produce a good argument to get more than others get.

Even when the contracts were modified to reduce the author's economic liability, the author might gain little from the customary alternative, another standard contract termed "profit-sharing" or "half-profits." In this agreement, the publisher was responsible for all costs associated with manufacture, advertising, and sale. He received half of the net profit after deducting up to 5 percent from the gross profit for bad debts. Tanzy (1961) suggests that this contract was preferred by the "astute publisher." From the publisher's viewpoint, the author had no financial investment—except of course the considerable time and effort spent writing the manuscript. This contract recognized the publisher's risk (capital) but not the author's (the labor invested in writing over months or years).

Half-profits contracts also risked alienating authors. A letter that Mrs. Humphrey Ward wrote to Macmillan in the late 1880s demonstrates the potential for estrangement between author and publisher implicit in profit-sharing. Mrs. Ward complained about the lack of profits on her first novel, *Miss Breverton*, which Macmillan had brought out on the half-profits system. She was "dismayed" that what she had thought was a "good first book . . . ends with a deficit of £22." In the same letter, she informed Macmillan that she was taking her second novel to another publisher who was not insisting upon this particular "standard contract." Mrs. Ward's second novel was the extremely successful *Robert Elsemere*.

Not all authors could afford to seek another publisher. Mrs. Ward was from an elite literary and academic family. Although her correspondence with Macmillan revealed her insistent interest in how much she would earn, she was not financially dependent upon Macmillan's offer. More typical were the authors who readily accepted the terms Macmillan gave them, even though some complained that they were not getting enough.

Mrs. Ward was an exception. Publishers had the upper hand. The difference in power was implicit in the tone of negotiations between publishers and authors. Through the 1880s Macmillan and Company bargained in a straightforward manner, while many authors' letters about money were studded with circumlocutions and excuses.

For instance, setting terms for three of Mrs. Oliphant's manuscripts, George Lillie Craik, a partner in the firm and its business manager, offered one price for the three and explained, "It is always uncomfortable to bargain but in this way we make one gulp of it [24 November 1881]." His sentence made it awkward for Mrs. Oliphant to request more money without seeming impolite. The person who can set the final terms is the person who can state it is "uncomfortable" to bargain, as seen in the following example.

Two years after Craik's letter to Mrs. Oliphant, the best-selling novelist

F. Marion Crawford requested more money. Unlike Craik, he was not direct but couched his request in economic metaphors. On 14 October 1883 he wrote to Macmillan: "Authors are rarely like agricultural capitalists who sow on a grand scale and can afford to wait a year for the sale of their crops. In fact, they rather resemble market government with the more modest 'nimble sixpenny' pretensions claimed for the hoe and the spade." We view this metaphor as a circumlocution because it was inappropriate. Although he defined authors as workers, Crawford chose to discuss conditions in England's agrarian South as opposed to her industrial North. Publishing was an industry. We must suppose that Crawford, who was noted for setting dramatic scenes, realized that he was beating around the bush.[8]

Publishers had economic power over authors because they were frequently an author's key source of income and served as his or her primary creditor. When an author received an advance, he owed either a manuscript or repayment. Also, "it was common . . . to borrow cash from one's publisher" (Sutherland 1976, 112). Throughout the 1860s, Henry Kingsley, the novelist brother of the even more successful Macmillan author Charles Kingsley, borrowed from Macmillan on a grand scale. In 1866, asking for yet another loan, he assured Macmillan that he would inherit on the death of his mother and his mother-in-law. In 1869 Kingsley wrote Macmillan about the possibility of foreclosure on his mortgage. Later that year, Kingsley made his life insurance policy over to Macmillan in exchange for an advance of £200, presumably against an overdue manuscript. After Kingsley's death, a relative wrote Macmillan asking for £5 so that Kingsley's widow would not lose her mortgaged furniture.

Business relationships frequently require flexibility. In this realm, too, publishers held sway, for they had available a third sort of standard contract that increased their alternatives but not those of authors. Alexander Macmillan preferred that contract, purchase of copyright. He generally purchased copyright for a first-edition run of 750 or 1,000 books to be published in the "three-volume library format." When Macmillan first explained this contract to Charlotte Yonge, he stressed its advantages to the author: "Most authors prefer this system as it is not open to the uncertainty of the half profit mode and the clear interest the publisher has in getting back his outlay quickly is supposed to give an impetus to his effort to the sale of the book. To the publisher it is far more pleasant as it leaves him [free] with regard to the advertising and other modes of quickening the sale of the book."

---

8. Crawford could also negotiate in a more straightforward manner, as shown below. In the example given there, Crawford did not receive the terms he requested.

Macmillan was being disingenuous. He did not mention that purchase of copyright facilitated the publisher's ability to issue a book in several formats. That ability was economically crucial in the 1850s when monthly magazines, designed for the middle-class and owned by the major publishing houses, began to serialize at least one novel in every issue.

Negotiations for Annie Keary's *Oldbury* demonstrate the publisher's need for flexibility. Initially, Macmillan offered Keary £200 to serialize *Oldbury* in his magazine—£100 on publication of the first episode in November and £100 on publication of the last in May. But George Grove, later author of the renowned dictionary of music and then editor of the magazine, had planned to start another novel in that November's issue. He declined to run *Oldbury* as scheduled.

Macmillan wrote to change his arrangement with Keary, who had looked forward to serialization in *Macmillan's Magazine* as "the height of my ambition." After reviewing Grove's position, Macmillan told Keary that George Lillie Craik had asked "his wife [the popular novelist Dinah Mulock] to read a considerable portion of it, as she takes much interest in you. . . . Both were very emphatic that it was not doing your book justice to publish it in a magazine at all" as this would too soon bare "the secrets of it . . . to the public eye." He added, "I am quite ready to publish the book early in the year and to fulfill the money arrangement" and assured Keary that the new arrangement would be better for her in the long run. Bur Keary had lost the opportunity for a larger readership and so, potentially, for greater interest in her subsequent novels.

In the search for profit, autonomy, and flexibility, publishers sometimes negotiated different kinds of contracts on different books by the same author. One contract might cover both magazine serialization and the library edition of a book. For instance, on 7 June 1875 Craik agreed to pay the popular novelist William Black "£750 for the right to publish *Violet the Rebellious* in the Magazine. . . . We are to pay £400 on its publication and the balance [of] £350 when the . . . book in three volumes is published."

Sometimes Macmillan contracted to publish some of an author's books on commission and to purchase the copyright for specific editions of others. For instance, when Charlotte Yonge joined Macmillan's list in 1863 she agreed that the firm could publish all her previous books on commission (as Parker had done) and could purchase the copyright to specific editions of her next few books. On 30 November 1863 Alexander Macmillan wrote: "We will give £200 for leave to print and publish an edition of 2000 copies [of *The Trial*]. We would propose that the leading [the space between the lines of type] should be taken out and the types made solid for a cheap edition uniform with *Heir of Redclyffe*. We are willing to go ahead with this at once."

As one might expect, Macmillan's proposal had economic consequences for his firm. Many of Parker's editions of Yonge's earlier books had been printed from plates owned by the author on the small pages used in cheap editions. Printing new library editions of Yonge's past work would require an investment in larger plates, and Macmillan had little reason to believe that such editions would sell well. Macmillan's plan fulfilled Yonge's wish to have her collected works published in a uniform format, while saving his firm money. Both the Yonge's collected works and, eventually, the library editions of Yonge's subsequent books appeared in a small format ("uniform with *Heir of Redclyffe*"), enabling Macmillan to issue future cheap editions without having to reset them.

By having many alternatives to offer, Macmillan might also tie an especially successful or promising author to the firm. For instance, as publishers do today if they can, Macmillan might write one contract for several books. On 24 November 1881 George Lillie Craik made the following offer to the ever-prolific and ever financially strapped Margaret Oliphant, who generally sold copyright on specific editions to receive immediate cash: "I understand you were to tell me if you could arrange with the newspaper to publish one of the novels for £300. If you can do so, we should be prepared to [publish] the three [in library format]: this newspaper one—the magazine one and a third to be published in library format and give you £1700 for them."

In this instance, Macmillan and Company did not reap the double profit of magazine serialization and book publication on all three books. (A newspaper was to serialize one novel, Macmillan was to serialize another, and the third would appear only as a three-volume novel.) Macmillan had good reasons for not offering to serialize the third novel. *Macmillan's Magazine* generally serialized two novels a year. If the firm contracted to serialize two novels that Mrs. Oliphant planned to write in succession, it might be promising Mrs. Oliphant all of the magazine's fiction pages for the coming year.[9] Subscriptions of readers who were not enthusiastic about Mrs. Oliphant's novels might lapse.

The publisher as flexible patriarch. Sometimes, flexibility improved the publisher's ability to woo authors who were either personal friends or economic assets to the firm. Then, Macmillan might tender contractual terms in an almost

---

9. She wrote so much so quickly that sometimes two different publishers would bring out two of her books in the same month.

offhand, patriarchal way. In the 1860s and 1870s this tendency was most pronounced in negotiations with women.

Macmillan had both a business and a social relationship with Annie Keary. With her sister, Keary had often received invitations to visit the ladies of the Macmillan family at their country home in Tooting. Macmillan's negotiations with Keary seemed to be infused with personal regard. On 7 November 1873 Macmillan addressed her as "My dear friend." He went on, "My wife reminded me this morning I had never definitely told you what we were to pay you for the copyright on your new story [second novel]." Macmillan assumed that there would be no negotiation about terms. He also presumed not only on friendship but also on his position as a male authority. We cannot imagine an author writing her publisher, "This morning, my husband reminded me that my manuscript is long overdue."

Patriarchal concern might even lead the publisher to offer more money than the contract provided for in order to cement ties with an author whose books brought profits to the firm. Macmillan knew that Charlotte Yonge donated her earnings to charity, a practice her parents had insisted upon before they would give her permission to publish. When he felt that his many requests for alterations in *The Three Pupils of St. John* had taken too much of her effort, he told her: "It occurs to me that you may have been wasting time otherwise valuable to you on these early chapters. I remember your benevolent aims. Shall I add £20 to the cheque to make up the way a little."

When Yonge's relationship with a coauthor was endangered by Yonge's misunderstanding of a contract, Macmillan again offered more money. On 22 July 1868 Yonge wrote,

> I am afraid I have been guilty of a misunderstanding and of leading [my coauthor] Miss Sewell into one, but I thought we were to have £200 for the copyright of the Historical Selections, and I must say I think it hardly compensation for all the trouble it has given.... I misled both Miss Sewell and myself so that we had agreed she should have £125 and I £75. I am sorry for the blunder, and I think that now—unless you would give us the £200 (which I really think that the copyright is worth) that a percentage on the price of each 100 would be the most satisfactory way.

Macmillan replied that the firm would have to "sell many thousands before we get our money back," a sale much more extensive than he felt likely, but he agreed to pay Sewell the requested £75.

Of course Macmillan may have offered more money because he shared

Charlotte Yonge's adherence to "muscular Christianity." In their correspondence, Macmillan expressed an interest in Yonge's editorial work for the *Monthly Packet*, a religious magazine for young people. But his view of religious projects was always tempered by commercial realism. He criticized one of Yonge's book proposals by saying, "Even among Church of England people the History of the Prayer Book is not the most attractive subject, though I do think it about the most useful."

Self-interest (Yonge still owned the plates to the novels that Parker had originally published) and patriarchal power expressed as kind generosity seem a better explanation. For Macmillan's generosity waned in Yonge's later life, when her work did not sell as well and she was supporting herself at least partially. In the late 1870s, in need of cash, she asked Macmillan to buy all her copyrights. Suddenly business seemed more important than religious sympathies. Craik, rather than one of the Macmillans, answered that letter offering a relatively low figure, for the popularity of many of her early books and so the worth of her copyrights had declined.

The Demise of the Circulating Library

Throughout the nineteenth century, publishing firms and author-publishers initiated a series of marketing attempts that might have undercut Mudie's Select Library and so decreased their dependence on this key distributor. In the 1830s Smith, Elder tried to issue romances for 6s. but succumbed to the demands of the already powerful circulating libraries (Griest 1970).

But Charles Edward Mudie did not have a commercial stick to wield against all challengers. Dickens bypassed Mudie's by having Chapman and Hall issue his books chapter by chapter, as eighteenth-century publishers had issued the work of earlier popular authors, selling bindings for an additional sum when it issued the last chapters. Chapman and Hall could afford to ignore Mudie's preferences. Printers who published books as a sideline, they had no other authors who sold as well and as consistently as Dickens. If Dickens flourished, they did.

W. H. Smith's railroad bookstalls sold paperbacks of popular eighteenth-century works but were eventually to sell the cheap editions of new novels and still later first editions brought out in paperback format. By the late 1860s rapacious readers ran to the railroad stations to buy recently issued sensation novels in paperback format. (Mudie, of course, disliked sensation novels, fiction about such forbidden matters as a wife's adultery. They offended his straight-laced sensibilities—though he carried such novels when they had moralistic endings.)[10]

Several social changes were implicit in the success of Smith's railroad stalls. As we have seen, some readers ventured to the railroad station to buy a paperback to read at home, whereas others read on trains. Bourgeois sensibilities also changed as new social groups joined the bourgeoisie. Middle-class men and women who read the paperback sensation novels that offended Mudie's taste were not from the same social backgrounds as the University of London students who had happily greeted Mudie's first Bloomsbury library. When Mudie's sensibilities and those of his subscribers were no longer the same, Mudie's hegemony over the publishers had to weaken. In part, this change arose from the sheer number of new readers as literacy spread.

The tastes of those new readers may also have enabled the existing elite to admit to reading sorts of novels they might previously have hidden in their homes. At least, the existence of sensation novels designed for the middle class might have enabled some of the educated elite to read them. To admit to doing so, elite readers would have insistently distinguished "good" literature from what we would today term "escapist fare" and would not have admitted to delving into the supposedly even "worse" fiction designed for the working-class. A sensation novel might have appeared minimally acceptable as "not serious reading," as it could claim derivation from the eighteenth-century Gothic subgenre.[11] These new reading habits also contributed to the decrease in Mudie's profits in the mid-1880s.

We cannot know how much Mudie's financial problems may have loosened his influence over publishers. But we do know that in the 1880s Mudie's Select Library no longer held sway over publishers and publishers developed new sorts of standard contracts with authors. These new contracts did not break the hold of publishers on authors; rather, publishers tried to take advantage of Mudie's problems to increase their power over authors.

After Mudie's 1894 announcement that his library was abandoning the three-decker, a representative of the Publishers Association visited the Society of Authors to describe the sorts of contracts publishers would now be giving.

10. In the early 1860s, for example, Mudie carried Mrs. Wood's *East Lynne*, whose plot revolved around a wife's adultery. Divorced, the wife suffered financially; deprived of her child, she despaired. By novel's end, the wife had come to understand the hideous nature of her crime and embraced mid-Victorian moral codes.

11. The refusal of these literati to admit reading certain books anticipates the practices of some twentieth-century intellectuals. Tuchman has overheard several intellectuals debate the merits of such best-selling American authors as Judith Kranz and Harold Robbins, while remaining purposively and steadfastly ignorant of the existence of today's romances.

Both organizations were new, formed around the collective interests of their respective members. Their very names indicated differing orientations toward power. The authors maintained a "society"—a group of people gathering around an avocation, much as scientists had first established learned societies. The publishers had an "association," connoting more impersonal business and professional connections. Although authors had an organization, the publishers continued to hold the power. The publishers' representative did not visit the Society of Authors to dicker; he went to inform authors that publishers would no longer be accepting three-decker novels.

Strength was explicit in the efforts of the Publishers Association to block the newly organized commercial book clubs, discussed earlier. Founded in the 1890s, these clubs sought to buy novels at a discount and to turn a profit by selling them at lower prices than bookstores did. The publishers feared that this new method of discounting books would lead once more to the hegemony of distributors over publishers. They did not want to reproduce their relationship with Mudie's Select Library. In the 1890s Frederick Macmillan led the publishers' successful attack on discounting. The strength of the publishers' position, both before and after the war against discounting, accounted for the interest of the Society of Authors in promoting the royalty contract.

Macmillan and the Royalty

To some authors at least, the proroyalty position of the Society of Authors was anathema. They were loyal to their publishers. The process by which one author, J. D. Shorthouse, became convinced of the benefits of the royalty system reveals both the strength of informal ties between authors and publishers and how much authors might benefit economically by signing royalty contracts.

Although Shorthouse published several novels with Macmillan, he is largely remembered as a one-book author. (The *DNB* introduces him as the author of *John Inglesant*, rather than characterizing him more generally as either novelist or author.) Shorthouse had published the first edition of *John Inglesant* himself, though Macmillan published all the subsequent editions.

As was typical of author-publisher relationships in the late nineteenth century, Shorthouse and Macmillan were on amicable terms. Macmillan knew Shorthouse well enough to advise him, on one occasion, to "go to Gladstone's breakfast" but was not close enough to get his first name right. Some years after Macmillan and Company had brought out *John Inglesant*, Shorthouse saw his work advertised and wrote to inform that his name was James, not John.

Shorthouse kept good track of the many editions of *John Inglesant*. As he assured Macmillan in April 1882 when acknowledging receipt of a £500 check, "the monetary success is far from a matter of indifference to me in these hard times." With a half-profits agreement, Macmillan reported assiduously to Shorthouse how many copies had been sold and sought ways to increase both the author's profits and its own. For example, in January 1882 Macmillan mailed Shorthouse the cheap one-volume edition of Charles Kingsley's *Westward Ho!* to encourage Shorthouse to permit a cheap one-volume edition of *Inglesant*.

Perhaps to maintain their cordial relationship, when Shorthouse joined the Society of Authors in 1891 he told Macmillan that he had visited the society to please his friend Sir Edmund Gosse. He wrote Macmillan that his visit had "not altered my opinion of Besant's wild statements" (18 May 1891). Sir Walter Besant had founded the society in 1889 and claimed that the royalty system favored authors.[12] Macmillan returned a friendly letter with clear political implications. He suggested that, as a member, Shorthouse could now advise the Society of Authors that their prejudice against the half-profits system was wrong.

Shorthouse did not convert the Society of Authors. It converted him. By 15 October of that same year, Shorthouse informed his long-standing publisher that he wanted to change his latest contract to the royalty system:

> I suppose I may conclude that you have satisfied yourselves that there is ultimately little difference between the two [plans] and that it makes little difference either to publisher or author which is adopted. I conclude this by your fixing the royalty at 1/6 of the published price [of 3s/6d for the cheap edition] and by your saying it was indifferent to you which [was] selected. But even if this be the case I think there are reasons why the royalty system is better and perhaps fairer for the author, both because he has no discretion as to expenses and because he has to depend for his profit upon a single book.... A study of the accounts you sent me makes me think that the royalty system is better for the author in the long run, especially on a lone prized book, and that 1/6 of the published price of 3s/6d on a book that sells at 2/6 less 6% only is a very *liberal* allowance to the author. (emphasis in original)

Shorthouse then reviewed for his publisher the costs of paper, printing, stereoplates, boarding (binding), and advertising the 1,578 copies of the cheap and latest edition of *Inglesant* and calculated what each of their half-shares of

---

12. Since Besant had relatively little leverage with his own publishers, his own contracts for novels did not use the royalty system.

profit should have been. His arithmetic revealed that he received nothing by the profit-sharing system but would have earned £175 on a 1/6 royalty. Besant and the Society of Authors had been right; Shorthouse wanted to ensure his future profits from his past work.

By the late 1880s both authors and publishers were beginning to realize that authors had the right to profit in the present from their work in the past—although publishers continued to have the upper hand in setting the terms of authors' profit. For most of the nineteenth century, English publishers and authors had lost money because of lax American copyright laws. In the absence of international copyright agreements, many American firms pirated British novels, although a few firms purchased sheets from British publishers. For decades both publishers and authors had bemoaned the American practices: the need for a strong international copyright agreement was one tenet to which both the Society of Authors and the Association of Publishers rigidly adhered. By stressing the right of British authors to profit from publication of their work in the United States, publishers could maintain more easily publishers' moral right to profit from their own investment in authors. (In 1891 Congress passed the Platt-Simmonds Act recognizing the copyright of British authors and so of the British publishers who held those copyrights.)

In little more than a decade, the notion of an author's right to profit on past work crept into Macmillan's correspondence. In two letters from George Lillie Craik to successful Macmillan authors, Craik responded to requests to sell old copyrights. We have seen that when Charlotte Yonge wanted to sell her copyrights in the late 1870s Craik quickly quoted a *figure*. In 1888, when F. Marion Crawford wanted to sell his copyrights, Craik quoted a *formula*. He advised Crawford.

> Generally it may be said that the value of a copyright is about three years purchase of the average return. We could not value your interest in the books we have at more than £200. We are prepared to give this sum, to send you a check for that amount at once, but we would [encourage] you to retain them on their present footing. While we could not give more than this sum, we think it possible, even probable, that [over time] they are of more value to you on the royalty terms. (9 November 1888)

Stressing as it does average value per year, Craik's letter was particularly pertinent to the author who claimed professional status. It suggests that authors, like publishers, could estimate future profits.

Yet several years earlier Crawford and Macmillan had signed modified "lease agreements," emphasizing immediate, not future, profits. In 1884 Macmillan had agreed to pay Crawford £1250 (more than $5000) for the American and British rights to *Zoroaster the Prophet* during the first year of publication. (Although the Platt-Simmonds Act had yet to be passed, Macmillan routinely dealt with several American publishers who honored English copyrights and, through their New York office, was an American publisher too.) In 1885 Macmillan struck a similar deal for *The Romance of a Lonely Village, or A Tale of a Lonely Parish*. Crawford understood that both he and Macmillan would be trying to get as much money as was possible from the books as quickly as possible. Milking the market for a good return in the first year—acting as a consumer-oriented publisher might—Macmillan could deplete the economic potential of those books in the next years, when Crawford was to receive a royalty.

Even granting Crawford's fervent desire to enter into these agreements, Macmillan does not seem to have been calculating Crawford's potential earnings on a three-year basis.[13] But Craik's 1888 formula did tell Crawford what his past work was worth and affirmed that the author's right to profit in the future from work in the past was limited by the publisher's marketing strategies, which then as now the author could not hope to control.

Although Crawford earned vast sums, he spent freely and was perpetually dependent on his publisher's payments to settle yesterday's bills. Such economic dependence decreases the leverage of even the most successful and acclaimed author when discussing contracts with a publisher. (Crawford had requested £2500 for the first year's lease to *Romance of a Lonely Village*; he received £1250.) In the mid-1880s, however, some best-selling authors were shrewd bargainers, more than capable of both advancing their monetary interests and attempting to control how Macmillan marketed their novels.

The Shrewd Professional

The shrewd professional author advanced his or her own interests by polite negotiation, such strong stances as threatening to find another publisher, use

13. Crawford's letters to Macmillan assume that the firm would realize as much profit as possible as quickly as possible. Arguing for the higher sum, Crawford had calculated, erroneously, that his novel *A Roman Singer* had probably sold 17,000 copies in four months and that his next book might sell 30,000 in one year. "Allowing that you receive £1000 for your first 2000 copies of the two-volume edition (sold at 11s 6p) and one dollar a copy for the remaining 28,000, the aggregate sum represented for the year is about 33,000 dollars. In view of such figures, and considering that you have sold enormous numbers of copies of *Mr. Isaacs* and *Dr. Claudius*, I do not think that the sum of £2500 for the first year of the present book is exhorbitant. After the expiration of twelve months, the usual royalty of 10 percent would continue to be [in effect] on further sales" (9 January 1885).

of a formal or informal agent (a paid literary representative or a family member), or some combination of these methods.[14] Through such methods the authors strove to gain an advantage in negotiations or to influence the firm's marketing decisions.

For instance, Mrs. Humphrey Ward, financially secure, bargained firmly and independently after the huge success of her *Robert Elsemere*, playing one publisher off against another. In early 1889, after a visit from her husband to discuss the possible terms of an American edition of *Robert Elsemere*, Frederick Macmillan appealed to her as the friend who had published her early books: "Mr. Ward ... thinks that Scribner meant to offer the sum named *in addition* to a royalty whereas our offer was *on account* of royalty. If he is right we have nothing more to say except that we do not understand how Scribner can expect to get his money back, but if I am right in thinking that Scribner meant this offer to be the same as ours I hope that you will let it come to us as the publishers of your first books" (letter to Ward, 25 February 1889).

Mrs. Ward then turned her attention to the early properties still housed at Macmillan's, asking politely whether the success of her later books warranted republication of her earlier works. In a letter written in 1889, when some authors were already using the royalty system, she asked Mr. Craik whether *Miss Breverton* and the children's book *Molly and Olly* could be put on royalty. She explained, "I should think that practically it would come to much the same thing, but as an arrangement I should greatly prefer it if it were the same to you."

Mrs. Ward was capable of indirection. She once asked Macmillan for the address of agent A. P. Watt, which she claimed to have misplaced. Mrs. Ward added that she would never think of using an agent herself in their "friendly" negotiations but wished to give the address to her sister, who had written a novel. Since many authors could have given Watt's address to Mrs. Ward, we may infer that she was threatening to use Watt.

In the late 1880s and increasingly thereafter, Macmillan had many dealings with A. P. Watt. Among others, Watt represented Kipling, whose poetry Macmillan published, and T. A. Browne (pseudonym "Rolf Boldrewood"), whose novels about Australia sold extremely well. Although the correspondence with the literary agent was always amicable, it was not based on friendship. Reading it, one feels certain that well-meaning businessmen are trying to work out the best deals possible, each realizing that the other party may

14. So far as we could tell, the names of London literary agents first appeared in Macmillan's ledgers in the 1880s. We assume that these middlemen began to ply their trade during that decade.

choose to do business elsewhere. The literary agent represented the demise of the writer as gentleman-author and the institutionalized recognition of writing as business.

Some authors bargained with Macmillan for a higher royalty percentage and sought to influence Macmillan's marketing strategies in order to justify their demands. After protesting that he was "no businessman," H. G. Wells argued the firm into a higher royalty on the cheap edition of his books than Macmillan normally paid. He wrote to encourage Macmillan to do more about advertising and to bring out agreed-upon new editions as soon as possible. He wrote to tell them that another firm had offered him a better deal. He wrote to ask whether Macmillan's challenge to book-club discounts would affect the sale of his work. He wrote to express dissatisfaction with his Italian publishers, with whom Macmillan frequently dealt. In short, Wells wrote about all aspects of Macmillan's business, now made *his* business, because he benefited directly from every copy sold at a better rate than did authors on the half-profits systems.

Unlike Mrs. Ward, Wells didn't bother to be polite or friendly:

> I am disappointed by your answer about the *Comet*. I really do not think the time has come to drop the book. . . . I do not think you have done all that could have been done to get it to the attention of its proper buyers and I look with dismay at my accumulating notes and copy for *Tono-Bungay*. In that I want to do all I can do in a novel, and I certainly wish I could feel that, for that, you will do all you can do *for* a novel. (22 November 1906)

Unlike an agent, the author interfering in business could claim, as Wells did in the letter cited above, "It's not merely a question of money payments, you know, it's the feeling of not being read or noted that demoralizes one." To be sure, other authors complained to their publishers about inadequate promotion, claiming that they were interested mainly in disseminating their ideas. However, Wells' tone was sharper than theirs; he truly could go elsewhere. Most other authors could not play one publisher off against another, and authors also differed in their ability to influence the production and promotion of their work.

Is a Standard Contract *Standard*?

A book contract is an impersonal agreement between a publisher and a writer. But written terms are subject to interpretation, and some aspects of a book's economic future are never ever written down. As Coser (1979) has shown, authors benefit most when members of a publishing firm decide to look out for them and have the bureaucratic power to do so. Today, if an author is displeased with the production staff's handling of his or her book, the author may appeal to the acquisitions editor who sponsored the book. That editor may have little bureaucratic power but is more likely to try to intervene for a friend or a successful author with whom the firm has had a continuing close relationship (Coser 1979; cf. Powell 1985).

We suppose that gender and social class are important factors influencing how and when publishers, editors, and authors strike up the friendships that protect the author. When an editor has bureaucratic influence, friendships might explain how books having identical contracts have dissimilar promotional fates. Promotional fates in turn influence sales and success. In the nineteenth century, when editors were men, male authors were probably more likely than females to strike up personal friendships with editors and publishers. Authors who were based in London or frequently visited London were more likely to go to the same parties as editors and publishers and so to establish these advantageous friendships. As we have seen, such authors were more likely to be men than women.

We cannot address the impact of such factors as social class and gender on the contracts and negotiations we have described. With the exception of Annie Keary and perhaps Henry Kingsley, we have been discussing Macmillan's contracts and negotiations with highly successful authors. We estimate that Crawford earned at least £14,400 from Macmillan between 1883 and 1907 and that Macmillan paid Mrs. Oliphant at least £10,125 from 1870 to 1891. In 1883 a British pound was worth more than $4.50, so Macmillan paid both Crawford and Oliphant more than $2500 (£500) a year for many years.

Not all writers received so much. In Shorthouse's letter informing Macmillan that he had attended a meeting of the Society of Authors and found Besant's statements "wild," he quoted Besant as having claimed that only fifty novelists earned as much as £2000 a year. Shorthouse also mentioned a petition designed by the Society of Authors to aid a woman novelist who had "published 58 novels in 31 years...[and had] never made more than £62 a year!!!" If Besant exaggerated, as Shorthouse thought, it may not have been by much. While coding entries of men and women writers listed in the *DNB*, we frequently read of the poverty of particular women in their later life, but not of the poverty of comparable men.

Unfortunately, we cannot systematically discuss the relationship between gender and the interpretation of publishing contracts. But we can suggest that, initially at least, the notion of professionalism did not encompass women novelists. At first, the Society of Authors excluded women from membership.

It leaders were not even familiar with the names of once-popular women authors; Thring (n.d.) paused in some correspondence to wonder about the identity of a Mrs. Riddell. Women came to early dinners of the Society of Authors by invitation only, and only the most successful, such as Mrs. Humphrey Ward and Mrs. Oliphant, were invited. Less well-known male authors could come on their own or could join.[15]

We can, though, infer that the distribution system that dominated the British novel for much of the nineteenth century did more than influence the content and style of some novels. It indirectly shaped the standard contract for Victorian novelists and so shaped the degree of their professionalism as well. Because in the 1880s professional activities were for men and because throughout the century publishers had the upper hand over authors, women—especially needy authors—probably came out second best.

15. Women could become members by 1889. The first five women admitted were "Miss C. M. Yonge, Mrs. Linton, Mrs. Humphrey Ward, Mrs. Flora Shaw, and Mrs. Ormerod." A resolution admitting women to the governing council was passed in 1896 (see Thring n. d., 47).

8
The Critical
Double Standard

ooks, like people, have careers. From its earliest origin as an idea in the mind of an author, editor, or publisher to its eventual dismissal or enshrinement by future critics and historians, a manuscript passes through necessary stages. It has a natural history.

We have tracked some stages of the natural history of fiction manuscripts received by Macmillan and company: submission, internal review, acceptance (or rejection), and contract negotiation. We cannot discuss such important matters as how the expected profit margin on a book was determined. Nor do we know what was actually earned by the various editions of novels that Macmillan accepted or what kinds of promotional efforts Macmillan made to place the novels it published in the right hands. But we can discuss literary critics' reception of some of the novels that Macmillan published.

In the first sections of this chapter, we address two questions about the reception of novels. First, did novels by women receive different sorts of reviews than those by men? If male and female novelists won fame for different kinds of accomplishments, as we demonstrated in chapter 6, reviewers' notions about what a woman and a man could write well must have been very different. Thus, we must expect that novels by women and men were subject to what Showalter (1977) has termed "the critical double standard."

Second, as the empty field phenomenon unfolded, how, if at all, did the standards applied to men's and women's novels shift? If critics participated in edging women out of the evolving high-culture novel as it passed through discernible stages, the critical double standard must have changed from one period to the next. Critics may have applied one kind of "critical double standard" as "male" realism edged out "female" romanticism and another kind of critical double standard—*but still a double standard*—as realism gave birth to modernism.

To concentrate our inquiry, we draw on reviews from two well-established journals, the *Athenaeum* and the *Edinburgh Review*. The reviews we consider were received by four novelists included in our *DNB* sample who were also linked to Macmillan and Company: George Eliot, George Meredith, Mrs. Oliphant, and Mrs. Ward. We have chosen these four authors because the data about them are particularly rich and because they represent different levels of accomplishment. In the Victorian period, Eliot and Meredith were considered first-rank; Oliphant and Ward were less esteemed but well received. Even though the critics presumably sought to distinguish merit from mediocrity, we expect that they would have applied a double standard based on gender to both the meritorious and the mediocre.

Not all of these authors had direct ties to Macmillan and Company. Mrs. Oliphant and Mrs. Ward published both fiction and nonfiction with Macmillan; Macmillan published Mrs. Ward's husband as well. Macmillan also published George Meredith's poetry, and John Morley was sufficiently friendly with Meredith to have sent the aspiring and rejected novelist Thomas Hardy to Meredith for advice. Morley was also friendly with George Eliot, in part as a result of his having published a favorable review of one of her books in *Macmillan's Magazine*. Eliot also occupies a prominent position in previous discussions of the critical double standard (Showalter 1977).

We did not follow the preferred practice of matching pairs of women and men, because the second-rank authors whom Macmillan published, such as Charles Kingsley and F. Marion Crawford, did not fall into the *DNB* sample. In the final section of this chapter, we do examine a matched pair, Margaret Oliphant and F. Marion Crawford, analyzing reviews of their works in the *Athenaeum* and the *Edinburgh Review* to ask a third question derived from our notion of the empty field phenomenon: Did Macmillan give equivalent contracts to authors whom critics gave equivalent reviews? Although critics may have used different criteria to identify a man and a woman as a "second-rank novelist," both would nonetheless be termed second rank. In an equitable world, both would receive equivalent contract terms for their novels. We believe, however, that Macmillan paid second-rank men more than second-rank women. As we explained in chapter 7, women were less likely to have personal relationships with the publisher or to be able negotiators, and because they appeared to be less financially secure than many men, they may have been more at the mercy of their publisher.

Dating Critical Suppositions about Women Writers

Since the early 1970s feminist literary critics have documented a difference in the expectations that critics have held for the work of women and of men. Some (for example, Ellman 1968; Stimpson 1979) have concentrated on twentieth-century criticism. Others (for example, Showalter 1977) have mined the nineteenth century. All agree that, in most criticism, what is virtue in a man is weakness in a woman. For instance, where a man's writing may be praised for its philosophic complexity, as were George Meredith's novels, a woman's may be damned for its pretentiousness, much as were George Eliot's late novels.

Differing expectations about the literary propensities and abilities of women and men began well before the rise of the novel as the prototypical bourgeois genre. Women who wrote and so challenged the assumption that literature was a male preserve were virtually barred from genres associated with the marketplace. In the early eighteenth century ladies were decried if they wrote comedies, since those plays often included scatological material. Critics offered up Aphra Behn, who wrote comedies and romantic fiction, as a woman who had scandalously desexed herself. Indeed, "the tradition of late eighteenth-century women writers developed from two groups that emerged earlier in the century: respectable women who wrote primarily for their own or their friends' amusement, and the faintly or frankly disreputable women who published for profit" (Halsband 1969 as cited in Poovey 1984, 36). Behn was in the latter group.

By the late eighteenth century, when the ideology of women as the gentler sex was gaining importance, critics extended the emerging industrial ideology of women's place to fiction. Defining ideology as conscious and unconscious beliefs governing social relations, Poovey (1984) demonstrates that by the end of the eighteenth century ideology had assigned to women's sphere the virtues associated with collectivity, which were threatened by the emerging industrial individualism.[1] As Joyce Tompkins explains:

> There was a very real belief in the civilizing function of woman in society, and to this was added the hope that womanly delicacy and purity, imported into literature, might supplement the robust virility of eighteenth-century utterance. The world of the novel in particular seemed incomplete; let the women now speak of their experience; let them contribute their native sense, their elegant simplicity, to the common stock, and complete the revelation of human nature. The contribution, it may be repeated, was to be emphatically feminine. (1961, 124)

---

1. Poovey's purpose is to show how ideology permeates literary style as well as social relations. The phenomenon she describes is comparable to the American cult of true womanhood, which flourished in the nineteenth century.

Like other eighteenth-century ideologues, critics argued that there were clear differences between women's hearts and men's hearts, women's minds and men's minds. Women's hearts—their feelings—were finer and more delicate than those of men. Conversely, their minds lacked rigor. By insisting on such intrinsic differences between women's and men's minds, the developing ideology made it seem impossible for women to write as men did. One may improve a woman's mind—that is, educate her to learn all she is capable of learning—but one cannot transform it into a man's mind.

Since women's and men's minds were supposedly different, women would necessarily write a different sort of literature than men did. Thus, Tompkins quotes a reviewer for the *Monthly* who expressed his "sincere admiration of 'the excellences of our female writers,' " but chided "authoresses" who "[tread] too much in the footsteps of men" and worried whether women could handle a love theme. As that reviewer saw it, the female heart experiences "the delicate sensibilities of which the rougher sex is seldom capable," and the "female mind combines the power to 'unfold sentiments of elegant love' with an instinctive care for perfect decorum" (quoted in Tompkins 1961). But love is not always elegant; nor is it always experienced with delicacy.

When women wrote novels with "sympathy, imagination, spontaneity, simplicity," critics viewed their contributions with "sympathetic indulgence." When they did not, they "forfeited the special consideration that women confidently claimed and critics seldom failed to show" (Tompkins 1961, 125). A "lady novelist" who lacked delicacy was a woman to be damned.

Within this critical double standard, reviewers additionally distinguished excellence, what deserved to be read, from mediocrity, what did not. Presumably, the ability to make this critical distinction was also a male attribute. Better educated, capable of reading history with enjoyment, men supposedly made analytic distinctions of which women were incapable.

At the turn of the century, novels themselves contained this ideological distinction. In *Northanger Abbey* (written between 1794 and 1799 and published in 1818), Jane Austen used it to establish the sympathetic gentility and sophisticated understanding of her hero, Henry Tilney. Consider the following passage in which Catherine Morland discusses books and learning with Tilney. Catherine uses the term "novels"; Henry emphasizes "good novels."[2]

Catherine introduces the topic of novels by observing that some scenery they pass as they walk is reminiscent of the south of France as described in Mrs. Radcliffe's *Mysteries of Udolpho*. She adds, "But you never read novels, I

2. We are grateful to Rachel Brownstein for calling our attention to this passage.

dare say?" to which Henry replies, "Why not?" Catherine explains, "Because they are not clever enough for you— gentlemen read better books." Henry objects, "The person, be it gentleman or lady, who has not pleasure in a *good novel*, must be intolerably stupid. I have read all Mrs. Radcliff's works, and *most* of them with great pleasure. The Mysteries of Udolpho, when I had once begun it, I could not lay down again;—I remember finishing it in two days—my hair standing on end the whole time."

Henry Tilney does more than distinguish good novels from all novels; he distinguishes those of Mrs. Radcliffe that he read with great pleasure from those he did not. He possesses a male ability, displayed through a vocabulary emphasizing the "niceties" of finer critical judgments. When Catherine Morland inquires, "But now really do you not think that Udolpho is the nicest book in the world?" Henry Tilney objects to the word "nice." He expands upon the word: "And this is a very nice day, and we are taking a very nice walk. . . . Oh! [nice] is a very nice word indeed!—and it does for everything. Originally perhaps it was applied only to express neatness, propriety, delicacy, or refinement; different people were nice in their ideas, in their sentiments, or their choice. But now every commendation on every subject is comprised in that one word."

Gender-stereotyping continues throughout this passage. Tilney goes on to prove his critical abilities by speaking of the pleasure to be derived from reading history, which, Catherine Morland comments, her father and brothers also enjoy. Recalling how history was essential material when she was taught to read, Catherine explains that reading history is instruction and torment to her. And so once more Catherine gives Henry Tilney the chance to display his analytic ability. He not only distinguishes between instruction and torment but adds the coup de grace: "Historians are not accountable for the difficulty of learning to read. . . . if reading had not been taught, Mrs. Radcliffe would have written in vain—or perhaps might not have written at all."

The assumptions implicit in this passage were often explicit in literary criticism. Expectations about the differential "hearts" and "minds" of women and men led cultural entrepreneurs to expect "strong writing" from the pens of men. Some early nineteenth-century critics even seemed to have a vested interest in attributing culturally valued novels by women to the men with whom the women were associated. Thus, in 1834 a reviewer for *Fraser's* "gloated" over his discovery of what he believed to be the true identity of the author of the powerful *Absentee Landlord* and its companion, *Castle Rackrent*. "Ay: it is just as we expected! Miss Edgeworth *never* wrote *the* Edgeworth novels. . . . all that, as we have long had a suspicion, was the work of her father" (quoted in Showalter 1977, 74; emphasis in original).

Similar prejudices were revealed when critics rendered judgments about novels published by pseudonymous authors. Indeed, disputes about the gender of such writers indicate how much critics cared about an author's gender and how much their assumptions about gender affected their interpretations of novels. Probably the most famous cases of changing literary interpretations involve Brontë's *Jane Eyre* (1847) and Eliot's *Adam Bede* (1859). Both novels were reviewed and debated in a somewhat later period than we have been discussing. In the 1850s critics were particularly adamant about the qualities and qualifications that men and women should bring to the novel—each in their own gender-stereotypic way.

Critics—including women who reviewed for literary journals—encouraged readers to wonder about the identity and morality of Currer Bell, Brontë's pseudonym. According to Showalter, again and again the reviews used such words as "sensual," "gross," and "animal." Following the lead that critics provided, readers were supposedly stunned by *Jane Eyre*. In her autobiography of Charlotte Brontë, Elizabeth Gaskell explained: "The whole reading world of England was in ferment to discover the unknown author. . . . Every little incident mentioned in the book was turned this way and that to answer, if possible, the much-vexed question of sex" (quoted in Showalter 1977, 92). Showalter adds, "The presentation of female sexuality and human passion disturbed and amazed readers. If Currer Bell was a woman, they could not imagine what sort of woman she might be" (ibid.). Furthermore, George Lewes commented, writing to publisher Blackwood about George Eliot's use of a pseudonym for *Adam Bede*, "When *Jane Eyre* was finally known to be a woman's book, the tone [of criticism] noticeably changed" (cited in ibid., 94).

Similarly, criticism of *Adam Bede* changed after the identity of its author became known. William Hepworth Dixon, editor of the *Athenaeum*, wrote what Showalter terms a "vicious note for the gossip column," which read: "It is time to end this pother about the authorship of 'Adam Bede.' The writer is in no sense a great unknown; the tale, if bright in parts, and such as a clever woman with an observant eye and unschooled moral nature might have written, has no great quality of any kind" (quoted in ibid., 95).

It is not so surprising that literary judgments of *Jane Eyre* and *Adam Bede* were revised after the gender of their authors was revealed. Although earlier critics had expected different qualities in novels written by men and women,

> The intense concentration on the proper sphere of the woman writer did not appear in criticism until the 1840s. . . . Through the 1850s and 1860s [when the episodes we have discussed occurred] there was a great

increase in theoretical and specific criticism of women novelists. Hardly a journal failed to publish an essay on women's literature; hardly a critic failed to express himself upon its innate and potential qualities. (ibid., 74)

As we have seen, Showalter believes that the 1840s, 1850s, and 1860s marked a decided increase in concentration on women writers. These dates affirm the emergence of the empty field phenomenon. As we have stressed, the empty field phenomenon begins to unfold when men realize that women are occupying a field that is beginning to bring social and economic rewards. Though women may not prevail, they are prevalent. According to Showalter, after 1840, when women writers—good writers, at that—were prevalent in England, Europe, and America, critics increasingly concentrated on the "phenomenon" of women writers. She suggests that the prevalence and success of women novelists in the marketplace threatened male critics. As she puts it, "One form of male resistance . . . was to see women novelists as being engaged in a kind of aggressive conspiracy to rob men of their markets, steal their subject matter, and snatch away their young lady readers, to see them as dominating *because of superior numbers rather than superior abilities*" (ibid., 75; emphasis added).

Showalter's explanation and our theory are congruent. We have stressed that when men recognized novel writing as an important activity, they began to invade the field and to identify the high-culture novel as their own preserve. During the 1860s and 1870s, women's novels were prevalent among the submissions to and acceptances by Macmillan. We also argued that the prevalence of women novelists from 1840 through 1880 was a key factor leading such literary figures as John Morley to formulate a distinction between the good "circulating library novel" and the high-culture novel submitted, respectively, by an "authoress" and by a man. In Morley's reviews for Macmillan (and in those of Macmillan's other readers as well) we saw the critical double standard, which Showalter identifies as another form of resistance to the prevalence of women novelists.

The fit between Showalter's theory and ours is not perfect. According to Showalter, midcentury criticism included emphasis upon the supposed biological distinction between the minds of the sexes. Sometimes it included the notion that by expending energy in the act of writing women depleted the physical reserve necessary for childbirth and other womanly functions. Morley and the other Macmillan readers did not emphasize biology in their reviews, but sometimes, they did use an emerging comparative method, assessing women novelists in terms of other women novelists and men in terms of other men.

In general, this comparative method supposed that women "had a natural taste for the trivial; they were sharp-eyed observers of the social scene; they enjoyed getting involved in other people's affairs" (Showalter 1977, 82). Critical emphasis on these innate traits "implied that women's writing was artless and effortless as birdsong, and therefore not in competition with the more rational male eloquence" (ibid.). For simplicity's sake, we are going to identify the period of criticism that emphasized women's artlessness as "the birdsong phase." It corresponds to the period of male invasion, 1840 through 1880.

Of course, not all criticism during the birdsong phase discussed women's artlessness. Some merely offered an implicit contrast between women's abilities and men's mental powers. For instance, Morley wrote about women's manuscripts that displayed "a practiced hand"—a term he applied in 1877 to Mrs. Alfred Phillips' *Benedicta*, which he felt had been written "by a more practiced hand than most" of the fiction manuscripts he read for Macmillan.[3] Though Morley might not have subscribed to the biological theory, the term "practiced hand" established a contrast between the hand that produces a *manuscript* and the educated, rational, knowledgeable, and hence artful "male mind." The term "practiced hand" also crops up in reviews in the *Athenaeum*.

Since our analysis of Morley's criticism for Macmillan harmonizes with Showalter's comments about midcentury criticism, we might expect Morley's reviews to anticipate the published assessments of the novels that Macmillan issued. Frequently they did, as seen in the in-house reviews quoted and summarized in chapter 4. Additionally, the terms in which Morley rejected this or that "authoress's" romance reproduced many tenets of midcentury criticism about women. But the concordance between Morley's work for Macmillan and published reviews of published novels does not necessarily confirm the operation of the empty field phenomenon. It does not speak to possible shifts in the critical double standard—changing expectations about what women and men should and do write. To consider this crucial issue, we turn to reviews published in two important Victorian literary journals, the *Athenaeum* and the *Edinburgh Review*.

The *Athenaeum* and the *Edinburgh Review*

Because such literary critics as Showalter (see especially 1977) have already mined nineteenth-century journals to define the critical double stan-

---

3. The contrast between artless song and artful rationality is implicit in the review *Benedicta* eventually received in the *Athenaeum*. That weekly's anonymous reviewer felt it "would be best described in novelist's language as a wealth of nonsense" (1878a, 505).

dard, we have chosen to examine reviews in only two periodicals: the weekly *Athenaeum* and the quarterly *Edinburgh Review*. By and large, the reviews that we have read fit the pattern of the critical double standard so ably analyzed by feminist literary critics.

Both the *Athenaeum* and the *Edinburgh Review* were established well before the advent of the empty field phenomenon. Young men who were staunch Whigs founded the *Edinburgh Review* in 1802. Though they frequently wrote in moderate tones, they cared passionately about politics. As its early editor Francis Jeffrey had once told Sir Walter Scott, who objected to the journal's "excessive" emphasis on party politics, "The 'Review' has but two legs to stand on. Literature is one of them, but its right leg is politics" (quoted in *Edinburgh Review* 1902a, 287). At the time, as Williams (1976) emphasizes, the term *literature* generally indicated nonfiction—a connotation it was to maintain through much of the nineteenth century. Most of the articles in this quarterly did indeed concern what we now call nonfiction, although each issue generally contained one article about "imaginative literature," either poetry or, more rarely in its early years, novels.

In its articles on the major political issues of the day, the *Edinburgh Review* offered serious, reasoned, and principled arguments intended to have a lasting impact; so, too, the tone of its discussions of poetry and novels was anything but transitory. The *Review* considered only serious literature. By the 1860s it featured articles on the state of contemporary literature. It did not contain brief reviews of just-issued works. Rather, its discussions of poetry and novels tended to be assessments of a literary school or of an author's cumulative works, offered after the publication of a much-discussed book, an author's collected works, a biography or upon an author's death or the anniversary of his or her birth or death. The *Edinburgh Review* rendered judgments when "we no longer have the strain of . . . excitement. The picture has now got into perspective, and the judgment has had time to form itself." (The comment is from the review of George Cross' edited volumes of George Eliot's letters and journals [1885, 516].)

The *Edinburgh Review* steadfastly maintained its home in Edinburgh, where it was published by Constable (see *Edinburgh Review* 1902a, 275–318). But it sold up to five-sixths of each edition in London, where it was issued by Longmans. In 1817 and 1818 it reached its greatest circulation, 13,500 copies (ibid., 289).[4] The Whig *Review* had a sufficient impact on London intellectual circles to prompt the establishment of the Tory *Quarterly* in 1809.

Founded in 1828, the *Athenaeum* appeared weekly. It was not a party

4. We do not know its circulation in the period we are discussing.

organ, and in many ways its judgments were utterly conventional. Thus, the title of a scholarly work about the periodical is *The Athenaeum: A Mirror of Victorian Culture* (Marchand 1941). The bulk of the *Athenaeum* was devoted to nonfiction and to cultural activities in London. But it included a regular column devoted to reviews of new novels, a gossip column that frequently featured items about novels and novelists, and occasional articles on the state of the novel. Unlike the *Edinburgh Review*, the *Athenaeum* was stuffed with advertising. Like the *Athenaeum*'s gossip column, those advertisements proclaimed that the *Athenaeum* was meant to reach readers who wished to stay au courant. The ads were generally publishers' announcements of just-issued novels and nonfiction, and after its founding, Mudie's announcements of the books recently arrived at its circulating libraries.

The *Athenaeum* reached a fair number of readers who were able to support a weekly subscription and to maintain a home library. In the 1860s its circulation was 7,200 copies, enough to have its reviews reach many readers but considerably lower than the 40,000 copies sold by *Punch*, which also addressed itself to the upper and middle classes (Altick 1957, 358).

Both the *Athenaeum* and the *Edinburgh Review* published unsigned reviews by women. Publishing in the *Edinburgh Review* in the 1830s, Harriet Martineau adopted "the mannish way of talking" (Haight 1968, 258, quoted in Showalter 1977, 59) so that readers would take her seriously.[5] By altering her customary style, Martineau affirmed that critical standards were male standards, as did Elizabeth Rigby when writing in the *Review*. In the 1860s Geraldine Jewsbury wrote reviews for the *Athenaeum*. Like her readers' reports for publisher Bentley, her assessments of novels by women accepted the critical double standard that, we have seen, *Athenaeum* editor William Hepworth Dixon heartily applied to George Eliot's *Adam Bede* once he learned that a woman had written it. Martineau, Rigby, and Jewsbury were women of ability. By conforming to the expectations of the men who paid them for their reviews (and to the readers who identified criticism as a male activity), they helped to solidify male hegemony. They helped to ensure that what men deemed "culture" would be viewed as universal culture.

By examining the treatment of George Eliot in the *Edinburgh Review*, one can see that its use of the double standard was more subtle than the *Athenaeum*'s, though still clearly present. Treatment of George Eliot is also par-

5. Kanter (1977) points out that token women often identify with the men they work with. Martineau did, though, express concerns familiar to twentieth-century feminists. For instance, although unmarried, she wanted to be addressed as "Mrs." instead of "Miss" because she felt the former term was used as an honorific (Yates 1985).

ticularly important because it is indicative of how critics dealt with women authors; if critics treated the very great harshly, lesser writers might expect even more stringent treatment, if not condescension. Examination of some criticisms of Eliot may help us to define changes in the sorts of criticism applied to women novelists.

George Eliot and the Edinburgh Review. Eliot's identity was revealed in 1860. In 1868, assessing her poem *The Spanish Gypsy* and consistently referring to the author as "he," critic R. Monckton Milnes opened his essay with seeming high praise.

> When a writer of recognized worth and distinction produces a work of a different character from those with which his name has been hitherto associated, he finds himself in serious competition, not only with a fresh class of authors, but with the very elements of his own fame. The unwillingness with which men can acknowledge that a man of active life can be a philosopher, . . . or an artist a critic, or a beauty a wit, easily renders them averse to the versatility of genius and the manifold capacities of superior minds. (*Edinburgh Review* 1868, 523).

Praise given, Milnes condemns—but without *directly* invoking Eliot's gender. Rather, he compares her to the greatest of men in order to conclude that Eliot should have stuck to the novel. "It is best, for an artist, in any capacity, who has tried and proved his power within the bounds of a certain form and style, that he should perfect himself therein, and not follow the temptation of new experiment and fanciful aspiration." The form that Eliot attempted "is destined to the highest and the highest alone . . . as yet to only three of mortal men—to Shakespeare, to Voltaire, to Goethe." Milnes implies that Eliot should have stuck to a genre more acceptable for women (and for "ordinary" men).

R. Monckton Milnes found much to dislike: The form of the poem is "peculiar. . . . There is . . . some injury to the sense of artistic completeness." Even the story is inferior to that of a good novel. As he put it, "The story might undoubtedly have been told as well in prose and, in fact, it reads like an old romantic novelette; but if George Eliot had ever conceived such a design, he must soon have seen that it was not worthy of his telling" (ibid., 525).

Five years later, the *Edinburgh Review*'s critic—again R. Monckton Milnes—praised *Middlemarch*. He never identified Eliot as a woman and again used the pronoun "he" in referring to her. Milnes began with high praise. He suggested that the "agitation of interest" with which those "even beyond the ordinary range of literary circles" awaited each volume of *Middlemarch* was almost equal to that with which "Cambridge youth had awaited new volumes of *Clarissa*." But then, failing to recognize the difference in intent among works about towns by other women novelists, Milnes favorably compared *Middlemarch* to work by Miss Mitford (*Our Village*), Mrs. Gaskell (*Cranford*), and Miss Martineau's "too didactic" *Deerbrook*. Although the terms he used were laudatory, ultimately Milnes praised *Middlemarch* for being both wholesome and instructive—as novels by women were supposed to be. "In *Middlemarch* another volume is added to the noble series of British works of fiction which is at once acceptable to 'girls and men' and which is so peculiarly our own. . . . George Eliot's new enterprise is to be hailed with gratitude for its healthy tone and honest purpose, as well as for the admirable interior action, which makes it almost independent of incident and moulds the outward circumstances to its own spiritual ends" (*Edinburgh Reivew* 1873, 263).

Eliot could not escape being compared to other women and to other women writers. Having internalized male standards (see Showalter 1977), even women novelists who wrote criticism during this period applied a critical double standard to Eliot. Thus, when Margaret Oliphant reviewed *George Eliot's Life as related to her Letters and Journals* for the *Edinburgh Reivew*, she called Eliot a "great writer" but insisted that greatness brought her a special responsibility as a woman. "What is wrong in any woman is more, not less, wrong in a woman gifted beyond her neighbors" (*Edinburgh Review*, 1885, 535). Mrs. Oliphant found Eliot's books to be so dissimilar to those of other women that it was difficult for her to understand how Eliot's pseudonym had been penetrated. Explaining why, she used terms associated with men:

> George Eliot's books remain (with the exception of the 'Mill on the Floss') less definable in point of sex than the books of any other woman who has ever written. A certain size, if we may use the word, and freedom in the style, an absence of that timidity, often varied by temerity, which, however disguised, is rarely absent from the style of women, seems to us to obliterate the distinctions of sex; and her scientific illustrations and indications of a scholarship more easy and assured than a woman's ordinary furtive classical allusions no doubt added greatly to this effect. . . . The history of her first great book . . . shows both the strength and weakness of a mind which was so little that of a critic, and which combined womanly prejudices so ineradicable with so much of the unscrupulous masculine intelligence." (ibid., 544)

Over the years, critics for the *Edinburgh Review* changed the standards applied to all novelists, to women novelists, and to George Eliot. During the decades that we have identified with the period of redefinition, the 1880s and 1890s, critics emphasized what today are called "literary values." Women were still compared to women, but critics used new terms to claim that women failed if they dealt with topics deemed suitable for men: some were said to have sacrificed "art." Thus, despite the *Edinburgh Review*'s earlier praise for her "masculine intelligence," an 1894 reviewer, Alexander I. Shand, damned Eliot's last books when he assessed Mrs. Humphrey Ward's philosophical *Marcella*. Shand explained that in the work of both women "The motives and aspirations of frail humanity are treated in the same philosophic and analytic temper. There is somewhat similar power in the delineation of highly wrought passion; there are scenes and passages of singular pathos, and sentences which are pregnant with *sententious wisdom*. But George Eliot in her earlier novels, *before she sacrificed art to philosophical enthusiasm*, invariably showed the genius of dramatic concentration" (*Edinburgh Review* 1894, 114; emphasis added).

Shand's terms are reminiscent of the earlier double standard applied to women. Women may feel philosophic enthusiasm, but men may display philosophic originality and depth.[6] Thus, when Leslie Stephen himself wrote Eliot's entry in the *DNB* he extended women's lack of philosophy to Eliot herself: "In philosophy, she did not affect to be an original thinker, and though she had an extraordinary capacity for the assimilation of ideas, she had the feminine tendency (and no one was more feminine) to accept philosophers at their own valuation" (1888).[7]

Yet Shand's 1894 review of *Marcella* struck a new note; it did not assume that Eliot sang artlessly like the bird. Her early works qualified as "art." For supposedly literary reasons—aspects of construction—her later works did not. Nor were these later works "birdsong." To emphasize this shift in the critical double standard, we will call the period of the 1880s and 1890s the phase of "dissonant construction."

The Phase of Dissonant Construction

We intend the term *dissonant construction* to carry two connotations. First, as the modern (and shorter) realistic novel replaced the three-decker, which had earlier been praised for its realism, critics placed new emphasis on

6. The *Athenaeum* also finds that *Marcella* is an attempt by a woman to think like a man. It asks "How is it that *Marcella*, despite its author's eloquence, her more than feminine art of reasoning, her breadth and depth of vision and view, remains an unsatisfactory work of fiction?" (*Athenaeum* 1894, 469–470).

7. Eliot believed her own work transcended that of silly lady novelists. Even in her early period, Eliot intended her work to provoke thought in those who did not simply read novels but were trained to think—men. (See Showalter 1975.)

construction and individuality, including new notions of admirable style. The twentieth-century reader who obtains mid-nineteenth-century novels in a one-volume binding may rarely appreciate the subtlety of construction that some three-deckers display. But the typical midcentury *Athenaeum* review rarely mentioned such matters as how authors used the end of each volume to mark key aspects of the novel. Nor did the critics of the *Edinburgh Review* dwell on these points.

Second, the term dissonant construction suggests a critical belief that technically women could not construct a book as well as men could. This belief may have had basis in reality as well as in prejudice. As the shorter one-volume novel replaced the three-decker, many writers were loath to switch to the modern form. Critics may have mistaken their refusal to change for an inability to change. But, whatever the cause, in the late 1890s such writers were out of tune with their times; they were dissonant.

Many female and some popular male novelists were among those who remained faithful to the three-decker. Morley and Mowbray Morris rejected many three-deckers by women. According to the Macmillan Archives, in the 1880s and 1890s women's fiction submissions were more likely than not to be three-deckers. In the 1890s even such traditional critics as Morley and Morris found many novels by women old-fashioned. Gettmann (1960) stresses that many women published by Bentley either could not or would not make the change to the newer form. The same theme, that women's novels were outdated, crops up in Thring's manuscript (n.d.) on the Society of Authors. Aspiring women novelists wrote to the society to learn where to place "ghost stories." Although Mrs. Molesworth's collection of ghost stories received a good review in the *Athenaeum* of 14 April 1888, such stories had lost much of their appeal.

Women who wrote 1860s-style ghost stories in the 1890s were out of tune with the times. But they may have been in structural positions that made it difficult to keep up with London literary circles. Even these women's expectations that the society could help them find a publisher for their work suggests that they were excluded from the mainstream of literary life. Initially, as we have seen, the Society of Authors did not accept women as members. The women who were invited to its annual banquets were well published and widely read. The women who wrote for help seem not to have realized that personal contact is vital to receiving help in literary affairs.

We have consistently emphasized that what helps an author find a publisher is personal networks, personal introductions, or personal sponsorship—someone to vouch for the quality of the author and the quality of the work. We assume that those sponsoring a novel took care to specify what they knew about its potential quality. As reported in chapter 4, when Mrs. Oliphant wrote Macmillan about Miss Dworkin's book, she praised Miss Dworkin's talents in art and music but added that she had not seen the manuscript (26 January 1875). Similarly, after reading parts of the Macmillan Archive Sutherland (1976) surmised that in the 1860s and 1870s the Macmillans were more likely to publish the work of authors personally known to them than to accept novels submitted over the transom.

Personal sponsorship was as important during the 1880s and 1890s, the period of redefinition, as it had been earlier.[8] Sponsorship accounted for Frederick Macmillan's acceptance of Maurice Hewlett's *The Forest Lovers* (1898) despite negative reviews by both Morley and Morris. As discussed in chapter 4, Mrs. W. K. Clifford had acted as broker for that manuscript. Her reputation and her statement to Macmillan that he was "throwing away a small fortune" and that "she had never felt more certain about the popularity of any book" (Morgan 1943, 149–150) accounted for its acceptance.

But it is one thing to say that some women were out of touch—were dissonant—and another for critics to expect that all or even almost all women would be writing old-fashioned, poorly constructed work. Often a stereotype has some (frequently problematic) relationship to the behavior of the group it characterizes. We term a set of beliefs a stereotype precisely because it does not consider the possibility of variation within a group. Much as the "birdsong phase" of criticism offered a stereotypic double standard, the "phase of dissonant construction" represented a critical double standard.

Those standards appear more starkly in the *Edinburgh Review* than in the *Athenaeum*. In the 1890s the *Athenaeum* was still resisting modernism. Although in 1904 it would heap praise upon Maurice Hewlett's *The Queen's Quair*, in July 1898 its reviewer expressed distaste for *The Forest Lovers*, which Mrs. Clifford had so admired. The reviewer found it to have "an irresponsible style of narrative" and suggested that the writing style "was an unconscious parody of Louis Stevenson" and aped George Meredith.[9] The critic felt that Hewlett had been "determined to be original at the price of common sense"—though he did concede that there was "some most excellent matter in the volume as well" (*Athenaeum* 1898, 93).

The reviewers for the *Edinburgh Review* did not completely endorse modernism either. They disliked the new styles of prose exemplified by the

8. See Powell (1985) on the importance of personal sponsorship in academic publishing today.
9. This reference to Meredith is reminiscent of Morley's comment about *The Forest Lovers*: "not everyone can draw the bow of the master."

novels of George Meredith, which elsewhere drew critical acclaim. Also, because shifts in critical fashions are gradual, criticism in the *Edinburgh Review* of the 1890s still drew upon some of the tenets of the earlier birdsong phase of criticism. Its July 1899 review by Stephen Gwynn of Mrs. Oliphant's oeuvre and her posthumous *Autobiography and Letters* expressed some previous suppositions with a new twist.

The new modernist twist assumed that great novelists were suffering individualists, dedicated to their art and passionately involved in the life of the imagination. Supposedly, this passionate involvement showed itself in the way a novelist "lives" in the characters he or she created. Stephen Gwynn was so convinced that "living with one's characters" was a hallmark of a great writer that he even sought to apply it retrospectively, claiming that Jane Austen and Walter Scott "must have spent innumerable hours in the company of [their] characters" (*Edinburgh Review* 1899a, 32). Other hallmarks of modernism included originality, confronting philosophic issues about the meaning of life, and artful construction of novelistic structure.

According to Gwynn, most women scarcely qualified as artists. For new reasons, Gwynn suggested that a good mother cannot write great novels. Rather than cite biology, as earlier critics had done, he explained that most of Mrs. Oliphant's novels, including her early Carlingford novels, failed because she "was a woman and a mother, and the innermost preoccupation of her mind—the point to which her fluctuating thoughts would always swing back—was her children" (ibid., 37). Because Mrs. Oliphant cared about her children, she did not have "the artist's passionate absorption in his work"; the "art of the novelist . . . needs that the artist should live in imaginary characters" (ibid., 36, 37).[10]

At first, Gwynn suggested, Mrs. Oliphant's cheerful and optimistic nature and her personal happiness prevented her from passionate involvement in her work. Happiness flawed her first Carlingford novels, written before her life was plagued by the deaths of those whom she loved. Gwynn argued, "Happiness seldom needs to find a voice—not until it is remembered happiness;

10. Stephen Gwynn felt that women without children were the best of the women writers. He troubled to point out that George Sands did not meet nineteenth-century standards of motherhood because she left her child to vacation with her lover and argued that Elizabeth Barrett Browning wrote her best poetry before she became a mother. Showalter (1977, 47) also notes that between 1800 and 1900 a "fairly constant proportion" of women writers, roughly 50 percent, were unmarried. And Olsen (1979) stresses the prevalence of unmarried and childless women among female writers. But they cite quite different causes than those suggested by Gwynn, namely the amount of time and energy required to keep a household running smoothly.

and in the days when the first Carlingford tales were being written Mrs. Oliphant was thoroughly happy" (ibid., 37). Later, she was much too involved in the lives and deaths around her to invest herself in her work.

But Stephen Gwynn found merit in Mrs. Oliphant's feminine style, though he did not use the word "feminine." In phrases reminiscent of the birdsong phase of criticism, the reviewer praised Mrs. Oliphant for writing "easily and sweetly" (ibid., 27). He noted that her style "certainly does not conform to the prevailing standards [which he disliked]. It does not keep one on the stretch with continual expectations of the unexpected word: it is never contorted or tormented, never emphatic, never affected."

While praising Mrs. Oliphant for not meeting the contemporary critical standards, Gwynn consciously or unconsciously condemned her as old-fashioned and ladylike. Her style was not artful. He observed:

> The words flow simply and smoothly, like the utterance of a perfectly well-bred woman, sometimes talking eagerly, sometimes with a grave earnestness, but more often with a delicate undercurrent of laughter in the tone; and the style answers by a sort of instinct to each inflection of the voice. She is thinking more about what she has to say than about the way in which she is to say it; and since the day when people listed to Mr. Pater and misunderstood Stevenson that has been to a certain school of critics an unpardonable sin. (ibid., 29)

Gwynn continued, "Style comes to some by grace of nature and Mrs. Oliphant was one of the fortunate who had none of the vehemences and eccentricities of temperament which make it difficult for the writer to arrive at a harmonious manner of expression; nor was she obliged to hide mediocrity under a solemn and elaborate vesture of language. What she had to say was interesting, and she arrived spontaneously at a manner of saying it perfectly suited to her purpose" (ibid., 29). In the late nineteenth century, if such virtues were not dismissed as mid-Victorian, they were dismissed as journalistic. Certainly, they were not art.

In the 1890s critics for the *Edinburgh Review* felt that an admirable style was neither that of a "well-bred woman" nor that of a man who sought to construct sentences that inspired wonder in his reader. It was a "manly" style, as explained in Stephen Gwynn's essay of October 1899, "Some Tendencies of Prose Style." Praising eighteenth-century writers, he set forth his notion of "manliness" and indicated characteristics of the style that others praised: "The more one reads of the best prose written nowadays... the more one is inclined to regret the eighteenth-century manner, luminous, not coruscant, aiming above all things at suavity and sanity, which by its *manly directness* charmed the reader into a belief that he too might have written the same things in just the same way, instead of filling him with wonder (as Mr. Meredith does) how on earth any human being could have cemented words and ideas together in such a jeweled but bewildering mosaic" (1899b, 375; emphasis added). Mrs. Oliphant's style displayed neither manly directness nor the glitter of a bewildering mosaic.

The ambivalence implicit in Gwynn's praise produced a final expression of the critical double standard; Mrs. Oliphant's work approached greatness when she was inspired to write as a mother who had lost children. But she may not even have recognized the potential greatness in what the reviewer felt to be her best work, the stories of the unseen that confront death with continuing love. (An artist, this critic implied, can identify his or her best work.)

Perhaps Gwynn found those stories great because they satisfied late Victorian notions that creativity springs from inspiration.[11] As he put it: "stories of the unseen she could only write—as she expressed it herself—when they came to her; they were not written to order or for money" (*Edinburgh Review* 1899a, 42). Through Christian faith, they transformed the experience that marked her life—death.

Perhaps Gwynn found these stories great because he saw them as an expression of motherhood, an activity in which the otherwise "failed" storyteller could excel:

> So she wrote in her faith; and the words will stir in many that faith in the faith of others which lives often when faith itself is dead or withered or torpid. Motherhood was the soul of her life; it was the hindrance, as we hold, to high achievement in the way of art which she chose in the outset; it was the inspiration of the wisest and most beautiful things that she wrote, things than which few have been written in her lifetime wiser or more beautiful. It made of her life the tragedy of happiness, but bestowed upon her memory a noble and tragic beauty. (ibid., 47)

Ultimately, Gwynn thought, Mr. Oliphant failed as an artist. But he did praise her for an attribute much valued in a Victorian woman—her unwavering faith in life. "Even under the weight of all this affliction, she never lost heart" (ibid., 35).

---

11. Critics were aghast when Trollope's posthumous *An Autobiography* emphasized how little he owed to inspiration and how much to hard work. In his essay for the *Edinburgh Review* (1884), Shand thought Trollope's autobiography might be valuable to men who wanted to make a career as an author rather than as attorney but certainly could not serve as a guide for artists. *An Autobiography* lowered critical evaluations of Trollope's oeuvre.

The reviewers for the *Athenaeum* did not find this greatness in Mrs. Oliphant, not even in her "inspired" stories of the unseen. They disliked the style. Writing of *A Beleaguered City*, one reviewer complained, it is "to be regretted that she has made the personages in whose mouth the story is put use that horrible Franco-English dialect." This reviewer found the setting confusing and the story, an expanded magazine article, too long and "extremely dull" (*Athenaeum* 1880, 150).

In contrast to critics associated with the *Edinburgh Review*, however, the *Athenaeum*'s reviewers adored the complex work of George Meredith. They admired Meredith's individuality and originality—his personal vision. Praising *Diana of the Crossways*, one reviewer felt, "Not since [Meredith's earlier] *The Egoist* has there appeared an essay in fiction at once so novel and so true, so personal and peculiar and, at the same time, so pregnant and convincing. . . . [*Diana of the Crossways* is] the work of a man of genius and a great artist. . . . The book is instinct with imagination, is quick with interest as life itself, is full of matter and movement as a corner of the actual world. . . . [It] affects the reader more powerfully than the spectacle of nature itself" (*Athenaeum* 1885, 339–340). This reviewer did not praise Meredith's characters as realistic and individualized delineations of known types, one common feature of the mid-Victorian realistic novel, although other *Athenaeum* critics applied those standards to Mrs. Oliphant's novels of the 1880s and 1890s. Instead, this 1895 reviewer lauded Meredith's main character, Diana Merion, as an "original creation."

Finally, the *Athenaeum* admired the literary style that the *Edinburgh Review* had so disliked. "Every sentence is packed with significance. . . . Mr. Meredith writes such English as is within the capacity of no other living man; and in epigram, as in landscape, in dialogue as in analysis, in description as in comment and reflection, he is an artist in words of whom his country may be proud."

Meredith's language is difficult. (In its 1879 review of the *Egoist*, the *Athenaeum* had used the term "obscure," explaining that Meredith's "cleverness gets in the way of his writing.") It demands that the reader work at a novel. Thus, it requires an educated reader, not the run-of-the-mill member of a circulating library, nor a well-bred lady, nor a young girl.

Complex language also demands an author who invents language and invents with language, as Virginia Woolf was to do. But not just any language. To achieve recognition from those who can make reputations, the author must play with the language of the educated critics. He or she (more likely he) must know the language appreciated by the club and must have lived a life whose remembered happiness and present (individualized) sufferings suggest a world in which club members might imagine they too live. That is not the world of the lady novelists of the Victorian era.

Two Victorian Best-sellers

On the life of Mrs. Oliphant, the *Edinburgh Review*'s Stephen Gwynn commented that she "was prosperous, yet others with half her talent and less than half her labour earned twice as much, for work not so good as hers" (*Edinburgh Review* 1899a, 26). Thus, we raise one last issue: were authors who were equally praised also paid equally? We turn once more to the Macmillan Archives.

In chapter 7, reviewing contractual relationships between Macmillan and novelists, we posited that Macmillan paid most to those who needed it least. Women novelists, the historical data suggest, were generally in a more precarious financial situation than men were. Among those whom Macmillan paid relatively well were two popular authors who were constantly in financial straits: Mrs. Oliphant and F. Marion Crawford. She supported sons and nephew through elite educations; he spent his earnings with a seeming enthusiasm that left him always needing more money.

We could not locate all the receipts, letters, and memoranda of agreement for some of the books that Mrs. Oliphant and Mr. Crawford are known to have published with Macmillan. But those we did locate indicate that the authors' financial relationships to Macmillan were not comparable. Oliphant published many of her 250 volumes of fiction and nonfiction with other firms, but from 1870 through 1891 Macmillan paid her at least £ 500 a year. Crawford published fewer books but more fiction with Macmillan. From 1883 through 1907 Macmillan and Company agreed to pay him at least £ 660 a year. Once Crawford had established his reputation, Macmillan and Company paid him more per novel than it did Oliphant, with the probable exception of Oliphant's *Young Musgrove* (table 8.1). Yet critics judged Crawford's and Oliphant's novels to be of roughly comparable quality.

Despite their disparate financial arrangements with Macmillan, Oliphant and Crawford seem to be the most comparable man and woman among the novelists that firm published.[12] For although one could argue that Oliphant

12. Among the pairs we rejected are Charlotte Young and Charles Kingsley, Henry James and Edith Wharton, Rolf Boldrewood and Mrs. Henry Wood. Charlotte Yonge and Charles Kingsley wrote too early to suit our purposes, and Yonge came to Macmillan only after Parker sold his list. Henry James and Edith Wharton seem comparable, but their relationships to Macmillan were even more disparate than those of Crawford and Oliphant.

Table 8.1: Macmillan's Payments to Margaret Oliphant and
F. Marion Crawford

	Amount (in pounds)	Date	Title(s) prompting payment(s)
Macmillan's	100	25 Jan. 1870	*Saints & Mystics*
Payments to	150	17 June 1870	*Lambs & Mystics*
Mrs. Oliphant	100	31 Dec. 1873	Don't know reason for payment
	500	1 May 1875	*Curate in Charge* [*The Curate*]
	360	14 July 1875	Book on Florence
	1,700	25 Nov. 1881	3 novels, can't tell titles
	500	1 Jan. 1877	*Young Musgrove* (installment)
	200	8 June 1877	*Young Musgrove* (installment)
	50	16 Aug. 1878	*Dress* (copyright)
	750	24 Oct. 1878	*He that will not when He may* (copyright, three payments to be made)
	150	5 June 1879	*St. Margaret of Scotland*
	1,000	23 Dec. 1880	A literary history (installments)
	75	18 Dec. 1882	Selections from Cowper
	300	23 June 1883	*Neighbors on the Green* (in *Cornhill Magazine*) and ghost stories (if Macmillan not repaid in four years, ghost stories become their property)
	400	25 Aug. 1885	*A Country Gentlemen* (copyright paid in installments)
	40	8 Oct. 1886	*A House Divided against Itself*
	400	2 Mar. 1887	*A Poor Gentleman*
	400	1887	*Joyce* (copyright after serialization in *Blackwoods* Magazine)
	600	24 Mar. 1889	Book on Edinburgh
	300	24 Oct. 1888	*Kirsteen, the story of a Scots family seventy years ago* (copyright)
	600	9 Nov. 1889	*The Heir Presumptive & the Heir Apparent*

	Amount (in pounds)	Date	Title(s) prompting payment(s)
	1,200	11 Mar. 1890	*Jerusalem & the Holy Land* [*Jerusalem*]
	10,125	Total from Jan. 1870 to Sept. 1881 (from Macmillan)	
Macmillan's	500	5 Mar. 1883	*Doctor Claudius*
Payments to	200	7 Aug. 1883	*Mr. Isaacs*
F. Marion Crawford	140	14 Oct. 1883	*Mr. Isaacs*
	350	26 Feb. 1884	Part payment of 850 for entire copyright of *Mr. Isaacs* and English edition of *A Roman Singer*
	1,250	10 Mar. 1884	*Zoroaster* (whole of copies sold in 2 volumes and 23,000 copies in one volume and royalty of 10% for every copy sold after that)
	1,250	10 Dec. 1885	*Romance of a Lonely Village* [*Romance of a Lonely Parish*] (same terms as for *Zoroaster*)
	700	18 Mar. 1887	On account of a 15% royalty on selling price of *Saracinesca* in U.S.
	4,000	20 May 1887	Rights in India and colonies for editions of *Zoroaster*, *Paul Patoff*, *With the Immortals*, *Crucifix*, and *Saracinesca* (each book for £500)
			£300 on unpaid balance of £700 for American sale of *Saracinesca* (£400 having been previously paid)

Table 8.1: (*continued*)

Amount (in pounds)	Date	Title(s) prompting payment(s)
		15% on English and American sale of *With the Immortals*, English sale of *Paul Patoff*, English and American sales of *Marzio's Crucifix* and English and American copyrights, including right to print *With the Immortals* in *Macmillan's Magazine* at £2 per page.
3,000	2 Apr. 1888	copyright of *Sant' Ilario*
200	21 Jan. 1889	copyrights (library editions?)
1,250	5 June 1890	copyright of *A Cigarette-Maker's Romance*
600	25 May 1893	*Marion Darche* (English copyright; 20% royalty on library editions and a 6s. edition; 6p on every copy selling less than 6s. Except for Macmillan's Colonial Library, for which Crawford receives £100 outright.)
1,000	20 June 1907	*The Diva* 25% royalty on 6s. edition, but 15% royalty if book price reduced to 3s 6p.; also 15% on Colonial Library, except Canada 6p. per copy sold (£500 on receipt of book and £500 on day of publication)
14,440		Total from Mar. 1883 to Sept. 1907 (from Macmillan)

Note: Some manuscript titles were changed when issued as books.

wrote so much that her work could not qualify as a scarce commodity and so was necessarily devalued, Crawford averaged from one to three novels a year for more than twenty-five years. The critical and financial arguments used to justify devaluation of Oliphant's books might be applied to him, too. So prolific an author could not claim large fees (though Crawford received them); so prolific an author could not achieve real depth and artistry.

Raymond Williams uses the term "outsiders" to encompass women novelists (Williams 1961). In his sense, Mrs. Oliphant was an outsider—admired, but peripheral to the power centers of cultural life. For instance, although she implored publishers to hire her as a salaried reader, she never obtained one of those prized positions.

F. Marion Crawford was an outsider too. Of American parentage, born and reared in Rome, where he mainly made his home as an adult, a resident of India for a while, Crawford was termed "American" by the British. And, as British reviews of American novelists made clear, with the exception of Henry James and possibly one or two other authors, Americans were outsiders from whom, as was the case with women, little of literary value could be expected.

Finally, both Oliphant and Crawford were considered sufficiently significant for their novels to be regularly reviewed by journals that aimed to identify literature of lasting value. Although the *Edinburgh Review* rarely surveyed the collected works of a novelist before his or her death, in 1906 it carried a twenty-page assessment of Crawford's popular novels (*Edinburgh Review* 1906, 61–80). In 1899 Stephen Gwynn had emphasized Mrs. Oliphant's status as outsider as a well-bred woman. In 1906 the *Edinburgh Review*'s critic judged Crawford as an American; the first two and half pages of the review discuss race, nationality, language, and creed, Americans and Britons, and American and British writers.

Just as Gwynn had placed Mrs. Oliphant solidly in the second rank, the 1906 critic deemed F. Marion Crawford second rank. To be sure, the 1906 reviewer demurred: "To attempt any definite assessment of a living writer is always a folly as well as an impertinence" (ibid., 79). But having recognized his folly he compared Crawford to Oliphant:

Macmillan was James' primary publisher, for he lived in England. James also had loose ties to Morley. Wharton lived in the United States, and Macmillan was only her British publisher. Boldrewood was an Australian novelist with no pretenses to high culture. Mrs. Wood's books came to Macmillan after her death, when her copyrights were included in Bentley's sale to Macmillan.

We should all agree that Mr. Crawford's place would never be above that class which falls short of the highest—to which are assigned writers such as Trollope and Mrs. Oliphant. Mrs. Oliphant is nearer his mark than the creator of Mrs. Proudie and Archdeacon Grantly; any of Mr. Crawford's characters will pale beside these robust Britons. . . . Whether the work of such novelists—the storytellers who are very good rather than great—will last, remains to be seen." (ibid.)[13]

Like the 1899 critic who assessed Mrs. Oliphant's work, the 1906 reviewer found virtues in Crawford's novels that were not generally appreciated by his contemporaries:

He writes simply, without grimace or contortion, and he is no maker of laboriously distinguished phrases; and so he has no chance of praise for his style. Again, he is not a novelist of problems or of purposes; he does not lend himself to discussion; and he avoids habitually the subjects treated by those who wish to write a "strong" book (as the cant phrase goes). Anyone who has written a novel will realise how much this abstention increases the difficulty, especially for a novelist who adheres to the old notion that the central theme must always be a love interest." (ibid.)

According to the 1906 reviewer, Crawford succeeded in his own terms. "The true object of the novel is, in his opinion, to afford a sort of pocket theatre, whose primary function—with which nothing must be allowed to interfere—is to amuse and to interest. . . . The novelist's business is to represent faithfully men and women in the various relations to life" (ibid., 80).

The critic ended his assessment: "We should say that [Crawford] has understood men and women very well. . . . And perhaps the true reason why we are always so ready to spend a couple of hours in his pocket theatre lies, not in the curious and varied nature of the entertainment, but in our confidence that we shall like some at least of the people on the stage, and feel ourselves in sympathy with the dramatist" (ibid.).

Thus reviews of the work of Mrs. Oliphant and Mr. Crawford in the *Edinburgh Review* are different in tone but similar in assessment. They do not suggest that one should have been paid more than the other.

Similarly, the reviews of these two novelists in the *Athenaeum* seem more alike than unlike. Both are praised for telling a good story and for creating

13. Again the reviewer compares novels to poetry: "Poets of no greater relative merit are still known by heart, though they died, perhaps, three hundred years ago" (Edinburgh Review 1906, 79). One implication is that novels merited comparison with poetry.

characters with individuality. Both received relatively short reviews, generally thirty to sixty lines. The *Athenaeum* published longer reviews of supposedly greater writers; for example, it devoted roughly 300 lines to praise of Meredith's *Diana of the Crossways*.

Like the *DNB*, the *Athenaeum* used social categories when discussing second-rank authors. Crawford was discussed as an American, Oliphant as a woman. Each was evaluated from the perspective of gender-appropriate expectations. He was compared to male novelists, especially Americans. She was primarily compared to other women. He was lauded for the "vigor of his thoughts" (review of *Dr. Claudius* in *Athenaeum* 1883, 727). She received praise for "a charming tale" (*The Curate in Charge*, reviewed in *Athenaeum* 1876, 196), "refinement of . . . humour" (*The Primrose Path*, reviewed in *Athenaeum* 1878b, 111), and "the tender beauty of the children" (*Young Musgrove*, reviewed in *Athenaeum* 1877, 769).

But these reviews do not explain why Crawford should have received larger fees than Oliphant. Provisionally, we infer that the critical double standard coexisted with a contractual double standard. Although authors who were financially needy (more likely women than men) generally had less bargaining power with publishers, men who claimed to be financially pressed received more money than women of comparable quality who did the same.

Perhaps Crawford received more money because his novels sold better than Oliphant's. Unfortunately, Tuchman located Macmillan's "edition books" (its ledgers specifying the size of the print runs of various editions of books, the date ordered, and the kinds of paper to be used) late in her last stay in London and did not copy out the information for Mrs. Oliphant's books. Records of Crawford's many books with Macmillan were voluminous. Many went through large and multiple printings of several editions. Some were electroplated, as was done when the publisher planned to print many copies and expected to order additional large printings in the future. For instance, in June 1907 Macmillan directed his printer to electroplate *The Prima Donna*, which the contract had identified as *The Diva*. (Crawford had received a £1000 advance according to a memo of agreement, 20 June 1907.) We do not know the size of the run of this first electroplated edition but in December 1907 Macmillan ordered 15,000 additional copies. Few novels received this treatment, and Mrs. Oliphant's work probably was not among them.

Because Macmillan sold more copies of each of Crawford's novels than of Oliphant's, we are tempted to say that Macmillan treated Oliphant and Crawford equally. Unless a publisher has decided that an author is absolutely first-rate, past sales are more pertinent than quality to contract provisions. Macmillan may have payed Oliphant less than Crawford because he feared another publisher might be issuing one of her books at the same time he was, undercutting Macmillan's potential sales. Even among Macmillan's contracts with other men, however, Crawford's contracts were unusual. The 1899 contract for Maurice Hewlett's *Richard Yea and Nay* (memo of agreement, 24 June 1899), for example, was comparable to the contract for Crawford's *The Diva* in that it specified a payment of £ 1000 on publication in advance of royalties of 25 percent in England, 20 percent in the United States, and 4*d*. on the first 3,000 copies of the colonial edition and 6*d*. on subsequent copies. The records do not specify that *Richard Yea and Nay* was electroplated, but Macmillan placed large orders with the printer: 7,500 copies on 25 September 1900 and another 5,000 copies on 10 October 1900.

Macmillan's edition books indicate general differences in the payments made to women and men for novels of approximately equal quality printed in runs of approximately the same size. Hewlett was a major writer. So was Edith Wharton, but Wharton did not get paid on as grand a scale as Hewlett. He received £ 1000 for American and British rights to *Richard Yea and Nay*. She received $1209 (roughly £ 250) for British and colonial rights to *House of Mirth* (Wharton letter to Macmillan, 4 November 1905). Hewlett had received a 25 percent royalty on British rights; Wharton received 20 percent. Macmillan had printed 7,500 copies of *Richard Yea and Nay* for the British market and 5,000 for the colonial. Between 20 September 1905 and 9 January 1906, he ordered 11,000 copies of *House of Mirth*, 8,000 for the British market and 3,000 for the colonies.

Perhaps Hewlett's advance was at least three times larger than Wharton's because he had agreed to include the American rights. (Scribner's had quickly sold 40,000 copies of the first edition of Wharton's *House of Mirth* in the United States). Two years after the publication of *Richard Yea and Nay*, in July 1901, Hewlett did reserve for himself the American rights on his next book for Macmillan, *The Queen's Quair*. Macmillan had agreed to give Hewlett an advance of £ 500 for the British and colonial rights (memo of agreement, 24 July 1901). If we assume that the British pound was worth $4.50, Macmillan would have paid Hewlett $2250, twice what Wharton received for *House of Mirth*.

Perhaps Wharton had yet to prove herself on the British market as Hewlett had already done. This objection is unfounded, according to the available data. On 10 October 1901 Macmillan ordered 5,000 copies of Wharton's *The Benefactress* from the printer. They must have sold, for on 16 November 1901 he ordered another 5,000 copies. It appears that Macmillan and Company wrote better contracts for men than for women.

Sociologists may find the data we have drawn on here to be impressionistic, even as they recognize that reviews cannot be subjected to statistically rigorous analysis. And we have not presented quantitative analyses of Macmillan's editions books. Yet our data are still telling. We infer that the reviews received by women and men did not justify disparate contractual terms. As expected, the data indicate that two very different literary journals reviewed the novels of Crawford and Oliphant with their authors' gender solidly in mind.

Our analysis implies more: the *Athenaeum*, the *Edinburgh Review*, and other literary journals expressed a critical double standard. Moreover, that double standard shifted in ways predicted by the empty field phenomenon. Despite the supposed plethora of women novelists, before the 1840s literary journals did not try to come to terms with them as a phenomenon; they merely applied different standards to women and men. In the 1840s and 1850s, as the reading public seemed to regard more women as important novelists, the literary journals sought to develop theories about the sorts of novels that women and men could and should write. Critics developed a full-blown ideology that, following Showalter (1977), we have termed "the birdsong phase of the critical double standard." As the cultural importance of the novel grew, as educated men sought to distinguish their novels from those preferred by the less elite, critics infused the term *art* with new meaning.

Art was philosophic; high-culture novelists imbued their plots and characters with purpose; their sentences, with surprising turns of phrase. Art was "constructed," self-reflexive, concerned with language, difficult. It was original and individual. It was modern. In this "phase of dissonant construction," the high-culture novel was suited to men.

9
The Case of
the Disappearing
Lady Novelists

n engrossing mystery should have heroes and villains, plots and subplots, and such emotions as greed and passion to provide psychological motivation. Our story has not presented these ingredients. We have not found the smoking gun used to commit the dire crime. We have not even found a corpse. There are still many women novelists, and some of them are critically acclaimed.[1]

We have, however, presented statistics which from one decade to the next indicate tendencies and trends, slow and sometimes small incremental changes. We have followed a trail of circumstantial evidence to a logical answer to our initial questions: Why does some literature supposedly transcend the ages and so constitute "culture," while other, once-popular books are no longer read?

We initially answered that the educated elite judges some books to be of lasting value. Usually when sociologists discuss the educated elite they are referring to specific groups within the upper class—namely those with cultural capital, whose identities are invested in maintaining the value of their cultural tastes as expressed in preferences and actions.

We have tried to imbue the term "educated elite" with a more refined meaning. Not just any member of the appropriate nineteenth-century class fractions defined culture. Mainly, men did so. Occupying positions as cultural brokers and cultural entrepreneurs, they argued among themselves about what sorts of literature should be valued. Resolving those arguments, they foisted their tastes upon other groups. Their definition of cultural traditions became the great tradition.

---

1. In an labeling process that recalls the critical double standard, however, they are more frequently praised as "women novelists" than as novelists who happen to be women.

Our initial question was broad. Our immediate answer was also drawn in broad strokes. To answer less abstractly, we have had to break our question into some of its component parts. How did men use their power to define cultural traditions? How did their practical literary activities relate to key aspects of the methods of producing and distributing literature in eighteenth- and nineteenth-century England? How did the these methods influence the degree of professionalism that writers enjoyed or might claim to possess? How did all of these changes affect the status of the novel? And, most particularly, how did the practical activity of men affect women novelists?

We have argued that from 1840 through 1917 the conditions under which literature was produced and disseminated changed. More literacy brought more literary opportunities. Increased industrialization led to the centralization and rationalization of the publishing industry in London. Aspiring men of letters who could move to London might hope, once there, to forge a career in literature. We inferred that they had more opportunities to do so than their female counterparts.

As opportunities changed, the novel changed. After 1840, when the major features of the literary system that was to dominate most of the Victorian era had fallen into place, some men increasingly understood that they could achieve social and economic rewards by writing novels. Literary critics and critical journals were troubled by the prevalence of women novelists, their standing in the marketplace, their presence among the esteemed writers of the day. In the 1840s and 1850s critics wrote and journals published articles about the "woman question" as it manifested itself in fiction. They applied different standards to women and men. Specific standards changed over time, but a critical double standard persisted. Over time, contracts changed too, but once again women were likely to come out second best.

Once it had become obvious that the novel was the prototypical genre of the age, men increasingly wrote novels. Some men wrote novels to achieve social and financial rewards. Other men, such as George Bernard Shaw (as quoted in chapter 3), "wrote novels because everybody [meaning other aspiring literati] did so then." Women increasingly wrote novels too. But the increase of fiction writing among men was more marked. Unlike men, women never possessed the power to define the nature of good literature; when women served as critics, they displayed their internalization of male standards as universal standards. Men were in a position to invade the field of novel writing where women had once been prevalent. From 1840 through 1917 men made the high-culture novel their own.

We joined our question about the identification of high culture to another query: Why and how does an occupation shift from having a preponderance of female practitioners to being performed mainly by men? Thus, our solution to the mystery "Where have all the lady novelists gone?" has theoretical consequences in two fields: the sociology of occupations and that branch of historically oriented literary criticism termed "gynocriticism" (Showalter 1984). For scholars in the sociology of occupations, we have presented a rare "pure case," a social history of shifting gender-concentration in an occupation mainly occupied before, during, and after the social change by middle-class people of the same race, ethnicity, and (mostly) national origin. For literary critics, we have provided material with which to think anew about the relationship of a literary subculture to the dominant cultural tradition.

Occupational Gender Segregation

We hope that our study has contributed to sociological studies of occupational gender-segregation in five ways.

A pure case. First, those who study occupational gender-segregation rarely have historical data on shifts in occupations in which almost all the incumbents have been drawn from the same social class and racial and ethnic group before, during, and after the shift. Without a pure case as a yardstick, measuring the relative contributions of race, ethnicity, class, and other external factors to shifting occupational gender-concentration is difficult.[2]

Multicausation and a male invasion. Second, most studies of changing occupational gender-segregation concern the entry of women into fields once largely occupied by men. By and large, such studies identify de-skilling, frequently caused by new technologies, as a key factor in opening male-dominated fields to women. According to these studies, when new technologies change the nature of the work necessary to produce a good or service, a job pays less, and men decamp from it.[3] Such studies would predict the converse when a

2. Some sociologists seek to circumvent the lack of a yardstick by introducing multivariate statistical analyses that enable them to control for race, ethnicity, and class. Case studies such as those we have provided in our analyses of the Macmillan records and the *DNB* biographies facilitate generalizations over a lengthy period. Although the sorts of multivariate analyses to which we have referred may also be historical, they are exceedingly difficult to perform and so are rarely undertaken.

3. Epstein's (1981) book on lawyers is an exception. She argues that the women's movement and new civil rights legislation led to lawsuits against major law schools and law firms, which were forced to conform to the laws they taught and argued. For a splendid short review of American and British literature on women's occupations and technology, see Hochwald (1985).

job becomes more complex—that men will desire it and attempt to edge women out. But little research related to the gender segregation of occupations addresses the issue of how a job becomes more complex and whether increased complexity is related to what we have termed the empty field phenomenon. We have tried to demonstrate that technology alone does not cause a re-valuation of the worth of a specific sort of work (although new printing technologies did contribute to the expansion of the publishing industry). Rather, we have emphasized that social change occurs through a series of homologies. Industrialism, revised taxation rates for both paper and windows, increased social mobility, new publishers, new technologies, and revamped distribution systems all arose at the same time and for some of the same reasons, but they did not cause one another. Together they contributed to the development of the nineteenth-century novel. Together they contributed to changes in the opportunities for literary work available to women and men.

In part, we have argued, these changes worked through transformations of ideologies. We have stressed three complementary ideologies: one that defined the novel as an important cultural form by stressing different forms of realism, one that stressed the right of authors to control the conditions of their work and so to claim the status of professionals, and one that enabled the cultural elite to devalue novels by women.

None of these ideologies was static. Rather, each changed as both the practical conditions confronting authors and the middle-class views from which they drew sustenance were transformed. Take the matter of women's (and mothers') supposed inability to write good novels. To explain why Mrs. Oliphant "failed" to become a great writer, the *Edinburgh Review*'s critic Alexander I. Shand argued that good mothers cannot be great novelists. Unlike earlier critics, Shand did not claim that the biological act of giving birth absorbed women's creativity. Rather, his statements obviously drew on mid-dle-class Victorian notions about an idealized mother, for they emphasized the feelings that a good mother should have. (She should be emotionally preoccupied with her children.)

Shand failed to offer rationalizations outside of the experience or ob-servational ability of middle-class Victorian men. For instance, he did not stress how the sheer physical work that a mother must undertake to care for young children and her home saps time and energy, as twentieth-century author and single mother Tillie Olsen (1979) was to do. For a middle-class Victorian author would have had servants to do physical chores, including those associated with caring for children. Nor did Shand stress the complicated task of coordinating a household, including supervision of servants, for that aspect of the work of middle-class women was and remains ideologically invisible to men.[4]

Temporal direction. Third, dating social change is a tricky matter. Sociologists and historians have debated whether the social status and economic rewards of an occupation change before, after, or while women (or men) enter it and men (or women) depart. Their debate matters. A better understanding of the temporal order of shifts in occupational gender-segregation would facilitate policy interventions to integrate women and men into the same jobs. By describing the institutional context and associated ideologies that men used to edge women out of the high-culture novel, we have shown that in our "pure case" men invaded *after* the social and economic rewards of being a novelist had become clear. But despite men's domination of literature throughout the lengthy period that we have considered, institutionalization of men's claims to the high-culture novel was not rapid. Simply to stress the importance of male domination is to ignore the substantive processes through which this social change occurred.

A useful metaphor. Fourth, we have offered a central metaphor, the process of gentrification, to highlight the power of dominant groups to dismiss (or sometimes not to notice) those whom they are replacing. It also suggests some similarities between processes occurring in quite different social arenas. Thus, we have underscored a point stressed by Everett Hughes (1971) throughout his studies of work and occupations, education, and race and ethnicity: an important factor in sociological explanation is understanding how seemingly dissimilar phenomena share common elements. Through comparison, we hope we have dismantled the gloss *male domination* by stressing how it depends upon both institutional contexts and cultural perceptions of groups claiming a share in social space.[5]

Men controlled the relevant institutions; we have inferred that their perception that novel writing was an empty field contributed to their invasion. But men's control of key institutions and their perceptions of women's contributions and abilities do not provide a sufficient explanation of the empty field phenomenon, any more than white control of American society and whites' perceptions of blacks and other colored minorities are sufficient to explain institutionalized racism. The concept of domination remains a gloss.

---

4. The ideologies we examined were suited to dismissing the novels of women belonging to the same social class as the men who expressed them.

5. Ethnomethodologists (see Garfinkle 1967) use the term *gloss* to indicate that the use of a concept sometimes detracts from the substantive processes it encompasses.

In the case of the Victorian novel, invasion occurred after the Victorian system of producing and disseminating literature had fallen into place. We have described how those changes occurred through a series of homologies. The factors involved in gentrification are necessarily different from those involved in the transformation of occupations, but these changes occur through comparable processes.

In the case of gentrification, real-estate developers who control urban markets encourage rentals and home ownership in urban areas that they define as increasingly desirable, as occurred in London's Hackney and New York's Soho. When rising costs have prevented members of the middle class from obtaining homes in neighborhoods already established as middle class, they invade the neighborhoods that real estate developers are promoting. Americans tend to desire home ownership because of their wish to achieve the American dream—material "progress" from one generation to the next—by increasing their assets. If parents owned their own home, adult children should too. If parents did not, adult children may prove that America is the land of opportunity by doing so.

Gentrification also depends upon other desires of middle-class fractions whose life-styles have been shaped by new economic conditions. For instance, the national economy increasingly requires both husband and wife to work. Families in which both husband and wife work in urban centers may find commuting problematic and so desire more proximity to their jobs than the suburbs can provide.

Finally, gentrification also draws upon the social invisibility of the poor minorities being displaced. As Gans (1962) showed decades ago, their neighborhoods are perceived as slums even though they are communally organized in complex ways.

The delineation of process. Even when invasion and succession[6] occur quite rapidly, as they sometimes do in the case of gentrification, the process we have termed the empty field phenomenon goes through stages: invasion, redefinition, institutionalization. At every stage, the socially dominant group prevails. Al-

---

6. When the sociological literature discussed whites fleeing new black neighbors and the spector of an integrated neighborhood, it abandoned the term "invasion and succession" as racially pejorative. We have retained the term to emphasize the power of upper-class real estate developers and white middle-class homesteaders to displace blacks and other minorities when they choose to do so. We argue that blacks did not invade; whites fled. In the case of gentrification, minorities do not flee; they are driven out. We wish to retain similar connotations in the case of the Victorian novel. Women did not flee the occupation; they did not stop trying to be respected novelists. Rather, the value of their novels was dismissed.

though women novelists were prevalent in the early nineteenth century, they never prevailed. As a group they never had the power to define the nature of good literature.[7] They never controlled literary opportunities or the production and distribution systems. At best, they might have tried to ward off an invasion, seeking to retain what had been their jobs by submitting their novels. But warding off an invasion requires both economic power and socially validated cultural capital. Men, we have inferred from our data, have been able to take advantage of opportunities in ways that women have not. Within a social class and across neighboring social classes, gender is crucial to both achievement and the recognition of achievement. Women must do more to earn less.

Both the historical and the sociological literature about occupational gender-segregation caution against overgeneralization. In our effort to delineate stages of social processes, we have attempted to heed their warnings. Sociologists urge researchers to decompose social categories to avoid foolish errors. Since national statistics may indicate that men are overwhelmingly the practitioners of a particular job, people may speak about occupants of a particular job as men and so try to explain that job's "maleness." In decomposing national statistics into information about local labor markets, one sometimes learns that in some regions almost all of that job's incumbents are women. In each region the job is gender-segregated, but its maleness is suspect.

Statistically defined occupations, as well, often merit decomposition into their constituent titles. Take the occupation of clerical worker defined by the United States census. It has more incumbents than any other job defined in the census, mainly because it encompasses a variety of different kinds of secretaries, typists, stenographers, file clerks, word-processors, and other job titles. Inspecting data about local labor markets and about the internal labor markets of some large corporations, one discovers a complex pattern of class, racial, and ethnic segregation in many of these titles that is worthy of analysis.

We have tried to describe the job of author by examining its constituent occupations in labor markets across time. In both the eighteenth and the nineteenth century, incumbents of the job of author and of its constituent job novelist were drawn from "regional labor *pools*." But after 1840 one labor *market*, London, was dominant. (Edinburgh, Oxford, and Cambridge are partial exceptions.) Men of letters sought to work in London; novelists, to sell their work in London. Before 1840, when London was a regional market, women fared relatively well compared to men. When it became a national market,

---

7. Recall that in Austen's *Northanger Abbey* Catherine Morland talks about "novels" and Henry Tilney about "good novels."

we inferred, men gained relative to women. We suspect that nonelite and local labor markets may often offer women better opportunities than more prestigious and national markets do.[8]

Although in both periods men controlled the specialties that mattered most to gaining opportunities for themselves and others, men were not a unified group. Frequently, the interests of male publishers and male authors differed. The vested interests of some publishers were anathema to other publishers. But men controlled nonfiction. Through that control men who were associated with elite publishers and periodicals were able to define good fiction. They could also define the relative worth of poetry and fiction. Men's ability to define literary hierarchies may be loosely compared to how (male) doctors controlled (female) nurses before nonmedical (male) administrators assumed authority over both groups. Doctors defined how nurses were to perform their tasks—indeed, how all medical work was to be performed and assessed (Freidson 1971).

Occupations and occupational specialties are ordered hierarchically, as are literary specialties. Men established and delineated the ideologies assessing the relative worth of forms of imaginative literature. The success of men's attempts to have their ideologies accepted as verities was not inevitable. Nor was their success in challenging specific institutional configurations. We saw that Smith, Elder tried to challenge the hegemony of the circulating libraries before it was possible to do so. We suspect that other challenges are now hidden from history because a later generation did not bring them to fruition.

Throughout this book, we have tried to refine the gloss male domination and to identify its constituent processes. Although the historical situation is more complex than the term male domination can ever indicate, the term does express what we infer to be a historical truth: Elite men defined lasting literary culture.

Contributions to Literary Criticism

"Gynocritics" (see Showalter 1984b) have assumed that men control culture. But we suspect that they have not fully appreciated the extent and subtlety of that control and so have mistakenly insisted that in the nineteenth

8. Our hypothesis may be read as a variant of dual labor market explanations that stress that women and other minorities stand the best chance of employment in "peripheral" rather than "core" sectors of the economy. American Ivy League colleges are a partial exception to our rule. Until relatively recently, these elite colleges were a very closed local labor market.

century women writers came into their own. Critics have probably made this argument because they have based their generalizations on the biographies and texts of both canonized nineteenth-century women writers and women writers whose works were popular in their day but have fallen into disfavor.

Because we have examined information different from that usually analyzed by literary critics, we have offered a different story. Using the Macmillan records, we have been able to explore the fate of submitted manuscripts. Since most fiction was rejected, we could learned, by gender, who dared to seek a literary career. Using data derived from the *DNB* and the *BMC*, we inferred that, although some women had achieved sufficient renown to be listed in the *DNB*, women born after 1814 had to work harder than men to achieve less acclaim. We also inferred that men were better able to take advantage of opportunities to derive income as "men of letters" than women were.

Our findings suggest some contradictions in the story offered by gynocritics. Like any body of serious scholarship, gynocriticism contains inconsistencies. It suggests that in the Victorian period women writers belonged to a "literary subculture" and came into their own.[9] In the Victorian period women writers experienced an authorial crisis hidden in their texts but available to sophisticated explication. Let us review some of the central ideas in this tradition of literary scholarship.

Gynocritical theories. Historically oriented feminist literary criticism has asked what male control has meant for both the activities of women novelists and the evaluation of literature by women. One answer has been that women novelists have participated in a literary tradition distinct from that of men.

First, such gynocritics as Patricia Spacks and Ellen Moers sought to prove the existence of a women's literary tradition. They did so in slightly different ways. Spacks (1975,7) suggested that women's activities have historically been peripheral to or at least "slightly skewed" from those that preoccupy men. Differences in women's and men's preoccupations, she argued, have led to differences in their writings. Women displayed a "female imagination."

Moers (1976) traced continuities in the works of women novelists. In part, she argued, these were created by the tendency of women novelists to study one another's work. Additionally, Moers stressed, some women faced similar conditions when they tried to write and developed similar solutions

---

9. Showalter uses the term "subculture." We find this term problematic. On the concepts *culture* and *subculture*, see Swidler (1986).

to those problems. For instance, faced with the cultural norm that women should not write imaginative literature and also with their unavoidable responsibilities during the day, some eventually acclaimed women novelists wrote at night so that their families either might not know that they were trying to be authors or would not feel that their literary activities were detracting from their familial duties.

Second, gynocritics attempted to refine the theories describing women's literary tradition, for Spacks' and Moers' arguments are problematic. Showalter (1977) has identified some of these problems. She suggested that women's literary tradition has displayed historical discontinuities because of characteristics of the dominant literary tradition. Like other readers, women are primarily familiar with novels incorporated in the dominant cultural tradition. Because the mainstream literary tradition has tended to ignore novels by women, in each generation women have had to discover anew the existence of the female literary tradition. Furthermore, even when they have been familiar with this tradition, many women novelists have been loath to identify with other women writers. Like George Eliot, they have wanted to be judged as novelists, not as women novelists.[10]

Additionally, Showalter rejected Spacks' notion of an intrinsically "female" imagination. She found that this notion smacked of the common stereotypes about women authors in its assumption that gender transcends social class and historical circumstances; that is, it suggests that across historical periods novels by women have more in common with one another than with novels by men of their own period. We, too, find this assumption flawed. All women in all historical periods simply do not share life circumstances; indeed, there are significant differences among women in any period.

Recognizing continuities among women, Showalter (1977, 13) offered a different solution to understanding women's literary tradition. Her solution addressed the relationship between women's literary tradition and the dom-

---

10. Eliot decried the quality of "silly novels by lady novelists." Showalter (1977, 12) described the unwillingness of women to identify with other women as "self-hatred." However, that term implies that women novelists *should* identify with other women novelists. Although as feminists we believe that women should understand and be sympathetic to the conditions and problems other women confront, we know that they often do not identify with other women. Drawn from different class fractions, racial and ethnic groups, women face very different life situations that may prevent them from sympathetically understanding one another. Because of her liaison with George Lewes, many middle-class Victorian women were critical of Eliot. Why should she be sympathetic to those who seemed to accept the norms used to ostracize her? Furthermore, we do not believe that in all historical periods women novelists want or should want to be judged as women writers. See Showalter (1984a).

inant tradition. She argued that in every period women were responsive to the main cultural tradition of their age, but their orientation toward it changed. Thus, she argued, from 1840 through 1880 women's novels were "feminine." They imitated "the prevailing modes of the dominant tradition" and internalized "its standards of art and its views of social roles." From 1880 through 1920 women's cultural tradition was "feminist." It protested "against those standards and values" and advocated "minority rights and values, including autonomy." Finally, from 1920 through 1960 it was "female." This phase involved "self-discovery, a turning inward freed from some of the dependency of opposition, a search for identity."[11]

But, concentrating on the expression, subversion, and transformation of ideas as ideas, Showalter did not explain *why* women's orientation changed from one period to the next. She did not delineate changes in the material conditions of all novelists, including men, that might have been associated with changes in both the dominant literary tradition and the orientation of women writers to that changing tradition. Rather, Showalter committed the common error: she assumed that despite male control of literature nineteenth-century women were coming into their own as professional authors.

Third, in order to uncover previously hidden psychological themes prompted by men's control of literary traditions, gynocritics addressed the women's literary tradition with the most respected weapons of male literary criticism. Drawing on Harold Bloom's notion of the "anxiety of influence," Sandra Gilbert and Susan Gubar (1979) attempted to describe the psychological tension supposedly experienced by all women writers of the late eighteenth and the nineteenth centuries. Bloom's theory was originally intended to apply to the problems of originality confronted by American male writers (see Baym 1985). Gilbert and Gubar argued that rather than experience an anxiety of influence, as men supposedly do, "already canonized nineteenth-century women writers" (Baym 1984a, 47) suffered an "anxiety of authorship" personified by a recurrent figure in their texts, the madwoman in the attic. This inarticulate figure served as the author's "double."

Although it is infused with psychological insights about a historical period, Gilbert and Gubar's work offers a self-contained interpretation invalidated by historical evidence. Baym (1984a, 47) criticized it by arguing,

> "The anxiety of authorship" ... is advanced as a historical concept, a fruitfully accurate description of the state of literature and attitudes toward it in a particular place at a particular time. But though advanced

11. Showalter recognized that her phases overlap. There are novels of each sort in each period and some women wrote novels in each of Showalter's classifications.

as a historical fact, the anxiety of authorship—except for Emily Dickinson—is demonstrated only by intra-textual evidence; thus *The Madwoman in the Attic* assumes the existence of the historical and literary situation which its textual readings require. Strikingly absent from the consideration of the historical moment is the appearance among women of a realizable ambition to become professional writers. Traditionally hermeneutic, Gilbert and Gubar concentrate on a hidden message—female anxiety of authorship—while reading past the surface evidence that their studied texts provide for the arrival of the woman professional author.[12]

In sum, during the Victorian era, the woman novelist had and had not "arrived."

Rethinking gynocriticism. Our findings cannot address the existence of a women's literary tradition; our data do not concern literary themes. But our findings may help to explain how women writers appeared to have come into their own, how women may nonetheless have suffered an anxiety of authorship, and how women's cultural tradition both drew on and differed from the dominant culture.

The first issue, the coexistence of the anxiety of authorship with women's increased prominence as authors, is relatively simple. The surface of a text may coexist with a contradictory subtext, much as in daily interactions a speaker's hostile body language may contradict her or his friendly words. An author may satisfy a variety of criteria deemed to indicate success and still experience the anxiety of authorship. Conversely, a writer may experience both financial and critical success, as George Eliot did, without feeling the authority of authorship. As Gilbert and Gubar define it, the anxiety of authorship arose because even the most esteemed women novelists had internalized the critical double standard expressed in variant forms during the eighteenth and nineteenth centuries. Although women wrote and wrote well, they knew that the cultural elite of their day insisted that women could not write as men did and should not even try.

Additionally, even though many women writers were successful, they were occupying an embattled field. In the early Victorian period, men were either dismissing their work as merely birdsong or dismissing their femininity. Later, men based their criticism on different criteria but nonetheless continued to dismiss their work or the meaning of their lives. Publications by other

---

12. In these comments on Gilbert and Gubar, Baym produced a variant of the error she criticized. She, too, made an unfounded historical assumption: like most other critics, she assumed that nineteenth-century authors were professionals.

women may have served as scant reassurance that women could write well, when their novels were damned or treated with critical condescension. Sheer numbers would not have been sufficient to allay the anxiety of authorship as described by Gilbert and Gubar.

The second issue, the relationship of women's literary tradition to the dominant tradition, is more complex. We believe that women fared best *before* the cultural elite defined the novel as an important genre. Particularly in the 1840s and 1850s, when novels by women helped to protest industrial conditions and to define the nature of community in an industrial age, women novelists flourished. Women published novels; many of them sold well and were widely read; some of them were critically praised as the work of women novelists.

The very success of women novelists helped to ratify the male critical judgment that the novel was an important genre. In the 1840s and 1850s the success of women also helped to spawn the rampant birdsong criticism that considered "the woman writer" in order to dismiss her potential contribution to the dominant culture. Women novelists' success in a genre increasingly deemed valuable created the impetus for men to edge them out.

We believe that women generally fare best *before* men have fully perceived the social and economic value of women's endeavors and so *before* men set standards and establish practices that formally exclude women. Once men have redefined a field as work for which they are better suited than women, most women will occupy at best provisional status.[13] Some may be invited as dinner guests, but all are excluded from membership.

Exceptions may be made. The work of some late nineteenth-century and early twentieth-century women was esteemed in its time and is still esteemed. Virginia Woolf is the perennial example of such an exception. But in general, as our analysis of the biographies in the *DNB* indicated, exceptions are rare. Once men have defined a field as important, women must do more and more to achieve less recognition than men, as was the case of the late women in our sample.

Our findings tend to confirm Showalter's delineation of the phases of a woman's literary culture. We have suggested some institutional transformations associated with these shifts. We deduced from the Macmillan data that during the period that Showalter identified as the "feminine phase" (between 1840 and 1880) men began to invade the novel. She indicated that during this phase, women imitated "the prevailing modes of the dominant

13. This generalization applies to several occupations, including movie director and computer programmer.

tradition" and internalized "its standards of art and its views of social roles." We inferred from our data that imitation did not prevent invasion. To the contrary, imitation might have *encouraged* invasion by suggesting to men that since they could be innovative, they might excel. Once critics began to emphasize that the novel might serve as a vehicle for the development of ideas, men's supposedly greater capacity for excellence seemed to promise a brilliant future for individual male novelists.

Showalter (1977) identified a second or "feminist" phase of the women's literary tradition, extending from 1880 through 1920. She suggested that it protested "against [the dominant] standards and values" and advocated "minority rights and values, including autonomy." We showed that during this period, men were also protesting mid-Victorian standards and mid-Victorian publishers' practices. They did so in the context of a changing publishing and distribution system. By the late 1880s the three-decker novel was no longer profitable. In the 1890s Mudie's Select Library abandoned it.

But men did not include women novelists in their protests. Why should they have? For from 1888 through 1917 we found that men were taking over the high-culture novel. Men redefined the nature of a good novel and institutionalized their gains. Critics identified women as outsiders. As in earlier periods, women who published criticism in the major literary journals expressed ideas upholding male critical standards as universal standards. Those standards gradually changed. Partially abandoning birdsong criticism, critics saw dissonant construction in women's work, not art.

Furthermore, men had no reason to admit women to their networks; women were attacking their power. Feminist novels decried the very social system, including the "universal" literary standards that men were establishing. Showalter (1977, 193–194) put it this way: "[The feminist writers] knew very clearly what they were *against*, but only vaguely what they were *for*. [They] were engaged in the kind of quarrel that, according to Yeats, leads to rhetoric but not poetry. Thus the writers of this period... have not fared well with posterity." To (re)admit women to the dominant literary tradition would have meant "devaluing" the novel that men had recently claimed as their own prestigious enterprise.[14]

We cannot prove that the institutional transformations we have discussed caused the phases that Showalter delineated, but they are associated with these phases. The congruence between our findings and Showalter's ideas is

14. Showalter cites Olive Schreiner as one of the feminist authors who did not fare well with posterity. During this period, Macmillan rejected Schreiner's problematic second novel as "ideological."

not fortuitous, for we drew heavily on Showalter's *A Literature of Their Own* when we developed ways of coding our data, defining literary periods, and analyzing nineteenth-century criticism.

But we do believe that our research has helped to explain nineteenth-century critics' formulation of the great literary tradition. By defining how men might have perceived the novel as an empty field and then acted on their perception, we have offered a new understanding of the dominant cultural tradition with which and against which the women's cultural tradition has defined itself.

We have stressed that authors are not professionals. Novelists do not define the nature of their work. Critics do, although in the nineteenth century, as is true today, some novelists were also critics. Authors do not control entrance to and departure from their occupation. Publishers do. Authors do not define how they will get paid. Publishers do, by defining markets, acceptable profit margins, and their own orientations toward production and consumption—whether they will seek long-term or short-term profits and novels that will be a critical or financial success. Like the readers whom they conceptualize as markets, publishers are stratified.

To understand the position of women authors, one must situate both male and female authors historically. One must understand, too, the stratified publishing and distribution system that some men created and that confronted women and other men who wrote. One must examine the processes through which elite men have defined universal culture. To say that men create culture does not suffice.

Some Speculations

We know how some of the activities of some men edged women out of writing the high-culture novel. But we cannot provide a documented answer to the question, "Where did all the lady novelists go?" Perhaps some talented middle-class women abandoned the novel for emerging empty fields and so made room for men to compete successfully against less able women authors. Our data do not enable us to determine the merit of this possibility. But it is a possibility. Vicinus (1985) carefully documents how communities of single women opened such new fields as higher education for women, nursing, and work in settlement houses. In the late nineteenth century many middle-class women also turned to social activism, including feminism. Had these new opportunities not been available, perhaps some of them might have become novelists.

Some women novelists born relatively early in the century shared backgrounds and political concerns with activists born somewhat later. The lives and activities of Elizabeth Gaskell, born in 1810, and Josephine Butler, born in 1824, are pertinent. Both were from religious middle-class backgrounds, and they had similar political beliefs.

Mrs. Gaskell's novels are infused with political concerns, including the position of women in Victorian society. *Mary Barton* revolves around the plight of farm laborers once they have become members of the industrial proletariat. *North and South* pits understandings of class relationships developed in England's industrial north against those of the agricultural south. Although its ending affirms Victorian morality, *Ruth* deplores the severe social punishment of an unmarried woman who bears a child. *Cranford* revolves around the plight of genteel unmarried ladies. Although with her husband, a Unitarian minister, Mrs. Gaskell tried to alleviate the problems of prostitution and poverty in England's industrial north, in her novels she "exposed . . . social evil, not from any expert knowledge of its causes or . . . its remedies, but from the purely human standpoint of pity for an individual case" (Gérin 1980, 41).

Mrs. Butler's life was infused with political concerns, especially feminism. Whereas Mrs. Gaskell "intervened in social life via the novel, Mrs. Butler intervened via political action" (Mary Evans 1987b). Perhaps as the nineteenth century wore on and Victorian women were "increasingly able to participate in social and intellectual life in general . . . they didn't, in a sense, *need* to write novels (after all, a private, enclosed and isolated activity) because they could enter the public world—or, at any rate, a small corner of it" (ibid.).

Perhaps some women turned to social action to prove themselves as "serious people—just as [some] men defined the novel in certain ways in order to legitimate writing and publishing as 'serious' occupations for bourgeois men." Our data supported these inferences about men. Evans (ibid.) suggests, "If we put these two things together—women 'disappearing' and men getting more exclusive about the novel—we might find the two [genders] doing the same thing, that is, turning their backs on affectivity and works of the imagination as the 'proper' concern of good bourgeois people. The novel becomes, therefore, transformed into serious reading so men can write it, and women—or talented, potentially literary women—desert fiction for 'real' life." She continues, "The iron law, the iron pen, and the iron fist of bureaucratic industrial capitalism are thus such as to limit works of the imagination for *both* [genders]. . . . Virginia Woolf is then significant because [she] defie[d] that central demand of serious bourgeois fiction—that it be realist" (ibid.). What we can safely infer is that during the nineteenth century, sometimes subtly and sometimes blatantly, elite men defined the high-culture novel and made it their own.

Appendix A
The Samples

Sampling problems often tell researchers about the topic they are studying. The challenges presented by the Macmillan Archives and the *Dictionary of National Biography* (*DNB*) confirm this general rule.

The Macmillan Archives capture characteristics of the publishing industry. They portray the growth of the publishing industry, including the increase in aspiring authors. Additionally, they affirm that the submission of manuscripts is somewhat seasonal. In some months Victorian publishers received more manuscripts than in others, just as today's academic journals report increased submissions during or immediately after college vacations, when professors have more time to write. Victorian publishers received more manuscripts on some topics during some months; for instance, Victorian authors familiar with the publication schedules used by many firms were likely to submit Christmas stories in the fall than in the spring.

To draw quickly a sufficiently large sample, Tuchman would have had either to sample (1) every "xth" manuscript from November 1866 through 1917, (2) the first 350 manuscripts in systematically selected years, or (3) every manuscript in specified entire years, enlarging the number of years sampled when in the chosen year Macmillan received relatively few submissions, as occurred in 1867 and 1877. The first method would have overrepresented the later decades; the second might have overrepresented some months. So Tuchman chose the third method.

Pseudonyms presented another problem. Fortunately, pseudonyms rarely appeared in these archives. We indentified the names of all but one of those pseudonymous authors using Halkett and Laing's (1971) *Dictionary of Anonymous Literature, A Biographic Catalogue of Macmillan and Company's Publications from 1843 to 1889* (1891), and the *Catalogue of the British Museum* (*BMC*). These last two reference books also helped us to identify mistakes in coding the genres of manuscripts and to learn that we had made few errors.

The sampling problems encountered working with the *DNB* were also revelatory. First, the *DNB* listed many men but few women. Thus, to amass enough cases we needed to identify the universe of women and to select a sample of men. This procedure has consequences for our analyses; we could not include standard tests of statistical significance. These tests permit one to generalize from a sample to the population (or "universe") from which it was drawn, but although the men were a sample the women we had identified were the universe.

Second, we had to decide how to choose the biographies we would code for later analysis. We decided to make our *DNB* sample as comparable as possible to the aspiring authors who had submitted manuscripts to Macmillan and Company. Most of the aspiring Macmillan authors had not written for a living. Thus, we determined to include in the *DNB* sample people who were not simply authors but rather who during their lives had published at least one piece of imaginative literature. In chapter 5 we discuss some of the consequences of that decision.

Using the indices to every volume of the *DNB*, we located the name of every woman who had her own listing in those tomes. We then read each biography to learn whether during her lifetime a woman had published any imaginative literature. We were also guided by the identification of the woman. Thus, originally, if the *DNB* listed a woman as someone whose "verses" had been published, we included her in our sample. This decision was also to have consequences, explained below.

We then had to devise a method to sample the men without reading every entry in the *DNB*. To do so, we added the total number of pages in the first 21 volumes and 2 supplements of the *DNB* and divided by 267 (the number of women we had found). Next, we leafed through each of the resulting 267 page spans until we found a man who met the qualifications we had applied to women. We continued this procedure until we had selected 267 men.

We then examined more closely the women and men whom we had selected and discovered that several women whom the *DNB* identified as "versifiers" were actually hymn writers and lyricists. There were no comparable men in our sample. Thus, we decided to reject any woman whose only writing had been words for music, although we accepted one woman, Jean Glover, described as a poetess whose work Robert Burns had put to music. This criterion eliminated several other women. Either too few men had been lyricists for one to fall in our sample or men who were lyricists did something more purely literary as well. As we gathered more information, we discovered that several other women whom we had originally included did not truly meet our criteria, and so they were discarded, too. All told, we discarded seven women. They could not be replaced, since we had already collected the names of all the women who qualified for the sample.

Because the statistical analyses we planned to execute did not require the same number of women and men and because our sampling procedure had been based on page spans, we retained a sample size of 267 for the men. Whenever we discovered that one of the men did not really qualify for the sample, we returned to the page span from which he had been drawn and took the next man who seemed to qualify. We had no problem locating replacements.

Many of our analyses, however, especially those in chapter 6, use fewer than 260 women and 267 men. Once we had specified periods to incorporate in the analyses, we learned that a greater proportion of the women than men would not be included in them, because women's biographies were more likely than men's to be vague about an author's year of birth. Thus, the initial analyses of the *DNB* biographies reported in chapter 5 consider 245 women and 262 men. Other analyses in chapter 5 are based on information about fewer authors because many biographies lacked pertinent details. Again, the *DNB* tended to report more details about the lives of men than those of women. Still more women were eliminated from the regression equations, either because we could not locate them in the *BMC* or because the number of novels or nonfiction they had published lay outside of the general pattern indicated by scattergrams. (These scattergrams plotted the amount of authors' fame against the number of books published in specific genres.)

All told, then, we started with information about 534 authors, used data about 270 women and 276 men, worked with information about 245 early and late women and 263 early and late men, included a higher proportion of the men than the women in some tabular analyses because of the pattern of missing information, and included 235 women and 241 men in the initial regression equations reported in chapter 6. As we argue was true of women's literary reputations, women were more likely than men to "disappear."

Sociological studies usually present statistics on the reliability of the coding. These are obtained by computing agreements and differences among people coding the same material. When we developed our code and trained coders, we calculated these statistics for our own use. Because at least three and as many as five of us worked at the same library table, we held group discussions of problematic coding decisions. Although we took frequent breaks, our work sessions were lengthy, and everyone made mistakes on seemingly nonproblematic items. The coder who made the fewest errors checked every protocol except those she had originally completed. The coder with the next fewest errors checked protocols that the best coder had originally completed. Again everyone discussed problematic items.

The *DNB* Sample

The indexes of the twenty-three volumes of the *DNB* use varying styles of citation from volume to volume. We have preserved all inconsistencies, citing each name as it appears in the index of the volume in which the author's biography appears and including pseudonyms here only when they appear in the index.

* Scored 4 on the Fame Index
† Scored 3 on the Fame Index
‡ Excluded from regression equations because the number of fiction or nonfiction publications lay well off the scatterplot for his or her group (see chapter 6)

Acton, Eliza (1799–1859)

Adams, Sarah Flower (1805–1848)

Alexander, Mrs. See Hector, Mrs. Annie French (1825–1902)

Aguilar, Grace (1816–1847)

Aikin, Lucy (1781–1864)

Alexander, Mrs. Cecil Frances (1818–1895)

Anspach, Elizabeth, Margravine of (1750–1828)

Arblay, Frances (Burney), Madame d' (1752–1840)*

Austen, Jane (1775–1817)†

Baillie, Joanna (1762–1851)†

Baillie, Marianne (1795?–1830)

Balfour, Clara Lucas (1808–1878)

Banks, Isabella, known as Mrs. Linnaeus Banks (1821–1897)

Bannerman, Anne (d. 1829)

Bartholomew, Ann Charlotte (d. 1862)

Barwell, Louisa Mary (1800–1885)

Bather, Lucy Elizabeth (1836–1864) known as Aunt Lucy

Baxter, Lucy, 'Leader Scott' (1837–1902)

Bayly, Ada Ellen, 'Edna Lyall' (1857–1903)

Benger, Elizabeth Ogilvy (1778–1827)

Bennett, Agnes Marie (d. 1808)

Berry, Mary (1763–1852)

Betham, Mary Matilda (1776–1852)

Blessington, Marguerite, Countess of (1789–1849)†

Blind, Mathilde (1841–1896)

Bowdler, Henrietta Maria (1754–1830)

Brand, Barbarina, Lady Dacre (1768–1854)

Brand, Hannah (d. 1821)

Bray, Anna Eliza (1790–1883)

Brightwell, Cecilia Lucy (1811–1875)

Broderip, Frances Freeling (1830–1878)

Brontë, Charlotte (1816–1855), afterwards Nicholls†

Burney, Fanny. See Arblay, Madame d'

Browning, Elizabeth Barrett (1806–1861)†

Brunton, Mary (1778–1818)

Bulmer, Agnes (1775–1836)

Burges, Mary Anne (1763–1813)

Burney, Sarah Harriet (1770?–1844)

Burrell, Sophia, Lady (1750–1802)

Bury, Lady Charlotte Susan M. (1775–1861)

Buxton, Bertha H. (1844–1881)

Cadell, Jessie (1844–1884)

Callcott, Maria, Lady (1785–1842)

Calvert, Caroline Louisa Waring [Louisa Atkinson] (1834–1872)

Cameron, Julia Margaret (1815–1879)

Cameron, Lucy Lyttelton (1781–1858)

Campbell, Harriette (1817–1841)

Carey, Rosa Nouchette (1840–1909)

Carne, Elizabeth Catherine Thomas (1817–1873)

Cartwright, Frances Dorothy (1780–1863)

Chapman, Mary Francis (1838–1884)

Charles, Mrs. Elizabeth (1828–1896)†

Charlesworth, Maria Louisa (1819–1880)

Chatelain, Clara de, née de Potigny (1807–1876)

Chatterton, Henrietta Georgiana Marcia Lascelles, Lady (1806–1876)

Clarke, Mary Victoria Cowden (1809–1898)†

Clive, Caroline (1801–1873)

Cobbold, Elizabeth (1767–1824)

Coleridge, Mary Elizabeth (1861–1907)

Coleridge, Sara (1802–1852)

Cook, Eliza (1818–1889)

Corner, Julia (1798–1875)

Costello, Louisa Stuart (1799–1870)

Craik, Mrs. Dinah Maria (1826–1887). See Mulock

Craven, Elizabeth, Countess of (1750–1828). See Anspach, Elizabeth, Margravine of

Craven, Mrs. Pauline Marie Armande Algae (1808–1891)†

Crewdson, Jane (1808–1863)

Cross, Mary Ann (1819–1880), 'George Eliot'*

Crowe, Catherine (1800?–1876)

Currie, Mary Montgomerie, Lady Currie, 'Violet Fane' (1843–1905)

Davidson, Harriet Miller (1839–1883)

De la Ramée, Marie Louise, 'Ouida' (1839–1908)

Dilke, Emilia Frances Strong, Lady Dilke (1840–1904)†

Dixie, Lady Florence Caroline (1857–1905)

Dorset, Catherine Ann (1750?–1817?)

Drane, Augusta Theodosia (1823–1894)

Eastlake, Elizabeth, Lady (1809–1893)

Eaton, Mrs. Charlotte Ann (1788–1855). See Waldie

Ebsworth, Mary Emma (1794–1881)

Edgeworth, Maria (1767–1849)*

Edwards, Amelia Ann Blanford (1831–1892)

Eliot, George, pseudonym. See Cross, Mary Ann (1819–1880)

Elliott, Charlotte (1789–1871)

Ewing, Juliana Horatia (1841–1885)

Falconer, Lanoe, pseudonym. See Hawker, Mary Elizabeth (1848–1908)

Fane, Violet, pseudonym. See Currie, Mary Montgomerie, Lady (1843–1905)

Fanshawe, Catherine Maria (1765–1834)

Farningham, Marianne, pseudonym. See Hearn, Mary Anne (1834–1909)

Fletcher, Mrs. Maria Jane (1780–1833). See Jewsbury

Ferrier, Susan Edmonstone (1782–1854)

Fothergill, Jessie (1851–1891)

Franklin, Eleanor Ann (1797?–1825)

Frere, Mary Eliza Isabella (1845–1911)

Fry, Caroline (1787–1846). See Wilson

Fullerton, Lady Georgiana Charlotte (1812–1885)

Gardiner, Marguerite, Countess of Blessington (1789–1849). See Blessington

Gardner, Mrs. (*fl.* 1763–1782)

Gaskell, Elizabeth Cleghorn (1810–1865)*

Gatty, Margaret (1809–1873)

Gerard, [Jane] Emily, Madame de Laszowska (1849–1905)

Gilbert, Mrs. Ann (1782–1866)

Gilchrist, Anne (1828–1885)

Glover, Jean (1758–1801)

Godwin, Mrs. Catherine Grace (1798–1845)

Godwin, Mrs. Mary Wollstonecraft (1759–1797)*

Gore, Mrs. Catherine Grace Frances (1799–1861)

Gosse, Emily (1806–1857)

Graham, Clementina Stirling (1782–1877)

Grant, Anne (1755–1838)

Green, Mrs. Eliza S. Craven (1803–1866)

Greenwell, Dora (1821–1882)

Grey, Mrs. Maria Georgina whose maiden name was Shirreff (1816–1906)

Guyton, Mrs. Emma Jane (1825–1887). See Worboise

Hack, Maria (1777–1844)

Hall, Anna Maria (1800–1881)

Hamilton, Elizabeth (1758–1816)

Hamilton, Janet (1795–1873)

Harding, Mrs. Anne Raikes (1780–1858)

Hardy, Elizabeth (1794–1854)

Hardy, Mary Anne, Lady (1825?–1891)

Harries, Margaret (1787–1846). See Wilson, Mrs. Cornwell Baron

Harrison, Susannah (1752–1784)

Harvey, Margaret (1768–1858)

Harwood, Isabella (1840?–1888)

Havergal, Frances Ridley (1836–1879)

Hawker, Mary Elizabeth, writing under the pseudonym of Lanoe Falconer (1848–1908)

Hawkins, Susanna (1787–1868)

Hay, Mary Cecil (1840?–1886)

Hearn, Mary Anne, 'Marianne Farningham' (1834–1909)

Hector, Mrs. Annie French, writing as Mrs. Alexander (1825–1902)

Hemans, Felicia Dorothea (1793–1835)*

Hodson, Mrs. Margaret (1778–1852)

Hoey, Mrs. Frances Sarah, 'Mrs. Cashell Hoey' (1830–1908)

Hofland, Barbara (1770–1844)

Howitt, Mary (1799–1888)

Hungerford, Mrs. Margaret Wolfe (1855?–1897)

Hunter, Rachel (1754–1813)

Hutton, Catherine (1756–1846)

Inchbald, Elizabeth (1753–1821)[†]

Inglis, Mrs. Margaret Maxwell (1774–1843)

Jenkin, Henrietta Camilla (1807?–1885)

Jevons, Mary Anne (1795–1845)

Jewsbury, Geraldine Endsor (1812–1880)

Jewsbury, Maria Jane afterwards Mrs. Fletcher (1800–1853)

Johnstone, Christian Isobel (1781–1857)

Kavanagh, Julia (1824–1877)

Keary, Annie (1825–1879)

Kelty, Mary Ann (1789–1873)

Kemble, Frances Ann. Afterwards Mrs. Butler, generally known as Fanny Kemble (1809–1893)

Kennedy, Grace (1782–1825)

Kingsford, Mrs. Anna (1846–1888)

Kirby, Elizabeth (1823–1873)

Knight, Ellis Cornelia (1757–1837)

Knox, Mrs. Isa, born Craig (1831–1903)

Lamb, Lady Caroline (1785–1828)

Landon, Letitia Elizabeth afterwards Mrs. Maclean (1802–1838)

Leadbeater, Mary (1758–1826)

Laszowska, Mme. de. See Gerard, Emily (1846–1905)

Lee, Harriet (1757–1851)

Lee, Holme. See Parr, Harriet (1828–1900)

Lee, Mrs. Sarah (1791–1856)

Lee, Sophia (1750–1824)

LeNoir, Elizabeth Anne (1755?–1841)

Levy, Amy (1861–1889)

Linskill, Mary (1840–1891)

Linton, Eliza Lynn (1822–1898)

Long, Lady Catharine (d. 1867)

Longworth, Maria Theresa (1832?–1881)

Loudon, Jane (1807–1858)

Lyall, Edna, pseudonym. See Bayly, Ada Ellen (1857–1903)

Lynch, Theodora Elizabeth (1812–1885)

Lyon, Mrs. Agnes (1762–1840)

Mackarness, Mrs. Matilda Anne (1826–1881)

Mackellar, Mary (1834–1890)

Manners, Mrs. Catherine, afterwards Lady Stepney (*d.* 1845). See Stepney

Manning, Anne (1807–1879)

Marcet, Mrs. Jane (1769–1858)

Markham, Mrs. See Penrose, Elizabeth (1780–1837)

Marryat, Florence, successively Mrs. Church and Mrs. Lean (1838–1899)

Marsh-Caldwell, Mrs. Anne (1791–1874)

Marshall, Emma (1830–1897)‡

Martin, Mary Letitia (1815–1850)

Martineau, Harriet (1802–1876)†

Meeke, Mrs. Mary (*d.* 1816?)

Menken, Adah Isaacs, formerly Adelaide McCord (1835–1868)

Meteyard, Eliza (1816–1879)

Miles, Sibella Elizabeth (1800–1882)

Miller, Mrs. Lydia Falconer (1811?–1876)

Mitford, Mary Russell (1787–1855)†

Morgan, Sydney, Lady (1783–1859)†

Montgomery, Jemima (1807–1893). See Tautphoeus, Baroness von

Mulock, Dinah Maria, afterwards Mrs. Craik (1826–1887)

Naden, Constance Caroline Woodhill (1858–1889)

Norton, Caroline Elizabeth Sarah (1808–1877)

O'Brien, Charlotte Grace (1845–1909)

O'Leary, Ellen (1831–1889)

Oliphant, Margaret Oliphant (1828–1897)

O'Meara, Kathleen (1839–1888)

Opie, Mrs. Amelia (1769–1853)†

Owenson, Miss Sydney (1783?–1859). See Morgan, Sydney, Lady

Pagan, Isobel (*d.* 1821)

Palmer, Alicia Tinda (*fl.* 1810)

Ouida, pseudonym. See De la Ramée, Marie Louise (1839–1908)

Pardoe, Julia (1806–1862)

Parker, Emma (*fl.* 1811)

Parr, Harriet (1828–1900), pseudonym 'Holme Lee'

Parr, Mrs. Louisia (*d.* 1903)

Parsons, Mrs. Eliza (*d.* 1811)

Parsons, Mrs. Gertrude (1812–1891)

Peacock, Lucy (*fl.* 1815)

Penrose, Mrs. Elizabeth (1780–1837), writer under the pseudonym of Mrs. Markham

Pfeiffer, Emily Jane (1827–1890)

Pickering, Ellen (*d.* 1843)

Pilkington, Mary (1766–1839)

Plumptre, Miss Anna or Anne (1760–1818)

Ponsonby, Lady Emily Charlotte Mary (1817–1877)

Porter, Anna Maria (1780–1832)

Porter, Jane (1776–1850)†

Power, Miss Marguerite A. (1815?–1867)

Price, Ellen (1814–1887). See Wood

Procter, Adelaide Ann (1825–1864)

Puddicombe, Mrs. Anne Adalisa, writing under the pseudonum of 'Allen Raine' (1836–1908)

Radcliffe, Ann (1764–1823)*

Raine, Allen, pseudonym. See Puddicombe, Mrs. Anne Adalisa (1836–1908)

Ramée, Mary Louise ('Ouida'). See De la Ramée

Ranyard, Ellen Henrietta (1810–1879)

Rathbone, Hannah Mary (1798–1878)

Richardson, Charlotte Caroline (1775–1850)

Riddell, Mrs. Charlotte Eliza Lawson, known as Mrs. J. H. Riddell (1832–1906)

Roberts, Emma (1794?–1840)

Roberts, Mary (1788–1864)

Robinson, Mary (1758–1800), known as 'Perdita'*†

Roche, Mrs. Regina Maria (1764?–1845)

Romer, Isabella Frances (d. 1852)

Rossetti, Christina Georgina (1830–1894)[†]

Rowson, Susanna (1762–1824)

Ryves, Elizabeth (1750–1797)

Saffery, Mrs. Maria Grace (1772–1858)

Sale-Barker, Lucy Elizabeth Drummond Davies (1841–1892)

Scott, Caroline Lucy, Lady Scott (1784–1857)

Scott, Harriet Anne, Lady Scott (1819–1894)

Sergeant, Adeline (1851–1904)

Sewell, Elizabeth Missing (1815–1906)[†]

Sewell, Mary (1797–1884)

Shelley, Mary Wollstonecraft (1797–1851)[†]

Sheppard, Elizabeth Sara (1830–1862)

Sheridan, Mrs. Caroline Henrietta (1779–1851)

Sheridan, Helen Selina, afterwards successively Mrs. Blackwood, Lady Dufferin and Countess of Gifford (1807–1867)

Sherwood, Mary Martha (1775–1851)[‡]

Shore, Louisa Catherine (1824–1895)

Simpson, Mrs. Jane Cross (1811–1886)

Sinclair, Catharine (1800–1864)

Skene, Felicia Mary Frances (1821–1899)

Smith, Elizabeth (1776–1806)

Smith, Sarah, writing under the pseudonym 'Hesba Stratton' (1832–1911)

Southey, Mrs. Caroline Anne (1786–1854)

Spence, Elizabeth Isabella (1768–1832)

Spender, Lily, usually known as Mrs. John Kent Spender (1835–1895)

Stannard, Mrs. Henrietta Eliza Vaughan, writing under the pseudonym of 'John Strange Winter' (1856–1911)

Stretton, Hesba, pseudonym. See Smith, Sarah (1832–1911)

Stepney, Catherine, Lady (d. 1845)

Strickland, Agnes (1796–1874)

Stuart-Wortley, Lady Emmeline Charlotte Elizabeth (1806–1855)

Tautphoeus, Baroness von, originally Jemima Montgomery (1807–1893)

Taylor, Jane (1783–1824)

Taylor, Louisa (d. 1903). See Parr, Mrs. Louisa

Thomson, Katharine (1797–1862)

Tighe, Mrs. Mary (1772–1810)

Toulmin, Camilla Dufour, afterwards Mrs. Newton Crosland (1812–1895)

Trench, Melesina (1768–1827)

Trollope, Frances (1780–1863)

Tucker, Charlotte Maria (1821–1893)

Veley, Margaret (1843–1887)

Wakefield, Mrs. Priscilla (1751–1832)

Waldie, Charlotte Ann, afterwards Mrs. Eaton (1788–1859)

Waring, Anna Letitia (1823–1910)

Webster, Mrs. Augusta (1837–1894)

West, Jane (1758–1852)

Williams, Helen Maria (1762–1827)

Williams, Jane (1795–1873)

Wilson, Mrs. Caroline (1787–1846)

Wilson, Mrs. Cornwell Baron, whose maiden name was Margaret Harries (1797–1896)

Winter, John Strange, pseudonym. See Stannard, Mrs. Henrietta Eliza Vaughan (1856–1911)

Wollstonecraft, Mary (1759–1797). See Godwin, Mrs. Mary Wollstonecraft

Wood, Ellen (1814–1887), better known as Mrs. Henry Wood

Woodrooffe, Mrs. Anne (1766–1830)

Worboise, Emma Jane, afterwards Mrs. Guyton (1825–1887)

Yearsley, Mrs. Ann (1756–1806)

Yonge, Charlotte Mary (1823–1901)[†‡]

——————————————— *Men* ———————————————

Adolphus, John Leycester (1795–1862)

Aidé, Charles Hamilton (1826–1906)

Albery, James (1838–1889)

Alford, Henry (1810–1871)[‡]

Anderson, Robert (1770–1833)

Anster, John (1793–1867)

Ashe, Thomas (1770–1835)

Ashe, Thomas (1836–1889)

Ayton, Richard (1786–1823)

Bald, Alexander (1783–1859)

Banim, John (1798–1842)[†]

Barnett, Morris (1800–1856)

Barrett, Wilson, originally William Henry (1846–1904)

Battine, William (1765–1836)

Bayne, Peter (1830–1896)

Beaumont, Thomas Wentworth (1792–1848)

Bell, Robert (1800–1867)

Beresford, James (1764–1840)

Bibby, Thomas (1799–1863)

Blacket, Joseph (1786–1810)

Blackie, John Stuart (1809–1895)[†]

Blackey, William Lewery (1830–1902)

Bloomfield, Robert (1766–1823)

Booker, Luke (1762–1835)

Bowles, William Lisle (1762–1850)

Bradstreet, Robert (1766–1836)

Brierley, Benjamin (1825–1896)

Briggs, John Joseph (1819–1876)

Brough, Robert Barnabas (1828–1860)

Brydges, Sir Samuel Egerton (1762–1837)

Buchanan, Robert Williams (1841–1901)[†]

Bulwer, Edward George Earle Lytton, Baron Lytton (1803–1873). See Lytton*

Burgess, Joseph Tom (1828–1886)

Burgon, John William (1813–1888)

Burns, Jabez (1805–1876)

Butler, Weeden, the younger (1773–1831)

Calder, James Tait (1794?–1864)

Cameron, William (1751–1811)

Card, Henry (1779–1844)

Carlyle, Joseph Dacre (1759–1804)

Carnegie, James, sixth de facto and ninth de jure Earl of Southesk (1827–1905)

Cary, Henry Francis (1772–1844)

Cayley, Charles Bagot (1823–1883)

Chatterton, Thomas (1752–1770)

Chenevix, Richard (1774–1830)

Chesney, Sir George Tomkyns (1830–1895)

Churton, Edward (1800–1874)

Clarke, John Randall (1827?–1863)

Clough, Arthur Hugh (1819–1861)[†]

Cochrane-Baillie, Alexander Dundas Ross Wishart, first Baron Lamington (1816–1890)

Collins, Charles Allston (1828–1873)

Conolly, Erskine (1796–1843)

Conquest, George (Augustus), whose real surname was Oliver (1837–1901)

Cope, Richard (1776–1856)

Cotter, George Sackville (1755–1831)

Cox, George Valentine (1786–1875)

Crocker, Charles (1797–1861)

Crowquill, Alfred, pseudonym. See Forrester, Alfred Henry (1804–1872)

Curwen, Henry (1845–1892)

Cyples, William (1831–1882)

Darley, George (1795–1846)

Davidson, John (1857–1909)

Davies, Robert (1769?–1835)

Davies, Walter (1761–1849)

Denison, William Joseph (1770–1849)

DeVere, Sir Aubrey (1788–1846)

Dircks, Henry (1806–1873)

Doubleday, Thomas (1790–1870)

Dovaston, John Freeman Milward (1782–1854)

Drummond, Sir William (1770?–1828)

Duffield, Alexander James (1821–1890)

Dunkin, Alfred John (1812–1879)

Dunmore, seventh Earl of. See Murray, Charles Adolphus (1841–1907)

Dyson, Charles (1788–1860)

Edwards, Henry Sutherland (1828–1906)

Edwards, John (1751–1832)

Egan, Pierce, the elder (1772–1849)

Elliott, Ebenezer (1781–1849)

Evans, Daniel (1792–1846)

Erskine, Sir David (1772–1837)

Everett, James (1784–1872)

Fawcett, John (1768–1837)

Field, Barron (1786–1846)

Finlaison, John (1783–1860)

Fleay, Frederick Gard (1831–1909)

Forrester, Alfred Henry, artist, best known under the name of Alfred Crowquill (1804–1872)

Forrester, Charles Robert (1803–1850)

Forsyth, William (1812–1899)

Forsyth, William (1818–1879)

Francis, Francis (1822–1886)

Fraser, James Baillie (1783–1856)

Frere, John Hookham (1769–1846)

Gall, Richard (1776–1801)

Geredigion, Daniel du o. See Evans, Daniel (1792–1846)

Gibson, David Cooke (1827–1856)

Gilbert, Sir William Schwenck (1836–1911)*

Gilfillan, George (1813–1878)

Godwin, George (1815–1888)

Gordon, Adam Lindsay (1833–1870)

Goulburn, Edward (1787–1868)

Grain, Richard Corney (1844–1895)

Grant, Johnson (1773–1844)

Greg, Percy (1836–1889)

Grieve, John (1781–1836)

Griffiths, Arthur George Frederick (1838–1908)

Grosart, Alexander Balloch (1827–1899)

Gurney, Archer Thompson (1820–1887)

Haliburton, Thomas Chandler (1796–1865)

Hamilton, Thomas (1789–1842)

Hankinson, Thomas Edwards (1805–1843)

Harper, William (1806–1857)

Hawker, Robert Stephen (1803–1875)

Haworth, Adrian Hardy (1767–1833)

Henley, William Ernest (1849–1903)[†]

Henry, James (1798–1876)

Heraud, John Abraham (1799–1887)

Herbert, Henry William (1807–1858), a writer under the name of Frank Forester

Hill, Pascoe Grenfell (1804–1882)

Hinds, Samuel (1793–1872)

Holland, John (1794–1872)

Hood, Thomas (1799–1845)*

Hort, Fenton John Anthony (1828–1892)

Howard, Edward (d. 1841)

Howell, John (1774–1830), called Ioan ab Hywel

Hughes, John (1842–1902)

Hunt, James Henry Leigh (1784–1859)[†]

Hyslop, James (1798–1827)

Irving, Joseph (1830–1891)

James, Charles (d. 1821)

Jennings, Hargrave (1817?–1890)

Johnson, Thomas Burgeland (d. 1840)

Jones, John (fl. 1827)

Keats, John (1795–1821)*

Kemble, Stephen or George Stephen Kemble (1758–1822)

Kennish or Kinnish, William (1799–1862)

Kent, Charles, whose full Christian names were William Charles Mark (1823–1902)

Kett, Henry (1761–1825)

Knapp, John Leonard (1767–1845)

Knox, William (1789–1825)

Landor, Walter Savage (1775–1864)*

Lathom, Francis (1777–1832)

Lear, Edward (1812–1888)

Le Grice, Charles Valentine (1773–1858)

Lever, Charles James (1806–1872)[†]

Liddell, Henry Thomas, first Earl of Ravensworth (1797–1878)

Linton, William James (1812–1898)

Lister, Thomas (1810–1888)

Lockhart, John Gibson (1794–1854)*

Lovell, George William (1804–1878)

Lyall, Sir Alfred Comyn (1835–1911)[†]

Lyle, Thomas (1792–1859)

Lytton, Edward Robert Bulwer, first Earl of Lytton (1803–1873)

MacCarthy, Denis Florence (1817–1882)

Maclaren, Ian, pseudonym. See Watson, John (1851–1907)

McKay, Archibald (1801–1883)

Macnish, Robert (1802–1837)

Major, John (1782–1849)

Mant, Richard (1776–1848)

Marriott, John (1780–1825)

Mason, James (1779–1827)

Mathews, Charles James (1803–1878)[†]

Mayhew, Augustus Septimus (1826–1875)

Mivart, St. George Jackson (1827–1900)

Meredith, George (1828–1909)*

Merivale, John Herman (1779–1844)

Miller, Hugh (1802–1856)

Mogridge, George (1787–1854)[‡]

Montgomery, James (1771–1854)[†]

Moore, Sir John Henry (1756–1780)

Morier, James Justinian (1780?–1849)

Morton, Thomas (1764?–1838)

Murray, Charles (1754–1821)

Murray, Charles Adolphus (1841–1907)

Nantglyn, Bardd. See Davies, Robert (1769?–1835)

Neale, John Mason (1818–1866)*

Nevay, John (1792–1870)

Newton, Robert, D. D. (1780–1854)

Nichol, John (1833–1894)

Nicoll, Robert (1814–1837)

Norton, John Bruce (1815–1883)

O'Brien, Cornelius (1843–1906)

O'Bryen, Dennis (1755–1832)

O'Donnell, John Francis (1837–1874)

Oliphant, Laurence (1829–1888)[†]

O'Reilly, John Boyle (1844–1890)[†]

Overton, Charles (1805–1889)

Paget, Francis Edward (1806–1882)

Pardon, George Frederick (1824–1884)

Parkinson, Richard (1797–1858)

Pater, Walter Horatio (1839–1894)*

Paynter, David William (1791–1823)

Pelly, Sir Lewis (1825–1892)

Pember, Edward Henry (1833–1911)

Percy, Thomas (1768–1808)

Pettitt, Henry (1848–1893)

Phillips, Samuel (1814–1854)

Planché, James Robinson (1796–1880)[†]

Polidori, John William (1795–1821)

Porter, James (1753–1798)

Praed, Winthrop Mackworth (1802–1839)

Proby, John Joshua, first Earl of Carysfort (1751–1828)

Quick, Henry (1792–1857)

Ramsay, John (1802–1879)

Reach, Angus Bethune (1821–1856)

Reed, Sir Edward James (1830–1906)

Reynolds, Frederic (1764–1841)

Richards, Alfred Bate (1820–1876)

Ritchie, Joseph (1788?–1819)

Robertson, William Bruce (1820–1886)

Rogers, Henry (1806–1877)

Rose, George (1817–1882)

Ross, William Stewart, known by the pseudonym of 'Saladin' (1844–1906)

Rushton, Edward (1756–1814)

Ruskin, John (1819–1900)*

Ryan, Richard (1796–1849)

St. John, Percy Bolingbroke (1821–1889)

Sandwith, Humphrey (1822–1881)

Scott, Andrew (1757–1839)

Scott, William Bell (1811–1890)

Sewell, William (1804–1874)

Sharp, Sir Cuthbert (1781–1849)

Shelley, Percy Bysshe (1792–1822)*

Shorthouse, Joseph Henry (1843–1903)†

Sillery, Charles Doyne (1807–1837)

Sinclair, William (1804–1878)

Smith, Albert Richard (1816–1860)

Smith, Sir William Cusac (1766–1836)

Sotheby, William (1757–1833)

Stables, William [Gordon] (1840–1910)‡

Stagg, John (1770–1823)

Stebbing, Henry (1799–1833)

Sterling, John (1806–1844)

Stewart, Sir Thomas Grainger (1837–1900)

Stirling-Maxwell, Sir William (1818–1878)†

Stowel, John (d. 1799)

Sturch, William (1753?–1838)

Sturgis, Julian Russell (1848–1904)

Symonds, John Addington (1840–1893)*

Tayler, Charles Benjamin (1797–1875)

Tennant, William (1784–1848)

Thomas, David (1760?–1822)

Thornton, William Thomas (1813–1880)

Tomlinson, Charles (1808–1897)

Townsend, William Charles (1803–1850)

Trollope, Anthony (1815–1882)†

Twiss, Horace (1787–1849)

Valpy, Richard (1754–1836)

Vandam, Albert Dresden (1843–1903)

Vedder, David (1790–1854)

Waddell, Peter Hately (1817–1891)

Walcott, MacKenzie Edward Charles (1821–1880)

Waller, John Francis (1810–1894)

Warburton, Bartholomew Elliott George, usually known as Eliot Warburton (1810–1852)†

Waring, John Burley (1823–1875)

Watson, John, who wrote under the pseudonym of Ian Maclaren (1850–1907)

Watson, Walter (1780–1854)

Webb, Thomas Ebenezer (1821–1903)

Wells, Charles Jeremiah (1799–1879)

Westall, Richard (1765–1836)

Westwood, Thomas (1814–1888)

White, Henry Kirke (1785–1806)

Whytehead, Thomas (1815–1843)

Wilkins, William Henry (1860–1905)

Williams, Griffith (1769–1838)

Williams, Isaac (1802–1865)

Willmott, Robert Aris (1809–1863)

Wingfield, Lewis Strange (1842–1891)

Wolfe, Charles (1791–1823)

Woodward, George Moutard (1760?–1809)

Wright, John (1805–1843?)

Yates, Edmund (1831–1894)†

Young, Andrew (1807–1889)

Appendix B
Additional Tables Relevant to Chapter 6

Table B.1: Means and Standard Deviations (S.D.) of Specified Variables for Four Groups of Authors

Specified Variables[1]	Early Women	Late Women	Early Men	Late Men	All Authors
Fame index					
Mean	0.914	0.674	0.798	1.012	0.848
S.D.	1.133	0.927	1.084	1.306	1.117
N	152	89	173	86	500
Family help[2]					
Mean	0.428	0.438	0.289	0.360	0.370
S.D.	0.496	0.499	0.455	0.483	0.483
N	152	89	173	86	500
Father's SES					
Mean	62.521	63.442	59.703	61.586	61.674
S.D.	15.178	10.340	17.443	13.205	14.787
N	121	77	118	70	386
No. books written					
Mean	14.262	23.195	13.125	18.470	16.234
S.D.	14.912	25.986	16.653	18.844	18.911
N	149	87	160	83	479
No. fiction books[3]					
Mean	8.530	18.233	2.519	6.566	7.945
S.D.	11.921	23.676	4.170	10.678	14.122
N	149	86	158	83	476

Table B.1 (*continued*)

Specified Variables[1]	Early Women	Late Women	Early Men	Late Men	All Authors
No. poetry books					
Mean	2.336	1.977	1.387	2.088	2.360
S.D.	3.571	3.779	0.774	3.357	3.606
N	149	86	158	80	470
No. plays					
Mean	0.624	0.253	1.639	1.854	1.105
S.D.	1.825	0.838	8.616	6.927	5.855
N	149	87	158	82	476
No. nonfiction books[4]					
Mean	4.832	4.954	7.913	10.048	6.787
S.D.	5.325	6.115	10.097	12.740	9.019
N	149	87	160	83	479

[1] 20 cases are excluded from this and subsequent tables, because the *DNB* gave only a tentative date of birth so we could not classify them as early or late authors. We excluded an additional 7 cases as "outliers," that is, authors who published so much that their inclusion would have distorted the results. These seven authors are Emma Marshall, 1830–1897; Harriet Martineau, 1802–1876; Mary Martha Sherwood, 1775–1851; Charlotte Yonge, 1823–1901; Henry Alford, 1810–1871; George Mogridge, 1787–1854; and William Stables [pseudonym Gordon Stables], 1840–1910. Of these seven authors, two women, Martineau and Yonge, scored 3 or 4 on the fame index.

[2] "Yes" was coded 1; "no," 0.

[3] For technical reasons, throughout this appendix all fiction variables are calculated using the number of fiction books published plus 1.

[4] For technical reasons, throughout this appendix all nonfiction variables are calculated using the number of nonfiction books published plus 1.

SES = socioeconomic status

Table B.2: Regression on Fame Index of Specified Variables for
All Authors

	beta	R^2	Adjusted R^2
Gender	0.022		
Period	−0.034		
Family help	0.188 *		
Father's SES	0.000		
No. fiction books	0.127 *		
No. poetry books	0.242 *		
No. plays	0.137 *		
No. nonfiction books	0.151 *		
		0.181	0.162 *
(N = 500)			

Note: Outliers have been excluded. (See table B.1, n. 1.) Because we redefined the variables fiction and nonfiction as the number of books published plus 1, the *bs* for all variables are not what they would have been had we entered raw scores, and so we have excluded them from this table. Gender, period, and family help are dummy variables coded as either 0 or 1. For gender, "male" equals 1; for period, "late" equals 1; for family help, the presence of family help equals 1.
* Significant at 0.001

Table B.3: Regression on Fame of Specified Variables for Four Groups of Authors

	beta	R^2	Adj. R^2
Early women (N = 152)			
Family help	0.229 *		
Father's SES	0.020		
No. fiction books	0.221 *		
No. poetry books	0.147 **		
No. plays	0.150 ***		
No. nonfiction books	−0.131 **		
		0.149	0.104 **
Late women (N = 89)			
Family help	0.089		
Father's SES	−0.169 ***		
No. fiction books	0.021		
No. poetry books	0.088		
No. plays	−0.082		
No. nonfiction books	0.396 *		
		0.240	0.171 **
Early men (N = 175)			
Family help	0.186 *		
Father's SES	−0.041		
No. fiction books	0.292 *		
No. poetry books	0.379 *		
No. plays	0.168 *		
No. nonfiction books	0.049		
		0.364	0.325 **
Late men (N = 86)			
Family help	0.255 *		
Father's SES	0.140		
No. fiction books	0.078		
No. poetry books	0.253 *		
No. plays	0.152		
No. nonfiction books	0.245 *		
		0.300	0.229 **

Note: Outliers have been excluded. (See table B.1, n. 1.) *bs* are not presented. (See
    table B.2, note.)
*   Significant at 0.001
**   Significant at 0.01
*** Significant at 0.05

Table B.4: Regression Analyses of Fame with Specified Variables

	Regression 1 No. Fiction Books			Regression 2 Square Root [No. Fiction Books]			Change in Adjusted R²
	beta	R²	Adjusted R²	beta	R²	Adjusted R²	
Early women (N = 152)							
Family help	0.229 *			0.230 *			
Father's SES	0.020			0.010			
No. fiction books	0.221 *			0.294 *			
No. poetry books	0.147 **			0.166 **			
No. plays	0.150 ***			0.149 ***			
No. nonfiction books	-0.131 **	0.149	0.104 **	-0.170 **	0.178	0.134 **	+ 0.030
Late women (N = 89)							
Family help	0.089			0.089			
Father's SES	-0.169 ***			-0.167 ***			
No. fiction books	0.021			0.061			
No. poetry books	0.088			0.098			
No. plays	-0.082			-0.083			
No. nonfiction books	0.396 *	0.240	0.171 **	0.386 *	0.242	0.175 **	+ 0.004

Table B.4 (continued)

	Regression 1 No. Fiction Books			Regression 2 Square Root [No. Fiction Books]			
	beta	R^2	Adjusted R^2	beta	R^2	Adjusted R^2	Change in Adjusted R^2
Early men (N = 175)							
Family help	0.186 *			0.190 *			
Father's SES	−0.041			−0.054			
No. fiction books	0.292 *			0.314 *			
No. poetry books	0.379 **			0.376 **			
No. plays	0.168 *			0.172 *			
No. nonfiction books	0.049			0.034			
		0.364	0.325 **		0.374	0.336 *	+ 0.011
Late men (N = 86)							
Family help	0.255 *			0.257 *			
Father's SES	0.140			0.136			
No. fiction books	0.078			0.079			
No. poetry books	0.253 *			0.252 *			
No. plays	0.152			0.150			
No. nonfiction books	0.245 *			0.245 *			
		0.300	0.229 **		0.300	0.229 **	0.000

Note: Outliers have been excluded. (See table B.1, n. 1.) *bs* are not presented. (See table B.2, note.)

*   Significant at 0.001

**   Significant at 0.01

***   Significant at 0.05

Table B.5: Comparison of Means and Standard Deviations of Fiction Variables for Four Groups of Authors

Specified variables	Early Women	Late Women	Early Men	Late Men	All Authors
No. fiction books					
Mean	8.530	18.233	2.519	6.566	7.945
S.D.	11.921	23.676	4.170	10.678	14.122
N	(149)	(86)	(158)	(83)	(476)
Square root [no. fiction books]					
Mean	2.468	3.617	2.736	2.089	2.251
S.D.	1.568	2.283	3.663	1.493	1.699
N	(149)	(86)	(155)	(83)	(476)

Note: Outliers have been excluded. (See table B.1, n. 1.)

Table B.6: Regression of Specified Variables on Fame for Three Groups of Specialists

	Novelists (N = 130)			Poets (N = 94)			Nonfiction authors (N = 151)		
	beta	R^2	Adjusted R^2	beta	R^2	Adjusted R^2	beta	R^2	Adjusted R^2
Gender	0.184 **			0.273 *			-0.017		
Born	-0.292 *			0.134			0.133 ***		
Family help	0.195 *			0.138			0.264 *		
Father's SES	-0.120			0.055			-0.002		
Square root [no. fiction books]	0.175 ***			0.219 **			0.178 **		
No. poetry books	-0.036			0.404 *			0.164 ***		
No. plays	-0.016			0.001			-0.111		
No. nonfiction books	-0.030			0.010			0.202 **		
		0.164	0.098 ***		0.318	0.228 **		0.254	0.192 *

Note: Outliers have been excluded. (See table B.1, n. 1.) bs are not presented. (See table B.2, note.)

* Significant at 0.001
** Significant at 0.01
*** Significant at 0.05

Table B.7: Means and Standard Deviations of Selected Variables for Novelists, Poets, and Nonfiction Authors

	Specialists		
	Novelist	Poet	Nonfiction Author
Fame			
Mean	0.946	0.766	0.894
S.D.	1.123	1.121	1.072
N	(130)	(94)	(151)
Gender			
Mean	0.162	0.574	0.728
S.D.	0.370	0.497	0.446
N	(130)	(94)	(151)
Period			
Mean	0.531	0.181	0.358
S.D.	0.501	0.387	0.481
N	(130)	(94)	(151)
Family help			
Mean	0.446	0.255	0.397
S.D.	0.499	0.438	0.491
N	(130)	(94)	(151)
Father's SES			
Mean	63.595	55.522	63.649
S.D.	11.289	19.026	13.126
N	(111)	(69)	(111)
Square root [no. fiction books]			
Mean	4.144	1.500	3.196
S.D.	1.976	1.251	3.784
N	(130)	(94)	(148)
No. poetry books			
Mean	21.046	4.925	1.685
S.D.	21.274	4.279	2.794
N	(130)	(94)	(143)
No. plays			
Mean	0.777	0.181	0.284
S.D.	1.718	0.733	1.017
N	(130)	(94)	(148)
No. nonfiction books			
Mean	0.492	1.872	13.987
S.D.	1.234	1.490	12.054
N	(130)	(94)	(151)

Note: Outliers have been excluded. (See table B.1, n. 1.) About dummy variables, see table B.2, note.

Table B.8: Regression on Fame of Specified Variables for All Authors

	Beta	R^2	Adjusted R^2
Gender	0.071 ***		
Period	−0.032		
Family help	0.251 *		
Novelist	0.107 *		
Poet	0.046		
Playwright	−0.001		
Nonfiction author	0.074		
		0.071	0.058 *
(N = 527)			

Note: *b*s not presented. (See table B.2, note.)
* Significant at 0.001
** Significant at 0.05
*** Significant at 0.01

Table B.9: Means and Standard Deviations of Selected Variables for All Authors

	Means	Standard Deviation
Fame	0.827	1.114
Gender	0.507	0.500
Period	0.351	0.478
Family help	0.359	0.480
Novelist	0.279	0.449
Poet	0.182	0.386
Playwright	0.032	0.177
Nonfiction author	0.292	0.455
(N = 527)		

Note: In this table every variable except fame is dichotomous; that is, the answer "yes" equals 1, and the answer "no" equals 0. Thus, the mean in every category except fame may be read as the percentage of persons in that category. For instance, 35.9 percent of the authors received family help; 50.7 percent were men; 35.1 percent were in the late period; 27.9 percent were novelists. The genre specialties do not add up to 100 percent, because we have omitted authors who did not specialize.

Appendix C
Authors' Contracts and Reviews

Table C.1: Authors Whose Macmillan Contracts and Reviews
Were Examined

Black, William
Boldrewood, Rolf (T. A. Browne)
Crawford, F. Marion
Hewlett, Maurice
James, Henry
Keary, Annie
Kingsley, Charles
Kingsley, Henry
Molesworth, Mrs. Mary
Oliphant, Mrs. Margaret
Shorthouse, J. H.
Ward, Mrs. Humphrey
Wharton, Edith
Wells, H. G.
Yonge, Charlotte

Table C.2: Authors Whose Reviews Were Located in the *Edinburgh Review*

Austen, Jane	Kingsley, Mary
Baillie, Joanna	Ledwidge, Francis
Black, William	Martineau, Harriet
Blackie, John Stuart	Meredith, George
Brontës (all three sisters)	Morris, William
Bulwer (Lytton), Lord	Norton, Caroline
Burney, Fanny	Oliphant, Mrs.
Butler, Samuel	Opie, Amelia
Byron, Lord	Pater, Walter
Cholmondeley, Mary	Praed, Winthrop Mackworth
Coleridge, Sara	Rosetti, Christina
Conrad, Joseph	Rosetti, Dante Gabriel
Craven, Pauline	Ruskin, John
Crawford, F. Marion	Scott, Walter
Disraeli, Benjamin	Shelley, Percy Bysshe
Edgeworth, Maria	Shorthouse, J. H.
Eliot, George	Sterne, Lawrence
Gaskell, Elizabeth	Swinburne, Algernon Charles
Hardy, Thomas	Thackeray, William Makepeace
Ingelow, Jean	Trollope, Anthony
James, Henry	Ward, Mrs. Humphrey (Mary A.)
Jameson, Anna	Wells, H. G.
Keats, John	Wollestonecraft, Mary
Kingsley, Charles	Yonge, Charlotte Mary

Table C.3: Authors Whose Reviews Were Located in the *Athenaeum* (Mainly Macmillan Authors and Authors Listed in the *DNB*)

Austin, Alfred	Macquoid, Katherine S.
Banim, John	Malet, Lucas (Mary Kingsley)
Barring-Gould, Sabine	Markham, Capt. A. H.
Black, William	Meredith, George
Boldrewood, Rolf (T. A. Browne)	Minto, William
Bulwer-Lytton, Edward George	Molesworth, Mrs. Mary Louisa
Burnett, Frances Hodgson	Murray, D. Christie
Clunnes, E. C.	Noel, Lady Augusta
Conway, Hugh	Norris, W. E.
Cooper, Katherine	Notley, F. E. M.
Corbett, Julian S.	O'Hara Family
Crawford, F. Marion	Oliphant, Mrs. Margaret
Ennis, Graham (Mrs. Molesworth)	Palmer, Lady Sophia
Fleming, George	Pember, E. H.
Hardy, Thomas	Phillips, Mrs. Alfred
Helps, Arthur	Riddell, Mrs. J. H.
Hewlett, Maurice	Shorthouse, J. H.
James, Henry	Sturgis, Julian Russell
Kavanaugh, Julia	Trollope, Anthony
Keary, Annie	Villari, Linda
Kingsley, Charles	Walpole, Hugh
Kingsley, Henry	Ward, Mrs. Humphrey
Lafargue, Philip	Wells, H. G.
Lever, Charles	Westbury, Hugh
Lowell, James Russell	Wharton, Edith
	Yonge, Charlotte Mary

Bibliography

The Macmillan Archives at the British (Museum) Library Student Room have been an important source of our data. A particularly rich collection, these archives include Manuscript Ledgers, recording the manuscripts submitted to Macmillan from November 1866 through 1935; Readers' Reports, copybooks containing most of the reviews of manuscripts sent to editorial consultants through the early twentieth century; "Editions Books," ledgers recording orders to Macmillan's printers for print runs of editions of the books issued by the firm; "Macmillan's Letters," carbon copies of handwritten correspondence concerning business matters from members of the firm; letters about business from members of the Macmillan family to one another; and letters of some (mostly famous or best-selling) authors to Macmillan, including memoranda of agreement about contracts and payments. We have supplemented our reading of this material with an examination of letters to and from members of the firm in the Berg Collection of the New York Public Library.

We also examined articles in The *Athenaeum* from the 1830s through 1920 and in the *Edinburgh Review* from the 1860s through 1910. In addition to quoting from the Macmillan Archives, we have cited the primary sources listed below.

Primary Sources Quoted

The *Athenaeum*
1876   Review of Mrs. Oliphant's *The Curate in Charge*. 67, 2519 (5 February):196.
1877   Review of Mrs. Oliphant's *Young Musgrove*. 70, 2616 (15 July):769.
1878a Review of *Benedicta*. 71, 2634 (20 April):505.
1878b Review of Mrs. Oliphant's *The Primrose Path*. 72, 2648 (27 July):111.
1878c Review of series "English Men of Letters." Ed. John Morley. 72, 2645 (6 July):11.
1879   Review of George Meredith's *The Egoist*. 74, 2714 (1 November):555–56.
1880   Review of Mrs. Oliphant's *A Beleaguered City*. 75, 2727 (13 January):150.
1883   Review of F. Marion Crawford's *Dr. Claudius*. 81, 2902 (9 June):727.
1885   Review of George Meredith's *Diana of the Crossways*. 85, 2994 (14 March):339–40.
1894   Review of Mrs. Ward's *Marcella*. 103, 3468 (14 April):469–70.
1898   Review of Maurice Hewlett's *The Forest Lovers*. 112, 3690 (10 July):93.

245

A Biographic Catalogue of Macmillan and Company's Publications from 1843 to 1889.
1891   London: Macmillan.

Catalogue of the British Museum (BMC).

Dictionary of National Biography (DNB). 21 vols., suppl. 1 and 2.

The *Edinburgh Review*

1868   [R. Monckton Milnes.] "The Spanish Gypsy." 128:523–38.

1873   [R. Monckton Milnes.] "Middlemarch." 137 (January):246–63.

1877   [Alexander I. Shand.] "Mr. Anthony Trollope's Novels." 146 (October):455–88.

1879   [C. Rachel Jones.] "The Worthies of Norwich (Collected Works of Dr. Sayers; Memoir and Correspondence of Sir James Edward Smith; A Memoir of the Life and Writing of the Late William Taylor, of Norwich; Memorials of the Life of Amelia Opie; Memoir of the Life of Mrs. Frye; The Autobiography of Harriet Martineau; Catalogue of the Pictures Exhibited at Burlington House in the Winters of 1877, 1878, including a Special Selection of the Works of the Principal Artists of the Norwich School)." 150 (July):41–76.

1884   [Alexander I. Shand.] "The Literary Life of Anthony Trollope." 159 (January):186–212.

1885   [Margaret Oliphant.] "The Life and Letters of George Eliot (George Eliot's Life as Related in her Letters and Journals, arranged and edited by her husband J. W. Cross)." 161 (April):514–53.

1892   [Rowland Prothero.] "David Grieve." 175 (April):518–40.

1894   [Alexander I. Shand.] "Marcella (Marcella. By Mrs. Humphrey Ward)." 180 (July):108–30.

1899a [Stephen Gwynn.] "The Life and Writing of Mrs. Oliphant (The Autobiography and Letters of Mrs. M. O. W. Oliphant; Passages in the Life of Margaret Maitland; Salem Chapel and the Doctor's Family; Miss Marjoribanks; Phoebe Junior: A Last Chronicle of Carlingford; A Beleaguered City; A Little Pilgrim in the Unseen; The Wizard's Son; Two Stories of the Seen and Unseen; The Land of Darkness; Fancies of a Believer; The Land of Suspense)." 190 (July):26–47.

1899b [Stephen Gwynn.] "Some Tendencies of Prose Style (Engish Prose, edited by Henry Craik; Style by Walter Raleigh; A Book of Enlgish Prose: Character and Incident. 1387–1649 by W. E. Henry and C. Whibley)." 190 (October):356–76.

1902a "The Edinburgh Review (The Edinburgh Review [1802–1902]; On the Authorship of the First Five Hundred Numbers of the 'Edinburgh Review' by W. A. Copinger; The First Edinburgh Reviewers by Walter Bagehot; The Rev. Sydney Smith's Miscellaneous Works, including his Contributions to the 'Edinburgh Review'; The Life and Letters of Lord Jeffrey; Selected Correspondence of the late Macvey Napier; Life and Letters of Lord Macaulay; Memoirs of the Life of Henry Reeve)." (October):275–318.

1902b "The English Novel in the Nineteenth-century (The English Novel: Being a Short Sketch of its History from the Earliest Times to the Appearance of 'Waverley.' By Walter Raleigh. Fifth Impression)." (October):487–506.

1906 "The Novels of Mr. Marion Crawford (Mr. Isaacs; Doctor Claudius; To Lee-ward; Paul Patoff; Saracinesca; Sant' Ilario; A Cigarette Maker's Romance; Don Orsino; Katharine Lauderdale; Corleone; In the Palace of the King; Marietta: a Maid of Venice; The Heart of Rome; Soprano: A Portrait; The Novel: What it is; Gleaning from Venetian History by Joseph Pennell)." (July):61–80.

1907 "The British Novel as an Institution (The Works of Mrs. Gaskell, the Knuts-ford Edition in eight volumes)." (July):110–27.

Eliot, George
1856 "Silly Novels by Lady Novelists." *Westminster Review* 66:442–61.

Lee, Sidney
1963–64 [1900] "The Dictionary of National Biography, A Statistical Account." In *Dictionary of National Biography* (1885–1911) 1:lxii–lxxviii.

Lists of the Publications of Richard Bentley and Son, 1829–1898 (microfiche).
1977 Cambridge: Chadwyck-Healey.

Morley, John
1917 *Recollections*. 2 vols. London: Macmillan.

Oliphant, Margaret O. W.
1855 "Modern Novelists—Great and Small." *Blackwoods* 77:554–68.
1897 *William Blackwood and Sons*. 3 vols. London: William Blackwood and Sons.

Stephen, Leslie
1898 "National Biography." In *Studies of a Biography*, 1:2–36. London: Duckworth.
1903 "Some Early Impressions—Editing." *National Review* 42:563–81.

Thring, G. H.
n.d. "History of the Society for Authors." British Museum Library Student Room Add. 56868 and 56869. Typescript.

Times (London)
1911 Obituary of Mowbray Morris. 28 June.

Other Books and Articles Cited

Altick, Richard D.
1957 *The English Common Reader*. Chicago: University of Chicgo Press.
1962 "The Sociology of Authorship: The Social Origins, Education and Occupations of 1,100 British Writers, 1800–1935." *Bulletin of the New York Public Library* 66:389–404.

Arnold, Matthew
1960 [1869] *Culture and Anarchy*. Cambridge: Cambridge University Press.

Basch, Françoise
1974 *Relative Creature: Victorian Women in Society and the Novel*. New York: Schocken Books.

Baym, Nina
1984a "The Madwoman and Her Languages: Why I Don't Do Feminist Literary Theory." *Tulsa Studies in Women's Literature* 3:45–60.
1984b *Novels, Readers, and Reviewers: Responses to Fiction in Antebellum America*. Ithaca: Cornell University Press.

1985 [1981] "Melodramas of Beset Manhood: How Theories of American Fiction Exclude Women Authors." *Feminist Criticism: Essays on Women, Literature and Theory*, ed. Elaine Showalter, 63–80. New York: Pantheon Books.

Becker, Howard
1982 *Art Worlds*. Berkeley: University of California Press.

Bernard, Jessie
1964 *Academic Women*. University Park, Penn.: Pennsylvania State University Press.

Black, Helen C.
1893 *Notable Women Authors of the Day: Biographical Sketches*. Glasgow: D. Bryce and Son.

Blakey, Dorothy
1939 *The Minerva Press, 1790–1820*. London: London Bibliographic Society.

Bleiler, E. F.
1977 Introduction to *The Collected Ghost Stories of Mrs. J. H. Riddell*. New York: Dover.

Bloom, Harold
1973 *The Anxiety of Influence*. New York: Oxford University Press.

Blotner, Joseph L.
1958 "Virginia Woolf." In *Cyclopedia of World Authors*, ed. Frank N. Magill with Dayton Kohler, 1170–73. New York: Harper and Brothers.

Bolithio, Hector, ed.
1950 "Mowbray Morris: A Late Victorian Man of Letters." *A Biographer's Notebook*. New York: Macmillan.

Bourdieu, Pierre
1980 "Production of Belief." Trans. Richard Nice. *Media, Culture and Society* 2:261–93.

1984 *Distinction: A Social Critique of the Judgment of Taste*. Trans. Richard Nice. Cambridge: Harvard University Press.

Burstyn, Joan
1980 *Victorian Education and the Ideal of Womanhood*. London: Croom Helm.

Cantor, Muriel
1981 *Prime-Time Television*. Beverly Hills: Sage.

Colby, Vinetta
1970 *The Singular Anamoly: Women Novelists of the Nineteenth Century*. New York: New York University Press.

Cole, Jonathan R.
1979 *Fair Science*. New York: Free Press.

Collins, Arthur
1928 *The Profession of Letters, 1780–1832*. London: George Routledge and Sons.

Coser, Lewis A.
1965 *Men of Ideas*. New York: Free Press.
1977 "Georg Simmel's Neglected Contribution to the Sociology of Women." *Signs* 2(Summer):869–76.
1979 "Asymetries in Author-Publisher Relations." *Society* 17:34–37.

Coser, Lewis A., Charles Kadushin, and Walter Powell
1982   *Books: The Culture and Commerce of Publishing*. New York: Basic Books.

Cousin, John W.
1910   *A Short Biographical Dictionary of English and American Authors*. New York:
E. P. Dutton.

Dalziel, Margaret
1957   *Popular Culture One Hundred Years Ago*. London: Cohen and West.

Davidoff, Lenore
1973   *The Best Circles: Society, Etiquette, and the Season*. London: Croom Helm.

Davies, Margery
1983   *Woman's Place Is at the Typewriter*. Philadelphia: Temple University Press.

DiMaggio, Paul
1982   "Cultural Entrepreneurship in Nineteenth-Century Boston: The Creation of
an Organizational Base for High Culture in America." *Media, Culture and
Society* 4(1):33–51.
1987   "Classification in Art." *American Sociological Review* 52 (4):440–55.

Donaldson, Norman
1974   Introduction to *Lady Audley's Secret*, by Mary Elizabeth Braddon. New York:
Dover.

Douglas, Ann
1978   *The Feminization of American Culture*. New York: Avon.

Edwards, P. D.
1980   Introduction to *Autobiography*, by Anthony Trollope, ed. Michael Sadleir and
Frederick Page. New York: Oxford University Press.

Ehrenreich, Barbara, and Deirdre English
1973   *Witches, Midwives and Nurses*. Old Westbury: Feminist Press.

Ellman, Mary
1968   *Thinking About Women*. New York: Harvest Books.

Epstein, Cynthia Fuchs
1981   *Women in Law*. New York: Basic Books.

Evans, Mary
1987a   *Jane Austen and the State*. New York: Tavistock.
1987b   Letter to Gill Davies, 30 January.

Fahnestock, Jeanne Rosenmayer
1973   "Geraldine Jewsbury: The Power of the Publisher's Reader." *Nineteenth-
Century Fiction* 28(3):253–72.

Freidson, Eliot
1971   *The Profession of Medicine*. New York: Dodd, Mead.
1986   "Knowledge and the Practice of Sociology." *Sociological Forum* 1(Fall):684–
700.

Gans, Herbert
1962   *Urban Villagers*. New York: Free Press.

Garfinkle, Harold
1967   *Studies in Ethnomethodology*. Englewood Cliffs, N. J.: Prentice-Hall.

Gérin, Winifred
1980   *Elizabeth Gaskell*. New York: Oxford University Press.
Gettmann, Royal
1960   *A Victorian Publisher: A Study of the Bentley Papers*. Cambridge: Cambridge University Press.
Gilbert, Sandra, and Susan Gubar
1979   *The Madwoman in the Attic*. New Haven: Yale University Press.
Gilligan, Carol
1982   *In a Different Voice*. Cambridge: Harvard University Press.
Gissing, George
1927 [1891] *The New Grub Street*. London: Nash.
Gitlin, Todd
1983   *Inside Prime-Time*. New York: Pantheon.
Graff, Harvey
1987   *The Legacies of Literacy*. Bloomington: University of Indiana Press.
Greer, Germaine
1974   "Flying Pigs and Double Standards." London *Times Literary Supplement* 26 July, 784–85.
1979   *The Obstacle Race: The Fate of Women Painters and Their Work*. London: Secker and Warburg.
Griest, Guinivere
1970   *Mudie's Circulating Library and the Victorian Novel*. Bloomington: Indiana University Press.
Griswold, Wendy
1981   "American Character and the American Novel." *American Journal of Sociology* 86(July):740–65.
1986   *Renaissance Revivals*. Chicago: University of Chicago Press.
Gross, John
1970   *The Rise and Fall of the Man of Letters*. New York: Collier-Macmillan.
Habermas, Jurgen
1974 [1964] "The Public Sphere: An Encyclopedia Article." *New German Critique* 3(Fall):49–55.
Haight, Gordon S.
1968   *The George Eliot Letters III*. New Haven: Yale University Press.
Halkett, Samuel, and John Laing
1971   *Dictionary of Anonymous Literature*, 7 vols. Brooklyn, N.Y.: Haskell House.
Hall, Stuart
1986 [1980] "Cultural Studies: Two Paradigms." In *Media, Culture and Society: A Critical Reader*, ed. Richard Collins, James Curran, Nicholas Garnham, Paddy Scannell, Philip Schlesinger, and Colin Sparks, 33–48. Beverly Hills: Sage.
Halsband, Robert H.
1969   "Ladies of Letters in the Eighteenth Century." In *The Lady of Letters in the Eighteenth Century*, ed. Irvin Ehrenpreis and Robert H. Halsband. Los Angeles: William Andrews Clark Memorial Library.

Hamer, D. A.
1968   *John Morley: Liberal Intellectual in Politics*. Oxford: Clarendon Press.

Harris, Ann Sutherland, and Linda Nochlin
1977   *Women Artists, 1550–1950*. New York: Alfred A. Knopf.

Hartsock, Nancy C.
1983   *Money, Sex, and Power*. New York: Longman.

Hemlow, Joyce
1958   *The History of Fanny Burney*. Oxford: Oxford University Press.

Hirsch, Paul
1972   "Processing Fads and Fashions." *American Journal of Sociology* 77(4):639–59.
1978   "Production and Distribution Roles among Cultural Organizations: On the Division of Labor across Intellectual Disciplines." *Social Research* 45(2):315–30.

Hochwald, Eve
1981   "Women, Technology, and Workplace Equity in the New York City Newspaper Industry." *New Political Science* 2(3):137–41.
1985   "Studying Technological Discrimination: Some Feminist Questions." *Feminist Issues* 5(Spring):55–64.

Holcombe, Lee
1973   *Victorian Ladies at Work: Middle-Class Working Women in England and Wales, 1850–1914*. London: Archon.

Hughes, Everett C.
1956   *Men and their Work*. Chicago: University of Chicago Press.
1971   *The Sociological Eye*. 2 vols. Chicago: Aldine Atherton.

Hunt, Felicity
1986   "Opportunities Lost and Gained: Mechanization and Women's Work in the London Bookbinding and Printing Trades." In *Unequal Opportunities: Women's Employment in England, 1800–1918*, ed. Angela V. John, 71–93. Oxford: Basil Blackwell.

James, Louis
1963   *Fiction for the Working Man, 1830–1850*. New York: Oxford University Press.

Jardine, Alice
1982   "Gynesis." *Diacritics* 12(Summer):54–65.

Jensen, Margaret Ann
1984   *Love's Sweet Return: The Harlequin Story*. Toronto: Woman's Press.

John, Angela V.
1986   Introduction to *Unequal Opportunities: Women's Employment in England, 1800–1918*. Oxford: Basil Blackwell.

Kanter, Rosabeth Moss
1977   *Men and Women of the Corporation*. New York: Basic Books.

Kapsis, Robert E.
1985   "Hollywood Genre Film Production." Paper presented at the eightieth annual meeting of the American Sociological Association, Washington, D. C., 26–30 August.

Kessler-Harris, Alice
1981   "Gender, Class, Race, and Ethnicity in the Nineteenth-Century Labor Force."
        Paper presented to the Women and Work Seminar at the Graduate School
        of City University of New York.
1982   *Out to Work: A History of Wage Earning Women in the United States*. New York:
        Oxford University Press.

Kraft, Philip
1979   "The Routinization of Computer Programming." *Sociology of Work and Oc-
        cupations* 6(2):131–38.

Lamont, Michèle
1985   "How to Become a Dominant French Philosopher: The Case of Jacques
        Derrida." Paper presented at the eightieth annual meeting of the American
        Sociological Association. Washington, D. C., 26–30 August.

Lang, Gladys Engel, and Kurt Lang
1982   "Artistic Reputations: The Case of the Disappearing Lady Etchers in Britain."
        *Contributions to the Sociology of the Arts: 10th World Congress of Sociology in Mexico
        City*, 202–11. Sofia, Bulgaria: Resident Institute for Culture.

Larson, Magali Sarfatti
1977   *The Rise of Professionalism*. Berkeley: University of California Press.

Laurenson, Diana
1969   "A Sociological Study of Authors." *British Journal of Sociology* 20:311–25.

Laws, Judith Long
1975   "The Psychology of Tokenism." *Sex Roles* 1(1):51–67.

Leavis, F. R.
1969   *The Great Tradition*. New York: New York University Press.

Leavis, Q. D.
1932   *Fiction and the Reading Public*. London: Chatto and Windus.
1969   Introduction to *Miss Marjoribanks*, by Mrs. Oliphant. London: Chatto and
        Windus.

Lerner, Gerda
1969   "The Mill Girl and the Lady: Changes in the Status of Women in the Age
        of Jackson." *Mid-Continent American Studies Journal* 10:5–14.

Lewis, Roy, and Angus Maude
1953   *Professional People in England*. Cambridge: Harvard University Press.

Lieberson, Stanley
1980   *A Piece of the Pie*. Berkeley: University of California Press.

Lorber, Judith
1984   *Women Physicians: Career, Status, and Power*. New York: Tavistock.

Lowenthal, Leo
1961   *Literature, Popular Culture and Society*. Palo Alto: Pacific Books.

Lukács, György
1964   *Studies in European Realism*. New York: Grosset and Dunlop.

Luker, Kristin
1985   *Abortion and the Politics of Motherhood*. Berkeley: University of California Press.

Lynd, Robert, and Helen Lynd
1956 [1929] *Middletown*. New York: Harcourt, Brace and Janovich.

Marchand, Leslie
1964   The Athenaeum: *A Mirror of Victorian Culture*. Chapel Hill: University of North
        Carolina Press.

Merton, Robert K.
1968   "The Matthew Effect in Science." *Science* 199:55–63.

Milkman, Ruth
1976   "Women's Work and the Economic Crisis: Some Lessons from the Great
        Depression." *Review of Radical Political Economics* 8(1):73–97.

Miller, Nancy
1980   *The Heroine's Text*. New York: Columbia University Press.

Modleski, Tania
1984   *Loving with a Vengeance*. New York: Methuen.

Moers, Ellen
1976   *Literary Women*. New York: Doubleday.

Morgan, Charles
1943   *The House of Macmillan*. New York: Macmillan.

Morley, John
1917   *Recollections* (2 vols.) London: Macmillan.

Mumby, Frank Arthur
1974 [1930] "From the Earliest Times to 1870." Part 1 of *Publishing and Bookselling
        from the Earliest Times to the Present*, by Arthur Mumby and Ian Norrie, 21–
        232. 5th edition. London: Jonathan Cape.

Neff, Wanda F.
1966 [1929] *Victorian Working Women: An Historical and Literary Study of Women in British
        Industries and Professions, 1832–1850*. London: Frank Cass.

Newton, Judith Lowder
1981   *Women, Power and Subversion: Social Strategies in British Fiction, 1778–1860*. Athens:
        University of Georgia Press.

Nochlin, Linda
1971   "Why Have There Been No Great Women Artists?" *Art News* (January):22–
        39, 67–71.

Olsen, Tillie
1979   *Silences*. New York: Delta/Seymour Lawrence.

Parker, Rozsika, and Griselda Pollock
1981   *Old Mistresses: Women, Art and Ideology*. New York: Pantheon.

Petersen, Karen, and J. J. Wilson
1976   *Women Artists: Recognition and Reappraisal from the Early Middle Ages to the Twentieth
        Century*. New York: Harper and Row.

Peterson, Richard A.
1974   "The Production of Culture: A Prolegomenon." In *The Production of Culture*,
        7–22. Beverly Hills: Sage.

Poovey, Mary

1984   *The Proper Lady and the Woman Writer: Ideology as Style in The Works of Mary Wollstonecraft, Mary Shelley, and Jane Austen.* Chicago: University of Chicago Press.

Powell, Walter W.
1985   *Getting into Print: The Decision-Making Process in Scholarly Publishing.* Chicago: University of Chicago Press.

Radway, Janice
1984   *Reading the Romance: Women, Patriarchy, and Popular Literature.* Chapel Hill: University of North Carolina Press.

Reader, W. J.
1966   *Professional Men: The Rise of the Professional Classes in Nineteenth-Century England.* New York: Basic Books.

Reskin, Barbara
1980   Review of Jonathan R. Cole's *Fair Science. Contemporary Sociology* 9(6):793–95.

Reskin, Barbara, and Patricia Roos
1987   "Status Hierarchies and Sex Segregation." In *Ingredients for Women's Employment Policy,* ed. Christine Bose and Glenna Spitze, 3–22. Albany: State University of New York Press.

Rich, Adrienne
1976   *Of Woman Born: Motherhood as Experience and Institution.* New York: Norton.

Rossi, Alice, and Ann Calderwood
1973   *Academic Women on the Move.* New York: Russell Sage Foundation.

Rothman, Sheila
1978   *Woman's Proper Place.* New York: Basic Books.

Ryan, Mary
1975   *Womanhood in America: From Colonial Times to the Present.* New York: New Viewpoints.
1981   *Cradle of the Middle Class: The Family in Oneida County, New York, 1790–1865.* New York: Cambridge University Press.

Shear, Jeff
1987   "A Lawyer Courts Best-Sellerdom." *New York Times Magazine,* 7 June.

Showalter, Elaine
1975   "Dinah Mulock Craik and the Tactics of Sentiment: A Case Study in Victorian Female Authorship." *Feminist Studies* 2:5–23.
1977   *A Literature of their Own.* Princeton: Princeton University Press.
1984a   "Women Who Write Are Women." *New York Times Book Review* 89, 16 December.
1984b   "Women's Time, Women's Space: Writing the History of Feminist Criticism." *Tulsa Studies in Women's Literature* 3:29–44.

Silver, Catherine Bodard
1973   "Salon, Foyer, Bureau: Women and the Professions in France." *American Journal of Sociology* 78(4):74–90.

Simmel, Georg
1984   *On Women, Sexuality, and Love.* Trans. Guy Oakes. New Haven: Yale University Press.

Sklar, Kathryn
1973   *Catharine Beecher*. New Haven: Yale University Press.

Smith, Dorothy E.
1979   "Toward a Sociology for Women." In *The Prism of Sex*, ed. Julia Sherman and Evelyn T. Beck, 135–88. Madison: University of Wisconsin Press.

Spacks, Patricia
1975   *The Female Imagination*. New York: Alfred A. Knopf.

Spender, Dale
1986   *Mothers of the Novel*. New York: Pandora Press.

Stimpson, Catharine R.
1979   "The Power to Name: Some Reflections on the Avante-Garde." In *The Prism of Sex*, ed. Julia Sherman and Evelyn T. Beck, 55–78. Madison: University of Wisconsin Press.

Supple, Barry
1978   "Material Development: The Condition of England, 1830–1860." In *The Victorians*, ed. Laurence Lerner, 49–69. London: Methuen.

Sutherland, J. A.
1976   *Victorian Novelists and Publishers*. London: Althone Press.

Swidler, Ann
1986   "Culture in Action: Symbols and Strategies." *American Sociological Review* 51:273–86.

Tanzy, Conrad
1961   "Economic Relationships of Novelists and Publishers in England, 1830–1880." Ph. D. diss. Ohio State University.

Tillotson, Kathleen
1962   *Novels of the Eighteen-Forties*. Oxford: Clarendon Press.

Tompkins, Jane
1985   "Masterpiece Theater: The Politics of Hawthorne's Literary Reputation." Chap. 1 in *Sensational Designs: The Cultural Work of American Fiction, 1790–1860*. New York: Oxford University Press.

Tompkins, Joyce M. S.
1961 [1932] *The Popular Novel in England, 1770–1800*. London: Constable.

Treiman, Donald
1977   *Academic Prestige in Comparative Perspective*. New York: Academic Press.

Trollope, Anthony
1980   *Autobiography*. Ed. Michael Sadleir and Frederick Page. New York: Oxford University Press.

Tuchman, Gaye
1974a "Prewritten Obituaries as Nominations to the Social Memory." Paper presented at the annual meeting of the American Sociological Association.
1974b "Women and the Creation of Culture." In *Another Voice*, ed. Marcia Millman and Rosabeth Moss Kanter, 171–202. Garden City, New York: Anchor.
1980   "Discriminating Science." *Social Policy* (May–June):59–64.
1982   "Culture as Resource: Actions Defining the Victorian Novel." *Media, Culture and Society* (Winter):3–18.

1984a "Consciousness Industries and the Production of Culture." *Journal of Communication* 33:330–41.

1984b "When the Prevalent Don't Prevail: Male Hegemony and the Victorian Novel." In *Conflict and Consensus: A Festschrift in Honor of Lewis A. Coser*, ed. Walter Powell and Richard Robbins, 139–58. New York: Free Press.

Tuchman, Gaye, and Nina Fortin

1980 "Edging Women Out: The Structure of Opportunity and the Victorian Novel." *Signs* (Winter):308–25.

1982 "The Decreasing Structure of Opportunities for Victorian Women Writers: Shifting Occupational Sex-Typing." A Report on NEH Grant RO–3254–78–1586.

1984a "Fame and Misfortune: Edging Women out of the Great Literary Tradition." *American Journal of Sociology* (July):308–25.

1984b "What Victorian Women Wrote: Novelists' Contracts with Macmillan and Company." A Report on NEH Grant RO–20470–83.

Tyack, David B., and Myra Strober

1981 "Jobs and Gender: A History of the Structuring of Educational Employment by Sex." In *Educational Policy and Management*, ed. Patricia A. Schmuck, W. W. Charters, Jr., and Richard O. Carlson, 131–52. New York: Academic Press.

Vicinus, Martha

1974 *The Industrial Muse: A Study of Nineteenth-Century British Working-Class Literature*. New York: Barnes and Noble.

1985 *Independent Women: Work and Community for Single Women, 1850–1920*. Chicago: University of Chicago Press.

Walbank, F. A.

1950 *Queens of the Circulating Library*. London: Evans Brothers.

Watt, Ian

1957 *The Rise of the Novel*. Berkeley: University of California Press.

Waugh, Arthur

1930 *A Hundred Years of Publishing*. London: Chapman and Hall.

Wertz, Richard, and Dorothy Wertz

1977 *Lying in: A History of Childbirth in America*. New York: Schocken.

White, Harrison C.

1982 Review of Jonathan R. Cole's *Fair Science*. *American Journal of Sociology* 87(4):951–56.

White, Harrison C., and Cynthia White

1965 *Canvasses and Careers: Institutional Change in the French Painting World*. New York: John Wiley.

Wilensky, Harold L.

1964 "The Professionalization of Everyone?" *American Journal of Sociology* 70 (September)137–58.

Williams, Raymond

1961 *The Long Revolution*. Harmondsworth, England: Penguin.

1976 *Keywords*. New York: Oxford University Press.

1977 *Marxism and Literature*. New York: Oxford University Press.

1980   "The Bloomsbury Fraction." In *Problems in Materialism and Culture*. London: New Left Books.

Wolff, Janet
1981   *The Social Production of Culture*. New York: St. Martin's Press.

Wood, Elizabeth.
1980   "Women in Music." *Signs* 6(2):283–98.

Yates, Gayle Graham, ed.
1985   *Harriet Martineau on Women*. New Brunswick: Rutgers University Press.

Zimmeck, Meta
1986   "Jobs for the Girls: The Expansion of Clerical Work for Women, 1850–1914." In *Unequal Opportunities: Women's Employment in England, 1800–1918*, ed. Angela V. John, 153–77. Oxford: Basil Blackwell.

Zukin, Sharon
1981   *Loft Living: Culture and Capital in Urban Change*. Baltimore: Johns Hopkins University Press.

Index

References to tables are printed in italic type.